An Assessment of the Global Impact of the Financial Crisis

An Assessment of the Global Impact of the Financial Crisis

Edited by

Philip Arestis

Rogério Sobreira

and

José Luis Oreiro

First published 2011 by
PALGRAVE MACMILLAN

Palgrave Macmillan in the UK is an imprint of Macmillan Publishers Limited, registered in England, company number 785998, of Houndmills, Basingstoke, Hampshire RG21 6XS.

Palgrave Macmillan in the US is a division of St Martin's Press LLC, 175 Fifth Avenue, New York, NY 10010.

Palgrave Macmillan is the global academic imprint of the above companies and has companies and representatives throughout the world.

Palgrave® and Macmillan® are registered trademarks in the United States, the United Kingdom, Europe and other countries.

ISBN 978–0–230–27160–9 hardback

This book is printed on paper suitable for recycling and made from fully managed and sustained forest sources. Logging, pulping and manufacturing processes are expected to conform to the environmental regulations of the country of origin.

A catalogue record for this book is available from the British Library.

Library of Congress Cataloging-in-Publication Data

An assessment of the global impact of the financial crisis / edited by Philip Arestis, Rogério Sobreira, and José Luis Oreiro.
   p. cm.
   ISBN 978–0–230–27160–9 (alk. paper)
  1. Global Financial Crisis, 2008–2009.   2. Economic history—21st century.   3. Globalization—Economic aspects.   I. Arestis, Philip, 1941–   II. Sobreira, Rogério.   III. Oreiro, José Luis.   IV. Title.
   HB3722.A87 2010
   330.9'0511—dc22

                         2010033937

10   9   8   7   6   5   4   3   2   1
20 19 18 17 16 15 14 13 12 11

Printed and bound in Great Britain by
CPI Antony Rowe, Chippenham and Eastbourne

Contents

List of Tables and Figures

Tables

Figures

Notes on the Contributors

Nigel F.B. Allington, Cambridge Centre for Economic and Public Policy and Bye Fellow and Director of Studies in Economics, Downing College, Cambridge University; Professor of Finance, Ecole de Management, Grenoble; Research Fellow Julian Hodge Applied Macroeconomics Research Group, Cardiff University. He is a member of the Conservative Party's Higher Education Committee and has published on European issues more particularly price and growth convergence, including 'One Market, One Money and One Price' in the *International Journal of Central Banking*, as well on gender wage differences and the economics of higher education. He is engaged on a major project to measure the efficiency of UK politicians which is yielding a series of journal articles that will be published as a single volume in due course. The most recent article is 'Moats, Duck Houses and Bath Plugs: Members of Parliament, the Expenses Scandal and the Use of Web Sites', forthcoming in *Parliamentary Affairs*.

Philip Arestis, Cambridge Centre for Economics and Public Policy, Department of Land Economy, University of Cambridge, UK; Professor of Economics, Department of Applied Economics V, Universidad del País Vasco, Spain; Distinguished Adjunct Professor of Economics, Department of Economics, University of Utah, US; Senior Scholar, Levy Economics Institute, New York, US; Visiting Professor, Leeds Business School, University of Leeds, UK; Professorial Research Associate, Department of Finance and Management Studies, School of Oriental and African Studies (SOAS), University of London, UK; and current holder of the British Hispanic Foundation 'Queen Victoria Eugenia' British Hispanic Chair of Doctoral Studies. He is Chief Academic Adviser to the UK Government Economic Service (GES) on Professional Developments in Economics. He has published as sole author or editor, as well as co-author and co-editor, a number of books, contributed in the form of invited chapters to numerous books, produced research reports for research institutes, and has published widely in academic journals.

Flavio Basilio is Assistant Professor of Economics at Universidade de Brasilia (UnB), Risk Management Assessor at Banco do Brasil (BB) and Member of the Brazilian Keynesian Association (AKB). He has published various articles in academic journals in Brazil.

Luiz Fernando de Paula is Associate Professor of Economics, University of the State of Rio de Janeiro (UERJ) and CNPq Researcher. He is currently President of the Brazilian Keynesian Association (AKB) and member of the editorial board for the *Brazilian Journal of Political Economy*. His publications include more than 70 articles on banking, financial fragility, economic policy, Post Keynesian theory, and the Brazilian economy in books and scientific journals, such as the *Cambridge Journal of Economics*, the *Journal of Post Keynesian Economics*, *Banca Nazionale del Lavoro Quarterly Review*, *CEPAL Review*, and the *Brazilian Journal of Political Economy*. He has also authored or co-edited ten books, including *Monetary Union in South America: Lessons from EMU* (2004) and *Financial Liberalization and Economic Performance in Emerging Countries* (Palgrave Macmillan, 2008).

Jesus Ferreiro is Associate Professor in Economics at the University of the Basque Country, in Bilbao, Spain, and an Associate Member of the Centre for Economic and Public Policy, University of Cambridge. His research interests are in the areas of macroeconomic policy, labour market and international financial flows. He has published a number of articles on those topics in edited books and in refereed journals such as the *American Journal of Economics and Sociology*, *Economic and Industrial Democracy*, *Économie Appliquée*, *Ekonomia*, *European Planning Studies*, the *International Journal of Political Economy*, the *International Labour Review*, the *International Review of Applied Economics*, and the *Journal of Post Keynesian Economics*.

Elias Karakitsos is Director of Guildhall Asset Management; chairman of Global Economic Research; and an Associate Member of the Centre for Economic and Public Policy, University of Cambridge. He was a Professor at Imperial College, Head of Economics for ten years and has acted as an advisor to governments and financial institutions, including Citibank, Oppenheimer, Allianz, Crédit Agricole and Standard Chartered. He is the author of five books/monographs, 90 papers in learned journals and more than 330 reports on financial markets.

John S.L. McCombie, Director, Cambridge Centre for Economic and Public Policy, Department of Land Economy, UK; Fellow and Director of Studies in Economics, Downing College, Cambridge; Director of Studies in Land Economy, Downing College, Christ's College and Girton College; Member, Centre for Globalisation Research, Queen Mary, University of London. He did both his undergraduate degree and his Ph.D. at the University of Cambridge. He was recently Specialist Advisor to the

House of Lords and is a consultant to the World Bank and the Asian Development Bank. He was an editor of *Regional Studies* and is currently an editor of *Spatial Economic Analysis*. He is a co-editor or co-author of 15 books, and the author of over one hundred articles in books and journals, including the *Cambridge Journal of Economics*, the *Economic Journal*, the *Manchester School*, *Oxford Economic Papers*, the *Journal of Regional Science* and the *Journal of Post Keynesian Economics*.

Özlem Onaran is Senior Lecturer at Middlesex University, Britain. She has formerly worked at the Vienna University of Economics and Business, Istanbul Technical University, the University of Applied Sciences, Berlin, and the University of Massachusetts, Amherst, where she is currently also a research associate at the Political Economy Research Institute. She has published widely in academic journals and books in the areas of globalisation, distribution, employment, investment, financial crisis, development, and gender.

José Luis Oreiro, Associate Professor of Economics at University of Brasilia (UnB), Level I Researcher at National Scientific Council (CNPq/ Brazil), Director of the Brazilian Keynesian Association (AKB) and Member of the Editorial Board of the *Brazilian Journal of Political Economy (REP)*. He has published more than 60 articles in academic journals in Brazil and other countries, three books as editor and contributed in the form of invited chapters to many other books. According to REPEC, he is among the top 10 per cent of academic economists in Brazil.

Jonathan Perraton is Senior Lecturer in the Department of Economics and associate of the Political Economy Research Centre, University of Sheffield, UK. He has published invited chapters to book and articles in academic journals, particularly on economic globalisation, comparative national capitalisms and economic methodology. He is also joint author (with David Goldblatt, David Held and Anthony McGrew) of *Global Transformations: Politics, Economics and Culture* (1999) and co-editor (with Ben Clift) of *Where are National Capitalisms Now?* (Palgrave Macmillan, 2004).

Felipe Serrano is Professor in Economics at the University of the Basque Country, in Bilbao, Spain and head of the Department of Applied Economics V at the University of the Basque Country. His research interests are in the areas of social security, the welfare state, labour market, innovation and economic policy. He is the author of a number of articles on those topics in edited books and in refereed journals such as *Economies et Sociétés*, *Ekonomia*, *European Planning Studies*, the *Industrial* *and Labor Relations Review*, the *International Labour Review*, the *International Review of Applied Economics* and the *Journal of Post Keynesian Economics*.

Ajit Singh is an Emeritus Professor of Economics at Cambridge University and Life Fellow of Queen's College. Since his retirement he has been appointed as a Senior Research Fellow at the Judge's School of Management at Cambridge. He is an author of 15 books and monographs and about 200 academic articles. Nearly a hundred of the latter have been published in refereed professional economic journals including the topmost ones. He has been a senior economic advisor to the governments of Mexico and Tanzania, working with the highest levels of government. He was elected as an academician of the British Academy of Social Sciences in 2004. In 2006 he was inducted into the Hall of Fame of the Economics Department at Howard University where he did his Master's Degree before goining on to do a Ph.D at the University of California, Berkeley. His main research interests are: (i) the theory of the firm, the stock market, corporate governance, corporate finance, take overs and mergers and the market for corporate control; (ii) de-industrialisation and structural change in advanced countries; globalisation employment and productivity in advanced and developing countries; and (iii) the industrial revolution of the third world and economic policy in emerging economies.

Rogério Sobreira, Associate Professor of Economics and Finance, Brazilian School of Public and Business Administration at Getulio Vargas Foundation and CNPq Researcher. He has published several articles in academic journals and invited chapters mainly on banking regulation, banking firms, investment financing and public debt management. He has co-edited five books, all in Portuguese: *Financial and Banking Regulation, Development and the Building of a Nation – Economic Policy, Development and the Building of a Nation – Public Policy, Fiscal Adjustment: The Case of Selected Countries* and *Monetary Policy, Central Banks and Inflation Targeting*. He is member of the Brazilian Keynesian Association.

Howard Stein is a Professor in the Center for Afroamerican and African Studies and also teaches in the Department of Epidemiology at the University of Michigan. He is a development economist, educated in Canada, the US and the UK, who has taught in Asia and Africa. He is the editor or author of more than 15 books and collections. His research has focused on foreign aid, finance and development, structural adjustment, health and development, industrial policy and rural property right transformation. His latest authored book is entitled *Beyond the World Bank Agenda: An Institutional Approach to Development* (2008). The book examines the evolution of the World Bank agenda aimed at explaining the failure of these policies in places like sub-Saharan Africa. The volume also generates alternatives based on institutional economic theory and applies them in the areas of state formation, financial development and health care.

Shujie Yao is Professor and Head of the School of Contemporary Chinese Studies at the University of Nottingham. Before joining Nottingham as Professor of Economics and Chinese Sustainable Development, he worked at the University of Oxford, Portsmouth and Middlesex as research fellow, lecturer, Professor and Chair of Economics. Professor Yao is an expert on economic development in China. He has published six research monographs, edited books, as well as produced more than 70 refereed journal articles. He was ranked eighth among the world's China scholars specialising in the study of the Chinese economy in a recent article published in the *Journal of Asian Economic Literature*. He is founding editor of the *Journal of Chinese Economic and Business Studies*, chief economics editor of *Xi'an Jiaotong University Journal* (Social Sciences), an editorial member of the *Journal of Comparative Economics*, *Food Policy* and the *Journal of Contemporary China*. Professor Yao is also coordinator of the China and the World Economy programme at the Globalisation and Economic Policy Centre at Nottingham and special chair professor of economics of Xi'an Jioatong University. He has had a wide range of consultancy experience with major organisations including the UNDP, FAO, World Bank, ADB, DFID, EU and the UNCDF, working in many less developed and transitional economies in Africa, Asia and Eastern Europe.

Ann Zammit's professional work has included university teaching, research, economic advisory work, journalism, documentary film production, and other policy-oriented activities. It involved work-ing for various periods in Turkey, Malta, Chile and elsewhere in Latin America, and in Eastern Europe. Such work has always focused on global development issues. She has been employed by various interna-tional institutions – the Organization for Economic Co-operation and Development (OECD), the Organization of American States (OAS), the UN Research Institute for Social Development (UNRISD) and the South Centre (an intergovernmental body of developing countries based in Geneva). Consultancy work has been undertaken for the International Labour Organization (ILO) and the United Nations Development

Programme (UNDP). She taught at the University of Chile, the University of Hull (UK), University College, London, and Ithaca College (London). Research was undertaken at the Institute of Development Studies, Sussex and the Latin America Bureau, London. Involved in establishing the International Broadcasting Trust (an innovative non-profit TV documentary production company) she contributed to the development of programme ideas on development issues and produced the accompanying print-backup. Recent research has focused on three areas: aspects of corporate governance and corporate social responsibility; global labour standards and other global employment issues; and macroeconomics and gender equality.

Jing Zhang is a lecturer at School of Contemporary Chinese Studies in the University of Nottingham. Jing was awarded a Ph.D. in Economics from the University of Birmingham. Her research focuses on the empirical studies of globalisation and the environment; more specifically on the impact of economic growth; foreign direct investment flows on the environment; the role played by the difference in environmental regulations in the foreign firm location choice; and the impact of corruption and government quality on foreign investment inflows and on the environmental regulations. Her current research interests include the implications of the financial crisis for China amongst others.

1
Introduction

Philip Arestis, Rogério Sobreira and José Luis Oreiro

Recent economic events have had a profound impact on the global economy. According to the *World Bank Economic Outlook* published in April 2010, the major advanced economies experienced a fall of 3.2 per cent of GDP in 2009 and are expected to record a moderate growth of 2.3 per cent in 2010. The impact of the crisis was stronger in Japan and euro area than in the United States, the centre of the financial crisis. Indeed, the US economy experienced a decline of 2.4 per cent in GDP compared to a 4.1 per cent fall in GDP in the euro area and 5.2 per cent in Japan. The United Kingdom is also projected to experience a huge fall of 4.9 per cent of GDP in 2010.

These numbers are in sharp contrast to those observed in developing countries. For instance, the Newly Industrialized Asian Economies (Korea, Taiwan, Hong Kong and Singapore) had a fall of only 0.9 per cent of GDP in 2009. For the rest of Asia, the numbers are even better. In the case of China and India, GDP growth of 6.6 per cent was recorded in 2009, and in 2010 the growth in GDP is expected to be 8.7 per cent. The ASEAN-5 (Indonesia, Thailand, Philippines, Malaysia and Vietnam) experienced only modest growth of 1.7 per cent in 2009, but is expected to have robust growth of 5.4 per cent in 2010. Even in Latin America the impact of the crisis will be weaker than has been the case in developed countries: South America and Mexico experienced a fall of only GDP 1.9 per cent in 2009. For 2010, this region is projected to achieve robust GDP growth of 4.1 per cent.

During the recent crisis the economic performance of developing countries has been rather curious. In fact, just one decade earlier, the East Asian Crisis had shown the fragility of the 'Asian Model' of growth compared to the 'Western Model' of capitalism. In 1994–95, the Mexico Crisis had a huge impact on some important Latin American economies, including Brazil. For a long time Latin America has been considered a region characterised by balance of payments crises, capital flight and high rates of inflation. But now things have changed. The 2008 financial crisis had hit the heart of capitalism, but the effects were much weaker at the 'periphery' of the capitalist system than in its centre. The relevant question is why.

One possible answer is that developing countries have learned from previous crises and have adopted policies that help to reduce their external fragility. Indeed, as can be seen in Table 1.1, developing countries recorded strong current account surpluses in 2007, one year before the crisis. This situation did not change significantly in 2008 and 2009. Why would being a capital-exporting country help to isolate the economy from the effects of a financial crisis abroad? The answer to this question is that current account surpluses are, in general, associated with a substantial accumulation of foreign reserves. This is especially important in avoiding a capital flight from a country in the face of a fall in exports and in foreign direct investment during an external crisis. Capital flight can have disruptive effects over a developing economy since it can produce a huge and sudden devaluation of nominal exchange rate. In general, this can have negative effects over the real output of these countries, essentially as a result of the fact that a significant share of liabilities of private agents and government are expressed in foreign currency, while their assets are denominated principally in domestic currency.

Another problem that can arise as a result of capital flight is an increase in the domestic rate of interest in an attempt by the Central

Table 1.1 Current account surplus as a share of GDP (selected countries, 2007–2009)

	2007	2008	2009
United States	–5.2	–4.9	–2.9
Euro area	0.3	–0.7	–0.6
Japan	4.8	3.2	2.8
United Kingdom	–2.7	–1.7	–1.3
Newly Industrialized Asian Countries	5.7	4.4	8.9
China and India	7.0	5.9	4.1
ASEAN-5	4.9	2.6	5.1
South America and Mexico	0.7	–0.3	–0.3

Source: IMF (2010).

Bank to avoid a substantial devaluation in the domestic currency. In this case, monetary policy will be used as a device to achieve an external balance, but its effect over the domestic economy will be to internalize the contraction of output occurring abroad by means of a reduction of domestic demand through interest rate increases. If the fiscal position of the country affected by a capital flight was not good before the crisis (for example, the country had a high public debt as a ratio to GDP), the increase in interest rate by the Central Bank would force the Treasury to reduce government expenditures in order to achieve or increase a primary surplus. This would be required to restore the 'confidence' of the financial system in the ability of the government to pay its debt. The combination of a monetary contraction with a fiscal contraction would produce a huge fall in domestic demand at the same time that external demand is falling as a result of the external crisis. The combined result of domestic and external demand contraction would be a huge fall in GDP, which will be higher than the one observed in developed economies. This is so since for the latter, fiscal and monetary policies would be conducted in order to reduce the output loss caused by the financial crisis instead of attempting to avoid a capital flight.

This reasoning shows that a current account surplus and the accumulation of foreign reserves are important for developing countries because they allow them to conduct anti-cyclical policies in the face of a financial crisis in developed countries. Stabilization of output is important for a robust growth in the long term due to its effects over capitalist animal spirits. Developed countries, then, should never pursue a growth strategy based solely on the accumulation of 'foreign savings'. This book presents, therefore, an extensive and widespread analysis of the crisis as it impacted on both developed and developing countries. It will show that the impact of this crisis is far from being homogenous in both the developed and the developing world. The most intriguing aspect of this crisis is the fact that the crisis had less of an impact on those economies responsible for the generation of the 'global savings glut', and more on those economies that are more dependent on foreign capital inflows. In connection with this aspect, the book also addresses the question of why this crisis has been so limited in magnitude and of such relatively short duration. Finally, it is shown that financial liberalisation alone cannot provide a full explanation of the crisis. It is necessary to take a good look at the size of the global financial sector and also to its related redistributive impact. Thus, one of the main lessons that can be learned from this volume is a profound need to implement policies that can guarantee financial stability.

In chapter 2 Philip Arestis and Elias Karakitsos continue the discussion by considering the origins of the current crisis along with policy implications. They concentrate on the US experience but also comment on the experiences in other countries. The focus of this chapter is on the emphasis attributed to the 'efficient market hypothesis' that all unfettered markets clear continously thereby making disequilibria, such as bubbles, highly unlikely. Indeed in this view, economic policy designed to eliminate bubbles would lead to 'financial repression', a very bad outcome in this view. Since the early 1970s when governments attempted and succeeded in implementing financial liberalisation initiatives, especially in the US and the UK, the focus has been on creating markets completely free from any policy interference. This is based on the belief that liberalised financial markets are very innovative, and sure enough they were. The experience with financial liberalisation is that it caused a number of deep financial crises and problems that were unprecedented in terms of their depth and frequency. However, most important for the purposes of this chapter, it was the US experience of financial liberalisation that is most telling in terms of the causes of the current crisis. Financial liberalisation alone cannot provide a full explanation of the crisis. The size of the financial sector is also of relevance. In this respect, it is important to note the enormous redistribution that had taken place in the countries at the centre of the crisis. For it was the case that a significant redistribution from wage earners to the financial sector had materialised prior to August 2007. Over the period prior to the 'Great Recession' and after the intense period of financial liberalisation, especially in the US, great strides were seen in terms of the development and extension of new forms of securitisation and the use of derivatives. This was a practice which led to the growth of collateralised debt instruments, especially in particular, in the form of collateralised mortgages. This financial architecture, along with the redistribution and the financial liberalisation alluded to above, were the main causes of the crisis. But there were, the chapter argues, contributory factors. Two of them are emphasized: the international imbalances, resulting principally from the growth of the Chinese economy, and the monetary policy pursued by countries over the period leading to the crisis. The chapter also discusses the clear policy implications that emanate from the crisis. It is concluded that one important policy that has not been addressed properly in recent discussions is that of financial stability.

Ajit Singh and Ann Zammit, in chapter 3, address the following main analytical questions concerning the global impact of the financial crisis: why has its impact been so limited in magnitude and of such relatively short duration. The world economy was hit by unprecedented shocks in the period leading up to the crisis. The financial system was the biggest casualty and seemed to be on the verge of a meltdown. This was due to the fall of the Lehman Brothers, to the dangerously high debt–equity ratio of the leading players in the financial market, and to the credit crunch indication that the banks were mutually suspicious. The securitisation of the subprime mortgage loans, together with financial globalisation, led to the worldwide financial crisis. In view of the uncertainty concerning the contamination caused by subprime mortgages in the securitised assets of most major financial institutions, the market value was no longer an accurate guide to asset prices. Individually and collectively, these shocks to the global economy were both quantitatively huge and qualitatively unprecedented. It was for these reasons that many students of the world economy expected the impact of the 2008 financial crisis to be quite severe, approaching the levels of the Great Depression of 1929. However, fortunately for the world economy this kind of outcome has not occurred to date. The highest recorded fall in advanced countries' GDP growth for a 12-month period during the Great Depression was 30 per cent in the US. Most countries rich and poor have escaped such catastrophic contractions in GDP; this is not an accident, since there are a number of positive long-term structural factors at work in the world economy, which have not been given adequate attention by commentators either at the time of the crisis or subsequently. These factors are: (a) the highly positive role of emerging countries in the world economy; (b) the unexpected co-operation between countries, which has taken place during this crisis and which stands in striking contrast to the 'beggar your neighbour' policies followed by nation-states in the 1930s; and (c) the political economy of the governance of the crisis which has meant that there has been coherence at the top level in the formulation and execution of economic policy. Despite the progress made so far (for example, saving the financial system from a meltdown) the world economy is still not out of the woods. The challenge is to create a new financial system, which maintains the dynamism of the old system while protecting the world economy from frequent bubbles, often caused by unwarranted euphoria or undeserved pessimism.

In chapter 4, Howard Stein argues that, in 2007, the IMF faced a 'crisis of identity' and huge cutbacks in spending. Lending from its General Resource Account (GRA), its major source of income, fell by an unprecedented 91 per cent from its peak in 2003 to a mere $6 billion – a level not seen since the 1970s. Similarly the International Bank for Reconstruction and Development (IBRD) saw its loans plummet by 40 per cent. In both cases middle-income countries were able to secure alternative sources of financing without any neoliberal baggage. This, many argued, helped to contribute to the global economic crisis. Like a phoenix rising from the ashes, the current crisis has resurrected the World Bank and the IMF. The Fund, for example, lent nearly $55 billion alone to European countries between November and April 2009 and another $78 billion since the creation of its Flexible Credit Line in March 2009. At the G20 meeting in early April 2009, the IMF received authority to triple its lending capacity to $750 billion and to expand its SDR allocation by an additional $250 billion. China and some other countries have gone further and talked of creating a new global currency based on SDRs administered by the Fund. At the same time, the IMF now claims that it has reformed its ways and made a greater commitment to regulation, counter-cyclical monetary and fiscal policy, social safety nets for the poor and moved towards *ex ante* from *ex post* conditionality. The chapter investigates these claims and whether the IMF and World Bank are part of the problem or the solution to the global economic crisis as it has affected developing countries.

In chapter 5 by Jonathan Perraton there is a discussion of the impact of the crisis in the euro area. In much comment the euro area has been perceived as being relatively insulated from the current crisis. Ireland and Spain apart, the member countries of the euro area typically did not experience house price booms comparable to those observed in the US and the UK. Indeed, the member countries financial systems were less Anglo-Saxon in character and were therefore assumed to be less vulnerable to a financial crisis. Externally, the euro area is in broad balance, with Germany in surplus and most trade conducted within the area itself. The European Central Bank (ECB), in particular, has been keen to portray the euro area as an 'innocent bystander' affected by problems generated elsewhere. This chapter provides a critical evaluation of these claims, examines the evolution of imbalances in key economies and assesses the performance of the macroeconomic framework of the ECB and the Stability and Growth Pact in response to the crisis. After reviewing macroeconomic developments, the chapter argues that significant imbalances had emerged in euro-area economies, with Germany being a major contributor to global payments imbalances and asset price bubbles emerging elsewhere. This has created stresses within the zone that the current macroeconomic policy framework has struggled to ameliorate. The official emphasis on supply-side measures, particularly labour market flexibility, has not succeeded in improving macroeconomic performance in the euro area. Indeed, wage increases running persistently below productivity growth in Germany and elsewhere may have aggravated imbalances. The euro-area macroeconomic framework has been sorely tested in the current crisis. Indeed, it may have limited the ability of the euro area to ensure coordinated reflation and the moves to restore 'business as usual' in the euro area macroeconomic policy framework risk stifling any recovery.

The impact of the crisis over developing countries is analysed by Jesus Ferreiro and Felipe Serrano in chapter 6. Although for the mainstream economic theory, developing countries are net importers of foreign capital, recent experience shows that they have become net capital exporters. This change of behaviour has given rise to the phenomenon known as 'global imbalance', a combination of two main elements: the deficit in the US balance of payments and the surplus in the balance of payments of developing economies. However, this interpretation hides the fact that the surpluses in the balance of payments are generated in only a small number of economies – more precisely, in raw material exporter countries and in some emerging Asian economies. The rest of the developing countries continue to be net importers of capital resources, and, consequently, they depend for their development and growth on the inflow of foreign capital. The aim of this contribution is to analyse the impact of the current financial and economic crisis on developing countries. The authors pay special attention to the recent evolution of capital inflows in developing countries. This analysis will be made for the different 'regions' of developing countries. The idea is that the crisis is having a smaller effect on those economies responsible for the generation of the 'global savings glut', and more impact on those economies, like the countries of Eastern Europe or Latin America, that are more dependent on foreign capital inflows. The analysis focuses principally on two kinds of capital flows: foreign direct investment inflows, and capital inflows emanating from banks in developed economies.

In chapter 7, Özlem Onaran discusses the effects of the current global crisis on Western and Eastern Europe, and reviews the policy reaction to the crisis. The main thesis of the chapter is that the decline in the labour share across the globe has been a major factor leading to the current global crisis. The chapter argues that global imbalances should also be interpreted in connection with the distributional crisis. The debt-led consumption-based growth of the US economy was financed by the surpluses of countries like Germany in Europe in addition to Japan or developing countries like China and South Korea, and the oil-rich

Middle Eastern countries. In Germany, current account surpluses and the consequent capital outflows to the US were made possible by wage moderation, which has suppressed domestic consumption and fuelled exports. Wage moderation in Germany created further imbalances within the West as well as between the East and the West. Thus, the high current account surpluses of the neo-mercantilists of the EU, i.e. Germany along with Austria, Netherlands, and Finland develop simultaneously with widening trade deficits in the other western EU countries like Spain, Greece, Portugal, Italy and Ireland. The low level of wages in Eastern Europe also did not save them from running high current account deficits thanks to the high level of imports from the international supplier networks of the European multinational companies as well as the high profits of these foreign investors (repatriated as well as reinvested). The fundamental problem of Eastern Europe was an excessive dependency on foreign capital flows in the absence of a development strategy backed by industrial policy, and as a typical consequence of this dependency a bust episode following the boom was an unavoidable outcome of reversals in capital flows. The mainstream policy reaction to the crisis has simply been efforts to return to the 'business as usual' strategy of neoliberalism. There is a clear unwillingness to address the distributional aspect of the origins of the crisis as well as the distribution of the burden of the costs of the crisis. The chapter concludes by discussing policy alternatives to this mainstream position.

In chapter 8 Nigel Allington and John McCombie reconsider the 'successes' of the Transition Economies, including those that entered the European Union (EU) in 2004, following the fall of Communism in 1989, namely the T8. It is now twenty years since the T8 became market economies and ten years since they entered the EU. Following the initial economic dislocation that occurred as these economies moved to a market economy, they experienced rapid growth until the 2007 crisis. The enhanced globalisation of capital flows, market liberalisation, and technology transfer that raised the levels of economic growth in the T8 is shown to have generated a considerable degree of convergence since 2004. The other transition economies in Central Asia had ten years of negative or slow growth until 2000 when their growth accelerated substantially. The T8 economies have now experienced a substantial economic collapse as an indirect result of the subprime crisis, whereas the other transition economies, with the exception of Kazakhstan, have not fared so badly. This chapter attempts to answer the question of whether for the T8 countries it is the transition process per se, or simply the transition economies that are in crisis. In other words, the question arises as to whether the institutional framework put in place after the transition has ameliorated or exacerbated the impact of the financial crisis. The economic ties with Western European economies are shown to have increased the severity of the crisis in the region. Paradoxically, the lack of integration with the advanced countries seems to have sheltered the other transition economies. A comparison is made between the recent economic performance of the T8 and the other transition economies and a number of policy implications are drawn.

The implications of the current financial crisis for China are discussed by Shujie Yao and Jing Zhang in chapter 9. The ongoing world financial crisis, which began in the US in 2007, is the most serious since the East Asian crisis of the 1990s. This chapter examines the causes and consequences of this crisis with a particular focus on its implications for China. Like the rest of the world, China has not escaped from the crisis as its trade and domestic production have been adversely dragged down by the economic recession in its key exporting economies, especially the US, the EU and Japan. However, China has not been hit as hard as its key competitors. While the key industrialised countries are suffering from massive economic shrinkage, China is still set to achieve a growth rate of 8 per cent in 2009. This crisis provides China with a 'once in a century' opportunity to achieve a much speedier economic convergence with the world's largest industrialized economies. It is expected to surpass Japan to become the second largest economy in the world by the end of 2010.[1] The crisis is also the catalyst for a shift in world power from the West to the East, making China increasingly influential in world economic and political affairs. China will become one of the key countries in leading the entire world out of the current crisis. The crisis provides China with opportunities to take advantage of low commodity prices, to move up the technological ladder of production, to improve its infrastructure, and to reduce regional income inequality. At the same time, China has to learn lessons from the developed countries to avoid becoming the potential centre of future crisis because of globalisation.

The impact of the current financial crisis on the banking system in Brazil is analysed by Luiz Fernando de Paula and Rogério Sobreira in chapter 10. The authors argue that the current financial crisis hit the Brazilian economy through two financial channels. The first was the capital flight from the stock market and (some) reduction in the domestic supply of credit. This was caused by the international credit crunch that impacted on the Brazilian big commercial and investment banks, with effects on the supply of interbank credit to the small and medium-sized banks; and, as a consequence, on the ability of the banking system to serve their clients' demand for credit. The second was the real channel – that is, the decrease in exports with impacts on the growth in GDP. Together with the adoption of counter-cyclical monetary and fiscal policies by the Brazilian government, the Brazilian banking sector remained sound in comparison to what happened in industrial countries. This soundness can be explained by some varied factors that include the still low development of the (mainly private) securities market, the banking regulation that prevented the development of toxic assets and low levels of banking leverage. The combination of still high interest rates with public indexed (and very liquid) bonds also played an important role in explaining this soundness. These factors helped to keep the domestic savings pretty stable with positive impacts on the supply of credit. The chapter thus analyses the role played by the Brazilian banking regulation in protecting the banking sector from being deeply affected by the crisis, as well as some characteristics of Brazilian banking behaviour in order to understand the Brazilian experience of the financial crisis.

Finally in chapter 11, José Luis Oreiro and Flavio Basilio show that a crisis took place in Brazil in the last quarter of 2008 because of the bursting of a speculative bubble in the exchange rate market in a setting characterized by the widespread use of exchange rate derivatives by non-financial firms. The speculative bubble was the result of growing confidence about the external robustness of the Brazilian economy in the face of the high level of international reserves, macroeconomic stability and the adoption of a floating exchange rate regime that was supposed to isolate the economy from external shocks. This growing confidence produced a huge exchange rate appreciation, which induced non-financial firms to seek alternative sources of income in order to compensate declines in their external competitiveness. One of the sources in question was the use of foreign exchange derivatives as a device for obtaining loans from the banking sector at lower rates. Following the bankruptcy of Lehman Brothers, the nominal exchange rate suffered a devaluation of 50 per cent in a few weeks, causing large losses for non-financial companies in Brazil because of the existence of these contracts. Estimates of the Bank for International Settlements (BIS) about these losses showed that they could have reached 2 per cent of Brazilian GDP. Although foreign reserves in Brazil were more than sufficient to stabilise the nominal exchange rate (US$200 billion just before the crisis), the Brazilian Central Bank allowed a sudden and huge devaluation of the domestic currency, with destabilising effects on the private sector. As a consequence of these losses, Brazilian banks reduced the rate of credit expansion, producing a large fall in the money supply (high-powered money and M1). Because of the substantial contraction of the money supply and banking credit, industrial output fell by 30 per cent in the final quarter of 2008, causing a contraction of almost 14 per cent of GDP. In order to avoid future problems related to exchange rate derivatives, the authors propose that this kind of financial instruments should be closely regulated by the Brazilian Central Bank.

We would like to thank the authors for their contributions. We would also wish to thank Taiba Batool and Gemma Papageorgiou at Palgrave Macmillan, and their staff, who have been extremely supportive throughout the life of this project.

Note

1. *New York Times*, 21 January 2010: http://www.nytimes.com/2010/01/21/business/global/21chinaecon.html.

References

International Monetary Fund (IMF) (2010) *World Economic Outlook Update*, January. Washington DC: International Monetary Fund.
World Bank (2010) *Economic Outlook*, November. Washington DC: World Bank.

2
Current Crisis in the US and Economic Policy Implications

Philip Arestis and Elias Karakitsos

1 Introduction

The purpose of this contribution is to discuss the origins of the current crisis along with policy implications, concentrating on the US experience. The focus is on the emphasis given to financial liberalisation in the US, where great strides were seen in the development and extension of new forms of securitisation and use of derivatives – a practice which led to the growth of collateralised debt instruments, especially in the form of collateralised mortgages. The experience of the US with financial liberalisation is most telling in terms of the cause of the current crisis. However, financial liberalisation alone cannot fully explain the crisis. The size of the financial sector is also important. In this respect, it is important to note the enormous redistribution that had taken place in the countries at the centre of the crisis. For it was the case that a significant redistribution from wage earners to the financial sector had materialised prior to August 2007. That redistribution, along with the financial liberalisation alluded to above, led to the new financial architecture of collateralised instruments. These were the main causes of the crisis. But there were, we argue, contributory factors. We isolate two of them: the international imbalances, mainly due to the growth of China, and the monetary policy pursued by countries over the period leading to the crisis.

There are clear policy implications that emanate from the crisis (see, also, Arestis and Karakitsos, 2010a). We suggest that an important policy that has not been addressed properly is that of financial stability (see, also, Goodhart, 2009). We, thus, discuss the latter policy at some length emphasising the recent pronouncements on this front by President Barack Obama that are summarised under the acronym of the 'Volcker Plan'.

We proceed as follows. After this short introduction in section 1 we discuss the origins of the crisis in section 2. The economic policy implications are discussed in section 3 before we summarise and conclude in section 4.

2 Origins of the current crisis

In discussing the origins of the current crisis we are very much aware of the limitations of current macroeconomics. Indeed, we agree with Minsky (1982), who argued about three decades ago that 'from the perspective of the standard economic theory of Keynes's day and the presently dominant neoclassical theory, both financial crises and serious fluctuations of output and employment are anomalies: the theory offers no explanation of these phenomena' (p. 60; see, also, Arestis, 2009, on the current crisis).

The current crisis, 'the Great Recession', has been caused by US financial liberalisation attempts and the financial innovations that followed them. That was greatly helped by significant income redistribution effects from wages to profits of the financial sector. Furthermore, the emergence of Central Bank independence along with the rate of interest instrument, focusing crucially on maintaining price stability, implied that the objective of financial stability was downgraded and responsibility over it became obscure. Two other factors, the international financial imbalances and the monetary policy pursued at the time, can be suggested as factors that promoted, rather than caused, the 'Great Recession'. We take the view that although these factors were important, they were not the original cause of the 'Great Recession'. They were accentuating the process of financial liberalisation and innovation rather than being part of the cause of the crisis. The rest of this section will attempt to explain the process just suggested.

2.1 Income redistribution effects

An important factor that contributed substantially to the 'Great Recession' emerged from the steady but sharp rise in inequality, especially in the US and the UK but also elsewhere. The share of national income taken up by profits had reached close to a post-Second World War high before the onset of the recession; while real wages had fallen even behind productivity. The declining wage and rising profits share were compounded by another long-term economic term: the increasing concentration of earnings at the top, especially in the financial sector. Figures 2.1 to 2.3 make the case vividly. Figures 2.1 and 2.2 make

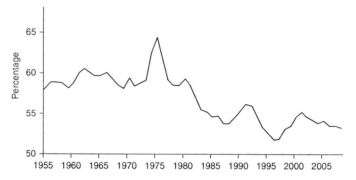

Figure 2.1 UK wages as a percentage of GDP
Source: Office for National Statistics.

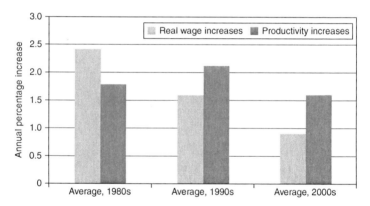

Figure 2.2 UK wages relative to productivity
Source: Oxford Economics.

the point in the case of the UK (both figures are from Lansley, 2010). Figure 2.1 clearly shows the falling share of wages, while Figure 2.2 shows clearly how wages fell below productivity. Figure 2.3 makes the case of the increasing shortfall of the real wage rate from productivity since the early 1970s in the case of the US. The real wage rate fell well behind productivity in the aftermath of the Second World War reaching its maximum shortfall of around 15 per cent during the Korean War. But the gap closed until the early 1970s when the real wage rate hit an all-time high increasing faster than productivity by more than 5 per cent

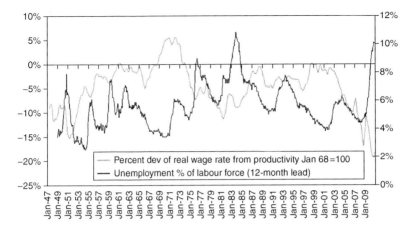

Figure 2.3 Percentage deviation of real wage rate from productivity (January 1968 = 100) and unemployment

in April 1972. In the aftermath of the first oil shock the real wage rate fell yet again behind productivity, suggesting that employees bore the brunt of the redistribution of income from the US to the oil-producing countries. Rising and high unemployment forced this redistribution of income. Unemployment soared from 3.5 per cent of the labour force in early 1970 to nearly 11 per cent in the midst of the 1980–82 recession. However, as the price of oil and unemployment fell in the 1980s the real wage rate caught up once more with productivity gains. By the spring of 1999, the time of the repeal of the Glass–Steagall Act, the gap between the real wage rate and productivity had once again been eliminated. Fluctuations in unemployment caused by the early 1990s recession and the subsequent anaemic recovery contributed to an oscillating real wage rate around productivity, but on an upward trend. Nonetheless, the real wage rate fell behind productivity following the burst of the internet and housing bubbles and the resultant increase in unemployment, hitting an all-time low of nearly –20 per cent in the aftermath of the collapse of Lehman Brothers in September 2008.

These unfavourable trends in the real wage rate are partly reflected in the wages and salaries of private and government employees. Figure 2.4 shows that wages and salaries as a percentage of GDP did not improve as much as the real wage rate in the golden post-Second World War era until the 1970s. The share of wages and salaries to GDP increased by only 3 per cent (from 50.5 per cent to 53.5 per cent) over that period. But from

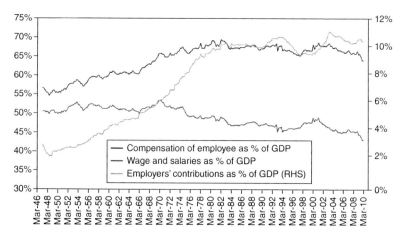

Figure 2.4   Compensation of employees and its components

the beginning of the 1970s until now the share of wages and salaries to GDP fell by an astonishing 9 per cent to 44.5 per cent by the end of 2009. Wages and salaries improved their share only in the period 1994–2001.

In spite of these unfavourable trends in the real wage rate and wages and salaries, since the 1970s, the compensation of employees, which includes in addition to wages and salaries employer contributions for government social security and employee pension and insurance funds, shows a more complicated picture. The compensation of employees improved in the post-Second World War era, increasing from 54.5 per cent to GDP in 1948 to nearly 70 per cent by the early 1980s (see Figure 2.4). But since then it has declined to 65.5 per cent. Hence, the net loss of the compensation of employees since financial liberalisation is only 3.5 per cent compared to 9 per cent in wages and salaries and a more than 10 per cent shortfall in the real wage rate to productivity. The smaller deterioration in the compensation of employees to wages and salaries, though, is partly due to higher employer contributions for government social security and employee pension and insurance funds. These contributions have more than quadrupled in the post-Second World War era from 2.3 per cent of GDP to 10.6 per cent (see Figure 2.4). Nonetheless, the share of employer contributions to GDP has increased by only a tiny fraction (i.e. 0.5 per cent) since the financial liberalisation of the early 1980s, thereby confirming the redistribution of income from employees to employers.

Figure 2.5 shows the increasing share of profits in relation to income in the case of the US, the rest of the world, and, more precisely, in the case of the financial sector. We note from Figure 2.5 that the bottom

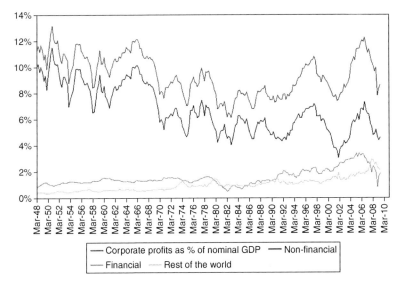

Figure 2.5 US profits as a percentage of GDP
Source: Arestis and Karakitsos (2010b).

of profitability at the end of 2001 hit an all-time low. This downtrend may be the result of shifting production abroad, which gathered pace in the era of globalisation, but also to the increasing challenge of the US from other industrialised countries, such as Japan, Europe and recently China. But the bleak picture of non-financial profitability is not shared by other subcategories. Financial companies in particular, have seen a sharp uptrend in their profitability since 1982, nearly a sixfold increase (see Figure 2.5). The financial deregulation, which had commenced in the 1970s but continued at that time, especially the repeal of the Glass–Steagall Act in 1999, both discussed below, certainly contributed to the long-term improvement of the profitability of financial companies. These developments are at the heart of the 'Great Recession' as they enabled the creation of liquidity that financed the housing bubble, but also the internet and other bubbles of less importance, such as commodities, shipping and private equity. Now that the house bubble has burst and deleverage is taking place, it is very likely that the long-term uptrend in the profitability of financial companies will be reversed.

Similar observations can be made in Europe, excluding the UK, although the rise in inequality is not as high as in the US/UK. The rising profits share aped financial institutions thereby increasing leveraging (debt to assets ratio) and high risk-taking in financial institutions.

This promoted the financial engineering based on the US subprime mortgages as explained in what follows in this section. These are important distributional effects, which are not accounted for by the prevailing view of theoretical macroeconomics and the economic policy implications of this framework, essentially monetary policy in the form of interest rate manipulation to hit the set inflation targets.

This redistribution was greatly helped by attempts at financial liberalisation in many countries around the world. Of particular importance for our purposes was the financial liberalisation framework in the US. Both the redistribution just referred to along with the financial liberalisation policies led to a period of financial engineering in the US, which spread worldwide to produce the current 'great recession'. We turn our discussion to financial liberalisation essentially in the US and the financial engineering there in an attempt to explain the origins of the current crisis.

2.2   US financial liberalisation and financial engineering

Financial liberalisation in the US began in the 1970s. More precisely in 1977, when the US started to deregulate its financial system. There was the deregulation of commissions for stock trading in 1977 to begin with, and subsequently investment banks were allowed to introduce unsecured current accounts. The removal of Regulation Q in the 1980s followed, that is removing the placing of ceilings on retail-deposit interest rates. The repeal in 1999 of the key regulation – the Glass–Steagall Act of 1933 (promoted by the US financial sector, using as their main argument the Big Bang of 1986 in the UK) – was the most important aspect of US financial liberalisation for the purposes of the question in hand. The final step in the process was the Commodity Futures Modernisation Act (CFMA) of December 2000, which repealed the Shad–Johnson jurisdictional accord, which in 1982 had banned single-stock futures, the financial instrument that allows selling now but delivering in the future. All these financial liberalisation attempts were important in promoting financial innovations in the US financial markets. We discuss their importance before we turn our attention to the financial engineering that emerged directly from them and caused the financial crisis of August 2009.[1]

When fixed commissions were in place, investment banks would book stock trades for their customers; deregulation meant greater competition, entry by low-cost brokers and thinner margins. Then, in the late 1970s, investment banks were allowed to begin to invade the commercial bank territory, through the creation of 'money market' accounts (current accounts that were unsecured). Removing Regulation Q allowed fluctuation in interest rates, thereby forcing commercial banks to compete for deposits on price, which led them to pursue new lines of business. Such new business was to respond to the investment banks' needs for short-term funding. It created, however, a financial crisis in the 1970s and 1980s when savings banks could not fund themselves in view of the narrowing of the margins of lending and borrowing rates. Investment banks moved into originating and distributing complex derivative securities, like collateralised bond obligations (normal investment bonds backed by pools of junk bonds). However, that was not a great success and the move collapsed in the second half of the 1980s.

However, that originate-and-distribute failure was followed by a new initiative of asset-backed and mortgage-backed securities, which gained a clientele in the 1990s. That was partially enabled by the relaxation of the 1933 Glass–Steagall Act in 1987 (see further details below), when the Federal Reserve Bank (the Fed) allowed 5 per cent of bank deposits to be used for investment banking, and then further promoted in 1996 when 25 per cent of deposits were allowed for the same purpose. This was followed, in 1997, the Broad Index Secured Trust Offering (BISTRO), a bundle of credit derivatives based on pools of corporate bonds, and later the Collateralised Mortgage Obligations (CMOs) based on pools of subprime mortgages and Collateralised Debt Obligations (CDOs) based on other debt. BISTRO was not a great success in view of the corporate sector's booms and recessions at that time. However, CMOs and CDOs, which were based on mortgages and other assets, became a success due to of the steady growth of the housing market. That was the first cause of the crisis: the originate-and-distribute model of securitisation and the extensive use of leverage.

This raises the issue of the difference between originate-and-distribute and originate-and-hold models. In the originate-and-hold model bank loans are held in the banks' own portfolios. In the originate-and-distribute (or originate-to-securitise) model bank loans are re-packaged and sold to other banks, foreign banks and the domestic and foreign personal sector. The latter model transfers the loan risk from the bank to whoever buys the Asset Backed Securities (ABS). Then the Commodity Futures Modernization Act (CFMA) of December 2000 emerged. This act deregulated single-stock futures trading, and provided certainty that products offered by banking institutions would not be regulated as futures contracts. CFMA enabled and legitimised credit default swaps (credit derivative contracts between two parties, whereby there is guarantee in case of default), thereby creating a potentially massive vector for the transmission of financial risk throughout the global system.

The apotheosis of the financial liberalisation in the US, however, had already come about with the repeal of the 1933 Glass–Steagall Act in 1999. The 1933 Act was designed to avoid the experience of the 1920s and 1930s in terms of the conflict of interest between the commercial and the investment arms of large financial conglomerates (whereby the investment branch tolerated high risks). The ultimate aim of the 1933 Glass–Steagall Act was to separate the activities of commercial banks and the risk-taking 'investment or merchant' banks along with strict regulation of the financial services industry. The goal was to avoid a repetition of the speculative, leveraged excesses of the 1920s and 1930s. Without access to retail deposits and with money market instruments tightly regulated, investment banks funded themselves using their partners' capital. The repeal of the act in 1999 changed all that: it enabled investment banks to branch into new activities, and it allowed commercial banks to encroach on the investment banks' other traditional preserves. It was not just commercial banks that were involved in that encroaching; insurance companies, like the American International Group (AIG), and hedge funds were also heavily involved.

The repeal of the Glass–Steagall Act in 1999 allowed the merging of commercial and investment banking, thereby enabling financial institutions to separate loan origination from loan portfolio; thus the originate-and-distribute model. Indeed, financial institutions were able to use risk management in their attempt to dispose of their loan portfolio. Actually, risk aversion fell sharply.[2] This was fostered by a new financial architecture in the form of securitisation and slicing risk through repackaging subprime mortgages, which were turned into CMOs and CDOs. Furthermore, financial institutions can now provide *risky* loans without applying the three Cs: Collateral, Credit history and Character (person or institution able to pay the loan off even in hard times). This fostered a new activity that relied on interlinked securities mainly emerging from, and closely related to, the subprime mortgage market. Subprime mortgage is a financial innovation designed to extend home ownership to risky borrowers. The term refers to borrowers who are perceived to be riskier than the average borrower because of their poor credit history. Rising home prices encouraged remortgaging, thereby expanding the subprime mortgage market substantially. The growth of loans in the subprime mortgage market was substantial. As a percentage of total mortgages we had the following phenomenal increase: 1994: 5 per cent;

1996: 9 per cent; 1999: 13 per cent; 2006: 20 per cent; 2007: 47 per cent. It should also be noted that between 1998 and 2007 mortgage debt as a percentage of disposable income increased by more than 50 per cent – from 61 per cent to 101 per cent.

Banks proceeded to set up trusts or limited liability companies with small capital bases, i.e. separate legal entities, known as Structural Investment Vehicles (SIVs). Parallel banking was thereby created outside the control and the regulatory umbrella of the authorities. This SIVs operation was financed by borrowing from the short end of the capital markets at a rate linked to the interbank interest rate. The short-term capital thereby raised was used by the SIVs to buy the risky segment of the loan portfolio of the mother company, mainly risky mortgages. The risky loan portfolio was then repackaged in the form of CMOs and CDO and sold to other banks and the personal sector. So long as the short-term rate of interest was lower than the long-term rate, and along with the high commissions charged, big profits were secured, and the housing market turned into a bubble. When the yield curve was inverted, that is long-term interest rates became lower than short-term rates, the sub-prime mortgage market simply collapsed. It occurred following a period of a policy of rising interest rates (mid-2004 to mid-August 2007) after a prolonged period of abnormally low interest rates (initially 1997–98 but more aggressively after the internet bubble of March 2000 but more so after November 2001, until central banks began to raise interest rates in 2005). It is true that after the internet bubble collapsed in March 2000 there was considerable fear, especially in the US, that this might lead to price deflation. This, along with the apparent world glut of savings (Bernanke, 2005), led to the period of low nominal policy interest rates as just suggested. The collapse of the subprime mortgage market by mid-2007 also meant the end of the housing boom and the burst of the housing bubble. Defaults on mortgages spread to investment banks and commercial banks in the US and across the world via the elaborate network of CMOs and CDOs.

The complex structure of the CMO and CDO markets complicated the task of credit rating institutions, which erroneously assigned AAA-status to many worthless papers. In fact some 80 per cent of the total value of CMOs and CDOs were rated as having AAA credit rating, thereby treated as completely safe (Goodhart, 2009). The overstated credit rating contributed to the growth of the CMO and CDO markets in the upswing but also to its downfall in the downswing. In the aftermath of the subprime crisis in the US, credit rating agencies were blamed for their high initial ratings of structured finance securities in that they did not reflect the true risks inherent in those securities. This unfortunate episode emerged in view of the credit rating agencies that rated only the credit default risk and not market or liquidity risk. For example, government debt with a rating of AAA had a different and superior overall quality as compared with the AAA of CMOs and CDOs. Many lenders who bought CMOs and CDOs were under the impression that all three types of risks were included in the rating of these tranches. They were, thus, confusing the AAA rating of government bonds and CMOs/CDOs. It may very well be the case, though, that rating agencies got this assessment of the credit default wrong. Although there is no evidence of this proposition, it may very well be the case that insufficient competition amongst the credit rating agencies means that they are not beyond reproach (Goodhart, 2009, chapter 2). A policy debate has been triggered about the need to strengthen the regulatory framework for credit rating agencies; the G20 London agreement of April 2009 contains relevant regulatory provisions.

The sale of CMOs and CDOs to international investors made the US housing bubble a global problem and provided the transmission mechanism for the contagion to the rest of the world. The collapse of the subprime market spilled over into the real economy through the credit crunch and collapsing equity markets in August 2007. Although it must be said that the first signs of the problem may be dated as early as March 2007, when US subprime investors announced major losses. Be that as it may, a breakdown of trust between the financial sector and households occurred, most specifically in the case of the subprime mortgage holders. As the losses on these mortgages and other toxic assets accumulated, banks lost trust between themselves, which led to the freezing of the interbank lending market in the second half of 2007. These problems further constrained the ability of the banking sector to lend to the real economy. Bank failures ensued, and are still taking place, which further eroded the ability of banks to lend. Then credit conditions in the real economy tightened further leading to corporate distress due to a lack of bank credit; trade credit provided between firms also dried up. This all emerged during the course of 2008, especially after the collapse of the Lehman Brothers in September 2008. Not only did the events just described take place within countries, but also amongst countries. All in all, a significant and synchronous global severe downturn is well with us by now: the 'great recession'. The seriousness of the economic situation can be further highlighted by the estimated $4.1 trillion losses in the world financial system, less than half of which has been formally written off. No wonder central banks around the world have initiated unconventional monetary policies to help their financial markets to overcome their financial difficulties (see, for example, Borio and Disyatat, 2009). Not to mention the attempts by governments around the globe, with different degrees of intervention and enthusiasm, to contain the depth of the crisis through 'stimulus packages', both fiscal and monetary, and to revive the real economy (see, for example, Arestis and Karakitsos, 2010a). The analysis so far has been concerned with the cause of the crisis. As mentioned above, two other factors contributed to the crisis and we turn our attention to these next. We begin with the international imbalances followed by a discussion of monetary policy aspects.

2.3 International imbalances

The process described so far was also accentuated by the international imbalances, which were built up over a decade or more prior to the crisis. The rise of China and of many other parts in Asia in particular, and the strategy they adopted to expand manufactured exports to create employment, produced high growth rates as a result. In some cases, that growth rate was more than double that of the developed world. Consumption was restrained in view of inadequate consumer finance, thereby creating a great deal of savings. Substantial trade surpluses emerged in these countries, which helped to keep total demand in line with supply. By contrast, countries importing these manufactured goods ran trade deficits and required low saving rates to balance their economies. As a result, high-saving countries created employment and low-saving countries enjoyed faster consumption growth in view of cheap imports.

The 'privilege' enjoyed by the US dollar as the world's currency encouraged and enabled that amount of savings to be channelled mainly into the US, helping to put downward pressure on US interest rates. Furthermore, the increasing allocation of manufacturing jobs to the relatively low-wage areas of Asia, and China in particular, where a well-educated low-cost workforce protected by the rule of law, and combined with developed world technology, helped to suppress the level of wages and hence lower inflationary pressures in the US and elsewhere. This, along with the channelling of savings into the US, also enabled the US low-to-mid-income households to increasingly rely on credit as a means of survival.

These factors, in particular the massive flows of capital into western financial markets, especially the US, pushed down interest rates, which along with the low interest rate policy pursued by the Fed over the same period, encouraged risk-taking on an extraordinary scale, and enabled US households to live well beyond their means. Low interest rates at the same time helped to push up asset prices, especially house prices, thereby enabling the financial sector to explode. Banks expanded their balance sheets substantially; and as King (2010) put it: 'In the five years up to 2007, the balance sheets of the largest UK banks nearly trebled. The build-up of risk came to threaten the stability of the entire financial system' (p. 4). The explosion of the banking sector enabled lending to households and businesses to expand substantially along with lending to other banks. All these imbalances created a more buoyant market for financial institutions thereby feeding the originate-and-distribute culture and machine (see Arestis and Karakitsos, 2010a for further details).

One important lesson follows from this experience, which is that the interests of the private financial sector are inconsistent with those of the economy as a whole. Consequently, the regulation of the financial sector by bodies accountable to the public should be carefully considered and implemented. Such required reform should, of course, entail regulation and relevant restructuring not merely of the domestic banking system but also of the international monetary system. We consider the issue of domestic regulation below. It is, though, imperative to consider the possibility of regulating the international monetary system at this juncture in view of the analysis in this subsection. Global imbalances contributed to previous crises, and were an important item on the agenda at the Bretton Woods conference in 1944. Indeed, Keynes (1980) recognised the asymmetry of the obligations imposed on the countries involved with the problem of adjusting international imbalances. Keynes (op. cit.) argues, 'To begin with, the social strain of an adjustment downwards is much greater than that of an adjustment upwards' but also

> the process of adjustment is *compulsory* for the debtor and *voluntary* for the creditor. If the creditor does not choose to make, or allow, his share of the adjustment, he suffers no inconvenience. For whilst a country's reserve cannot fall below zero, there is no ceiling which sets an upper limit. The same is true for international loans if they are to be the means of adjustment. The debtor *must* borrow; the creditor is under no such compulsion. (p. 6)

In terms of the current international imbalances they have been allowed to continue for a long period in view of the privileged position of the

US as the issuer of the world's reserve currency. The 'great recession' experience clearly implies that designing an international monetary system to avoid the problems alluded to by Keynes (1980) is long overdue.

A way forward is Keynes's (1980) proposal for an International Currency Union (ICU) with member central banks holding 'clearing accounts' in a new institution, the International Clearing Bank (ICB). The latter would issue 'bank money', the bancor. Each national currency would have a fixed, but adjustable, relation to the bancor. Residual international transactions would be settled through these accounts. The object of the ICB would be to maintain balance-of-payments equilibria between each of its members and the rest of the world. Persistent over-drafts and credits in the ICB's accounts would reflect deficits and surpluses in the balance-of-payments accounts of the countries involved. The aim of the ICU framework should be to bring simultaneous pressure on surplus countries to reduce their surpluses, and on deficit countries to reduce their deficits. This aim was reflected in the rules designed to govern the quantity and distribution of bancors. An important ingredient of this proposal is the suggestion 'that central control of capital movements, both inward and outward, should be permanent feature of the post-war system'; and this should be 'part of a uniform multilateral agreement by which movements of capital can be controlled *at both sides*' (Keynes, 1980, p. 52). Under current arrangements the best mechanism whereby this can be achieved is through the IMF in close collaboration with the G20 (which produces almost 90 per cent of global GDP). In April 2009, the G20 agreed to a new policy coordination framework with the IMF. This could become the platform for a new initiative along the lines just suggested.

2.4 Monetary policy

The other feature suggested earlier is the particular monetary policy pursued over the period of the financial innovations as described above. More specifically, this feature springs from the focus of economic policy, and monetary policy in particular, on price stability, and inflation targeting as the main framework of this type of policy, at the exclusion of any other objectives. Monetary policy is thereby geared to frequent interest rate changes as a vehicle to controlling inflation. It should be noted, though, that the US monetary authorities never pursued inflation targeting as the theoretical framework requires. The constitution of the Fed requires the pursuit of monetary policy for the achievement of a number of objectives, not merely that of price stability. The latter objective is required by the inflation targeting theoretical framework and adopted by the inflation targeting countries. Still, manipulating the rate of interest has been at the forefront of monetary policy in the US.

The impact of this policy has been the creation of enormous liquidity and household debt in the major economies, which reached unsustainable magnitudes and helped to promote the current crisis.[3] This was particularly so after the burst of the IT bubble in March 2000 when central banks, led by the Fed, pursued highly accommodative monetary policies to avoid a deep recession. Looking at debt statistics (see, BIS, 2008, p. 29), we find the following: between 1998 and 2002 outstanding household debt, including mortgage debt, in the UK was 72.0 per cent of GDP; between 2003 and 2007 it shot to 94.3 per cent of GDP; in the same periods, outstanding household debt jumped from 76.7 per cent to GDP to 97.6 per cent of GDP in the case of the US; and in the euro area from 48.5 to 56.6 per cent respectively. This suggests that while monetary policy did not have a role in causing the crisis it was, nonetheless, largely responsible for its promotion and continuation.

It should be clear that the dominant argument that increased liquidity is always beneficial may not be so wide-ranging. Diminishing marginal utility and associated increased financial activity relative to real economic activity along with speculation create increasing dangers of destabilising herd. This implies that an 'optimal level' of liquidity is evident. However, there is a serious complication in that although 'an optimal level of liquidity, with increased liquidity and speculation valuable up to a point but not beyond that point' there is nonetheless 'the complication for practical policy makers that the point of optimal benefit is impossible to define with any precision, that it varies by market, and that we have highly imperfect instruments through which to gain the benefits without the disadvantages' (Turner, 2010, p. 28). As alluded to above, the enormous liquidity created over the period in view of the monetary policy pursued at the time, must have surpassed the 'optimal level' to which we have just referred.

It is also important to note that the credit part of liquidity was particularly important in promoting the 'Great Recession', as Schularick and Taylor (2009) show. It is the case, though, that policymakers and proponents of the current macroeconomic paradigm, the 'New Consensus' theoretical framework in Macroeconomics, do not take credit and money seriously; they have no role to play in monetary policy. Indeed, the proponents believe firmly that macroeconomic outcomes are independent of any financial factors. They ignore that 'financial factors can have a strong, distinct, and sometimes even dominant impact on the economy' (Schularick and Taylor, op. cit., p. 1).[4] The credit system, though, could potentially have a role in producing financial instability, closely related to the proposition that 'financial crises are credit booms gone wrong', which is often attributed to Minsky (1977). Interestingly enough, Schularick and Taylor (2009) produce evidence that supports this view. Utilising a linear probability model, along with a probit model, conclude 'that a credit boom over the previous five years is indicative of a heightened risk of a financial crisis' (p. 20), and that 'the use of credit aggregates, rather than monetary aggregates, is of crucial importance' a result that leads to the further conclusion that 'credit is a superior predictor, because it better captures important, time-varying features of bank balance sheets such as leverage and non-monetary liabilities' (p. 22). An important implication of these results for monetary policy purposes is that to the extent financial stability is the focus of monetary policy, then a better instrument to focus on is credit aggregates in view of its superior power to predict incipient crises. Even policymakers recognise the importance of the 'credit view' of financial crises. For example the Chairman of the UK's Financial Services Authority has expressed a firm interest in this view along with the suggestion of the importance to regulate credit (see, for example, Turner, 2009).

As a result of these developments, the transmission mechanism of monetary policy has changed: the build up of household debt and asset holdings has made household expenditure more sensitive to short-term interest rate changes. Furthermore, the current high debt levels, combined with the difficulties in the 'real' sector, imply that lenders and equity holders stay away from the marketplace; not forgetting the presence and magnitude of toxic assets, which pose real problems that still need to be sorted out. The dangers with this type of conduct of monetary policy are clear: frequent changes in interest rates can have serious effects: low interest rates cause bubbles; high interest rates work through applying economic pressures on vulnerable social groups. There are, thus, severe distributional effects (see Arestis and Karakitsos, 2010a, for further details).

It should also be noted that monolithic concentration on price stability does not guarantee the stability of the economy (King, 2009; IMF, 2009). In fact, it can lead to economic instability (see, also, Blanchard et al., 2010; Karakitsos, 2010). Indeed, asset bubbles are often preceded by price stability. A few examples make the point very well: the US 1929; Japan 1990s; South East Asia 1997; the US again 2007. In all these cases, price stability was followed by the burst of a bubble. Central banks should move beyond price stability. It is also relevant to note at this point that focusing on interest rate variations to prick a bubble cannot be relied upon. This is so for the simple reason that since such an attempt would require quite substantial changes in the rate of interest, the rest of the economy is bound to be seriously and adversely affected.

We have argued elsewhere that targeting net wealth might be a more appropriate variable to focus on, rather than inflation, for monetary policy purposes (Arestis and Karakitsos, 2010a).[5] A wealth target deals with the consequences of the rise and fall of asset prices on the economy and is not a target of asset prices per se – equities or houses. Net wealth is an ideal variable to monitor (and control) bubbles simply because it is at the heart of the transmission mechanism of asset prices and debt to consumption. Economic policy should be tightened/loosened as the ratio of net wealth to disposable income, over a period of time, is above/below a predetermined threshold. This would allow asset price booms, but it would prevent them from becoming bubbles that will ultimately burst with huge adverse consequences for the economy as a whole. Such an approach will also help regulate financial engineering, since the central bank will monitor the implications of financial innovations as they impact net wealth, even if it is ignorant of them (as in the case of SIVs). Financial engineering is so complex that central banks have a tough time in measuring, monitoring and controlling the total liquidity in the economy. A net wealth target will check the consequences of this liquidity, while not impeding the financial engineering of the banks.

3   Economic policy implications

3.1   Preliminary observations

The obvious initial policy implication is the focus on monetary policy to meet the single objective of inflation should be abandoned. Monolithic concentration on price stability can lead to economic instability (see, also, Blanchard et al., 2010). Coordination of monetary and fiscal policies is vital, along with discretion in applying them. Fiscal policy should be used both in the short term and in the long term to address demand issues. Monetary policy should focus on financial stability.

Financial stability should incorporate both macroprudential and micro-prudential instruments. Both instruments should be under the banner of the policymakers avoiding rules and employing judgement and thus dis-cretion. The macroprudential toolkit should account for the failures of the system: low levels of liquid assets; inadequate levels of capital with which to absorb losses; an overly large financial sector; too leveraged a sector with high risks to the taxpayer and the economy. Thus, macroprudential financial instruments should be able to control the size, leverage, fragility and risk of the financial system. Microprudential instruments relate to the structure and regulation of individual banks. Banks that are 'too big to fail' should be cut down in size; guarantees to retail depositors should be limited to banks with a narrower range of investments; risky banks to taxpayers and economy should face higher capital requirements; large and complex financial institutions can be wound down in an orderly manner; and large banks should not be allowed to combine retail banking with risky investment business. Possibly, combining all the elements just suggested.

These policies should also include 'green elements', in particular because 'green fiscal measures' in the form of 'green investment' as well as 'green-efficiency' measures are most suitable and feasible under current circumstances.

Financial stability appears to be a new type of economic policy, and as such it requires further investigation, especially so in view of the recent initiatives by the US president. This is a very welcome sign. We turn our attention to this development in what follows.

3.2 Financial stability

On Thursday 21 January 2010, President Barack Obama took an important initiative in the right direction in terms of his 'Volcker Rule', which states that 'banks will no longer be allowed to own, invest, or sponsor hedge funds, private equity funds, or proprietory trading operations for their own profit, unrelated to serving their customers'. This amounts to curbing the size and scope of activity of the largest US banks in an attempt to prevent future financial crises. The plan includes limits to the size of banks and restrictions on riskier trading. This is a way of reducing the vast US bank balance sheets built up over the years and also of tackling the contentious issue of the US financial system that is replete with institutions that are 'too big to fail' and have to be rescued by the authorities when crises emerge. The plan contains three important constituent elements.[6]

The first is that size matters. No financial firm should be allowed to become 'too big to fail'. A financial institution that it is too big to regulate and manage is 'a systematically dangerous institution'; such institution should not be allowed to grow.

The second is essentially to eliminate proprietary investments (namely to prohibit banks that take insured deposits from running their own trading operations) and also ownership of hedge funds by banks. This is to avoid the potential for conflicts of interest when a bank is working on behalf of its customers and making its own investments. In this way, deposit-taking banks will not be able to engage in leveraged proprietary trading (i.e. using own funds in investments in search of excess returns), a highly profitable, but exceptionally risky form of business.[7] Nor will they be allowed to own, invest in or sponsor hedge funds or private equity funds. Institutions, whose downside risk is publicly insured, either directly or indirectly, and because they can blackmail the country when they go down, should not undertake this kind of activity. Financial institutions should be limited to investing their customers' funds. In other words, the President's proposals forbid any bank holding deposits that are guaranteed by the government to operate hedge funds, private equity funds or trade on its own account.

The third element is that there must be a restructuring of the financial sector. There are viable small and medium-sized banks that did not fail as a result of the subprime debacle. The big financial institutions serve no public purpose and they are dangerous. US should restore the protections that helped to secure safety under the Glass–Steagall Act.

One might make a couple of comments on these proposals. The obvious point is that the President's proposals appear to be a return to the principles underlying the Glass–Steagall Act of 1933. And this is certainly the modern way forward in terms of Paul Volcker in his written testimony to the Senate Banking Committee on 2 February 2010 clarified this particular point. He suggested that

> The first line of defence… must be authority to regulate certain characteristics of systematically important non-bank financial institutions. The essential need is to guard against excessive leverage and to insist upon adequate capital and liquidity. It is critically important that those (non-financial) institutions… do not assume a public rescue that will be forthcoming in time of pressure.

It, thus, appears to be the case that the crude separation of commercial and investment banks of the Glass–Steagall Act of 1933 is replaced by an equally crude split of the banking business from proprietary trading, hedge funds and private equity. And that banning proprietary trading may well prove to be the modern equivalent of the Glass–Steagall division.

Another point that might be added to these elements is that the US Federal Deposit Insurance Corporation (FDIC) should take the lead to audit all those bad mortgages and mortgage-backed securities at their value. And big banks should be made to shrink under FDIC supervision. It should be noted, though, that the 'Volcker Plan' is narrower than the 1933 Banking Act. The latter did not allow retail banks to underwrite and distribute the securities of private companies. It limited retail banks' ability to invest in securities on their own account and they were not allowed to own brokerage houses. The 'Volcker Plan' aims to limit risky behaviour by not allowing retail banks to engage in proprietary trading. Retail banks are also prohibited from owning or indeed sponsoring hedge funds or private equity funds. It is also the case that the number of institutions in the 'Volcker Plan' is small, four or five have been suggested, and a couple of dozen worldwide. All these are institutions that generated significant revenues from proprietary trading.

Interestingly enough, the ban on proprietary trading presents a unique opportunity for trading revenues to the non-bank sector. Several banks are also active in trading actual shipments of oil, gas, industrial metals and other physical assets. Part of this trading is also speculative in terms of current and future prices. Unlike banks, commodity-trading companies face no rules in their operations. Consequently, the 'Volcker Plan' could present a chance for the trading houses to enlarge their market share in that banks are likely to cut back on this type of trade. However, it is the case that banks are the main dealers of derivatives used to hedge risks in specialised commodity markets. Cutbacks of this type are bound to restrict the liquidity provided by the banks, which is in much demand from the trading houses.

The opponents, the Wall Street institutions lobby, are geared up to fight the President's plan. The Financial Services Forum (FSF), in particular, which represents 18 US top banks, has argued that the President's proposals misdiagnose the causes of the financial crisis; that the proposed separation of commercial banking from investment banking is too complicated and too costly to achieve; that the proposals put jobs at risk, damage US competitiveness and might even threaten growth in the US economy. It has also been proposed that proprietary trading should be limited to a percentage of overall assets or business. Tackling the 'too big to fail' institutions should be undertaken instead through more effective supervision. Establishing a new authority able to wind down failing financial institutions, rather than forcing them to shrink, can achieve this objective. The most frequently used argument against the proposals is that they are far too complicated. Surely though, they cannot be more complicated than the creation of the CDOs, as described and discussed in section 2.1 above. Indeed, compared to the CDOs that caused the crisis, the new proposals are delightfully simple.

No longer would the banks be able to blur the distinction between commercial and investment banks. In any case, ultimately there does not appear to be clear reasons why giant banks are important to the US economy.

An interesting development is that the FDIC and the Bank of England have signed a memorandum of understanding, a cooperation agreement, on 22 January 2010. The aim is to coordinate the unwinding of troubled financial firms and in the process to protect members of the public who rely on multinational financial companies.[8] This is the beginning of what is actually required. Namely, international co-operation to resolve the most complex financial institutions. In this context, the suggestion by King (2010), the Governor of the Bank of England, to merge the G20 and the IMF in an attempt to stop imbalances developing in the world economy is very relevant and apt. This could be achieved, according to King (op. cit.) if the G20 were to metamorphose into a Governing Council for the IMF. The ultimate aim is to endure coordination of economic policy so as to avoid unsustainable imbalances. The IMF and the FSF have proposed taxing large companies to create a global insurance fund. This would be used to rescue relevant institutions in serious difficulties. The counter argument is that such a fund would encourage banks to undertake even riskier activities in the knowledge that they can be rescued. The Basle Committee on Bank Supervision has actually raised capital requirements for proprietary trading and is considering extending it further for the largest institutions.

4 Summary and conclusions

We have dealt with the origins of the current crisis along with its consequences in terms of economic policy. In so doing we have highlighted a number of implications. This analysis suggests that there are economic lessons that emanate from the recent crisis. We discuss these briefly along with their implications for the future conduct of economic policy. In doing so, though, we should not forget Minsky's (1986) dictum: 'instability is determined by mechanisms within the system, not outside it; our economy is not unstable because it is shocked by oil, wars or monetary surprises, but because of its nature' (p. 172). This is an important message, which is the backbone of the analysis of this contribution. Finally, we discuss policies that direct attention to the banking sector as in the recent proposals of the US President, in the form of the so-called 'Volcker Plan'.

Notes

1. Prior to the financial liberalisation period, from around the late 1930s to the early 1970s, there had been direct controls on bank lending and exchange controls on international flows, which may very well have contained the level of innovation and efficiency in the banking sector. But as Bodo et al. (2001) demonstrate that period was free from serious banking crises.

2. This underpricing of risk came about by low-risk spreads whereby the differentials between risky assets and safe assets declined substantially. It came about particularly over the long period 2001–05 of unusually low nominal, and very low real, interest rates. But even over the longer period of the late 1980s/early 1990s to 2007 macroeconomic risks were reduced substantially in view of the 'great moderation' or 'great stability' era of low and stable inflation and steady growth.

3. Interestingly enough, at the 2010 Financial Crisis Inquiry Commission Alan Greenspan argued that the house-price bubble and the subsequent global financial crisis were not caused by the low overnight interest rates of the central banks but by the low long-term mortgage rates. Nor would an attempt by the Fed to rein on the subprime mortgage industry have succeeded; this is so simply because, as Alan Greenspan argued, the Congress would have blocked it – given the widely held view that the industry was bolstering home ownership across the US. In Alan Greenspan's view, higher capital and liquidity requirements for banks and increased collateral requirements for financial products would restrict losses to equity holders only; taxpayers will not be at risk. The severity of future crises would thereby be mitigated.

4. See Arestis (2009) for a comprehensive critique of the 'New Consensus Macroeconomics'.

5. Net wealth is defined as the assets (financial and tangible) less the liabilities of the personal sector, which include mortgage debt and consumer credit.

6. The proposals discussed in the text are broadly similar to those of the former Federal Reserve Bank Governor, and currently Chairman of the Economic Recovery Advisory Board, Paul Volcker. It is for this reason that the proposals of President Barack Obama have been labelled as 'The Volcker Plan'. The proposals require legislation and are likely to be modified in the Congressional negotiations.

7. Proprietory trading refers to the amount of financial investments undertaken by banks with their own cash (and thus bearing the risk of trading losses), in addition to their traditional 'acceptance of deposits and provide loans' activity. Financial investments are held prinarily because they provide more liquidity than loans since, unlike loans, they could be readily sold if needed. Over the past twenty years or so, however, this form of investment has increased substantially – primarily because of their higher expected returns. This form of investment has also been used to create or invest in hedge funds. During the 'Great Recession' banks have suffered a great deal of losses in their proprietory investment and trading books.

8. The US Congress is debating as to whether FDIC should be given the authority to dismantle a wider range of troubled financial institutions – FDIC currently only has authority over depository banks.

References

Arestis, P. (2009) 'New Consensus Macroeconomics and Keynesian Critique', in E. Hein, T. Niechoj and E. Stockhammer (eds), *Macroeconomic Policies on Shaky Foundations – Whither Mainstream Economics?* Marburg: Metropolis-Verlag.

Arestis, P. and Karakitsos, E. (2010a) 'Subprime Mortgage Market and Current Financial Crisis', in P. Arestis, P. Mooslechner and K. Wagner (eds), *Housing Market Challenges in Europe and the United States.* Basingstoke: Palgrave Macmillan.

Arestis, P. and Karakitsos, E. (2010b) *The Post 'Great Recession' US Economy: Implications for Financial Markets and the Economy.* Basingstoke: Palgrave Macmillan.

Bank for International Settlements (BIS) (2008) *Annual Report,* June. Basel, Switzerland: Bank for International Settlements.

Bernanke, B. (2005) 'The Global Saving Glut and the U.S. Current Account Deficit', *The Sandridge Lecture, Virginia Association of Economics.* Richmond, VA. Lecture available at: http://www.federalreserve.gov/boarddocs/speeches/2005/200503102/default.htm.

Blanchard, O., Dell'Ariccia, G. and Mauro, P. (2010) 'Rethinking Macroeconomic Policy', IMF Staff Position Note, SPN/10/03. Washington, DC: International Monetary Fund.

Bordo, M., Eichengreen, B., Klingebiel, D. and Martinez-Perio, M.S. (2001) 'Is the Crisis Problem Going More Severe?', *Economic Policy,* 32, 51–82.

Borio, C. and Disyatat, P. (2009) 'Unconventional Monetary Policies: An Appraisal', *BIS Working Paper No. 292,* Monetary and Economic Department, November. Basel, Switzerland: Bank for International Settlements.

IMF (2009) *World Economic Outlook,* October 2009. Washington, DC: International Monetary Fund.

Karakitsos, E. (2010) 'Bubbles Lead to Long-term Instability', in G. Fontana, J. McCombie and M. Sawyer (eds), *Macroeconomics, Finance and Money: Essays in Honour of Philip Arestis.* Basingstoke: Palgrave Macmillan.

Keynes, J.M. (1980) 'Activities, 1940–1946: Shaping the Post-War World. The Clearing Union', *Collected Writings Vol. 25.* London: Macmillan.

King, M. (2009) Speech at the Lord Mayor's Banquet for Bankers and Merchants of the City of London at the Mansion House, 17 June. Available at: http://www.bankofengland.co.uk/publications/speeches/2009/speech394.pdf.

King, M. (2010) 'Speech', University of Exeter, Tuesday 19 January.

Lansley, S. (2010) 'Unfair to Middling: How Middle Income Britain's Shrinking Wages Fuelled the Crash and Threaten Recovery'. Available at: http://www.tuc.org.uk/economy/tuc-f0.cfm?themeaa=touchstone.

Minsky, H.P. (1977) 'The Financial Instability Hypothesis: an Interpretation of Keynes and Alternative to Standard Theory', *The Challenge Magazine,* March–April, 20–7.

Minsky, H.P. (1982) *Can 'It' Happen Again: Essays on Instability and Finance.* Armonk, NY: M.E. Sharpe.

Minsky, H.P. (1986) *Stabilizing an Unstable Economy.* New Haven, CT: Yale University Press.

Turner, A. (2009) *The Turner Review: A Regulatory Response to the Global Banking Crisis.* London: Financial Services Authority.

Turner, A. (2010) 'What Do Banks Do? What Should They Do and What Public Policies are Needed to Ensure Best Results for the Real Economy?' Speech given at the CASS Business School, 17 March. Available at: http://www.fsa.gov. uk/pubs/speeches/at_17mar10.pdf.

Schularick, M. and Taylor, A. (2009) 'Credit Booms Gone Bust: Monetary Policy, Leverage Cycles and Financial Crises, 1970–2008', *NBER Working Paper No. 15512*. Washington, DC: National Bureau of Economic Research.

3
The Global Economic and Financial Crisis: Which Way Forward?

Ajit Singh and Ann Zammit

1 Introduction

This chapter provides a review and commentary on the current financial and economic crisis. It considers important analytical and policy issues from a global and North–South perspective. The analytical issues include the reasons for the better than expected performance of the world economy following the early period of acute crisis, the role of global financial imbalances, and whether or not economic theory has been helpful in explaining the causes of the crisis. It is argued that close international cooperation and policy coordination are essential to continued recovery and improvement in the distribution of the fruits of growth. Cooperation and financial regulation are particularly necessary in order to prevent international contagion and cascading sovereign debt defaults.

It is generally accepted that the acute phase of the current global financial and economic crisis began in September 2008, with the demise of Lehman Brothers – a leading US investment bank. Eighteen months later, and in the context of the continuing global economic and financial crisis, the following issues require careful analysis:

- Why the world economy has performed so much better than most analysts had expected at the beginning of the crisis.
- Which economic theories, if any, have been helpful in explaining the course of the crisis to date.
- To what extent, if any, were regulatory deficits in the field of finance and global financial imbalances responsible for the crisis?
- How should the world's financial system be organised so as to secure maximum sustainable and equitable growth for the real world economy?

- The question of government debt and of the danger of inflation.
- Other salient policy issues that have come to the fore, including that of the drawing down of sovereign debt.

While the economic significance of the above issues is self-evident, not all can be treated satisfactorily in a single paper, hence only a relatively few issues will be examined in detail.

2 Economic and financial crisis and the global economy

It is generally agreed that difficulties associated with the housing segment of the US property market were the immediate cause of the crisis (see, for example, International Monetary Fund (IMF), 2008a).[1] Complex financial instruments that incorporated subprime house mortgages lost their value as the housing bubble burst following ten years of continuous price rises based on expectations of a continuation of such increases. This housing bubble occurred despite the fact that during the previous two decades the supply of housing had increased appreciably (Solow, 2009). In brief, house prices had risen because interest rates were low and credit was easily available, and prices were expected to continue to increase, much as in the case of the classic tulip mania and bubble in the early seventeenth century when, at its peak, the price of a tulip bulb in Holland was equivalent to that of a three-storey townhouse.

Housing bubbles have occurred many times before in American economic history without leading to an acute economic and financial crisis, let alone in the rest of the world. This episode was different in that it was accompanied by a bubble in US share and other asset prices. Moreover, the bursting of the US housing bubble led to a fall in share prices not only in the US but also around the world. This was due to the much closer integration of world stock markets resulting from the financial globalisation that had occurred in the previous two decades. It is interesting to note that bank losses due to the failure in the subprime mortgage market are estimated to have been around US$250 billion. The consequent financial crisis led to a sharp fall in aggregate world stock market capitalisation of the order of US$26 trillion in one year – nearly one hundred times larger than the losses associated with sub-prime mortgages.[2] Robert Solow (2009) notes that the combined result of the housing and the stock market shocks was a fall in US household wealth from US$64.4 trillion in mid-2007 (before the crisis) to US$51.5 trillion at the end of 2008. Thus US$13 trillion of household wealth disappeared in the space of about one year. As Solow (2009, p. 5) rightly observes:

> Nothing concrete had changed. 'Buildings still stood; factories were still capable of functioning; people had not lost their ability to work or their skills or their knowledge of technology. But a population that thought in 2007 that they had 64.4 trillion dollars with which to plan their lives discovered in 2008 that they have lost 20 per cent of that.'

Many economists date the acute phase of the present crisis to the bankruptcy of Lehman Brothers USA in September 2008. Whether or not the collapse of this important financial institution was the root cause of the crisis, it certainly provided the trigger. In a comparison of the crisis of the 1930s and that beginning in 2008, Christina Romer, currently Chair of the US Council of Economic Advisers, observes: 'In 2008, the U.S. financial system had similarly survived the initial declines in house and stock prices... but the outright failure of Lehman Brothers proved too much for the system. As has been described by many others, the breakdown in funding relationships in the weeks following Lehman's collapse was almost unfathomable. The financial system truly froze...' (Romer, 2009, p. 3).

3 Short- and long-term causes of the crisis

In addition to the literature on the failure of the subprime mortgage market, there is by now a relatively large literature on the other short-term as well as long-term 'causes' of the current economic and financial crisis, referred to above. It is too soon after the events to expect a consensus to emerge on the causes of the crisis – except perhaps on the observation that it had multiple causes. The diverse contributions on this topic have been succinctly and most helpfully summarised by Aiginger (2009, Table 1). For reasons of space only some of the causes listed in Table 3.1 are discussed in the following sections.

3.1 Deficits in regulation

It is widely agreed that a major long-term factor in the making of the crisis was the lack of government regulation, both national and international, of financial institutions in the US and worldwide. In turn, this regulatory deficit appears to have arisen from an ideological faith in the virtues of the free market. It was believed not only that

Table 3.1 Summary table of the causes of the economic and financial crisis

Trigger:	Unsecured loans to US home owners Politically welcomed, cleverly sold Bundled, rated and passed on
Regulation Failures	Underestimation of risks and belief in self-regulation Overwhelmed by innovations and internationalisation Pro cyclciality were supported by rules (mark to market valuation, Basel 2) Oligopoly structure of rating agencies, incompatibilities; stock market listing Neglect of cumulative systemic risks Insufficient regulation of the derivative market, SPV, Hedge Funds
Inflated Expectations of Returns:	Heterogeneity of profits across to countries/businesses/ activities New forms of equity substitutes Leveraging of banks, the firms an consumers
Imprudent in incentive systems/ risk management:	Bonus for short term success, stock options Over-leveraging and hybrid capital Illusion about the benefits of mergers and firm size (market wide oligopolies) Speculation as an attractive career Higher earnings in financial capital relative to real capital Risk free promises from advisors, pension funds in mathematical model
Macro-economic imbalances:	Savings surplus of the emerging Asian countries, oil producers Triple deficit in the USA: trade, budget and savings Insufficient reduction in money supply after the recovery in 2002 Reinvestment of rent-seeking capital in the USA
Aggravating factors:	Bubbles in currency, raw materials, oil and foods stuffs Specialised plus just-in-time relationships with purchasers/subcontractors Short-term view regarding profits; accounting rules; and analyst's reports Shortages of raw materials, energy, food stuffs Unequal income and wealth distribution Provision of loans and then selling them on ('originate to distribute')
Weakness in coordination	IMF, Work Bank, G7, competition policy, tax havens Underestimation of systemic risks

Source: Aiginger (2009).

the market was always efficient but that it was also self-correcting (see further Ormerod, 2010).

Alan Greenspan, the former Chairman of the US Federal Reserve (Head of the Central Banking System and the chief regulator of US monetary policy) in a speech given in April 2005 outlined how innovation had brought about a multitude of new products, speaking approvingly of how such 'improvements have led to a rapid growth in sub-prime mortgage lending' (Greenspan, 2005).

The *New York Times*, reporting on Greenspan's evidence before a 2008 US Congressional Committee, wrote '... Mr. Greenspan conceded error on regulation, stating that he had "put too much faith in the self-correcting powers of free markets... refused to accept blame for the crisis but acknowledged that his belief in deregulation had been shaken"' (Andrews, 2008).

In testifying before the 2010 US Congress Financial Crisis Inquiry Committee (established to investigate the subprime mortgage crisis) Greenspan defended himself against the dual charge that he was responsible for the housing bubble due to his low interest rate policy and for not puncturing the bubble before it had reached a level that would cause serious systemic difficulties. Greenspan suggested that his critics had short memories as many of them had earlier applauded subprime mortgages as being of tremendous benefit to low-income Americans. Furthermore, he suggested that at the time many people would have questioned whether there was indeed a housing bubble and asked how, in any case, the Federal Reserve would know the answer to this question better than the market. He also told the committee that regulators were helpless to stop the economic meltdown and the subprime mortgage crisis (Greenspan, 2010).

The net result of this mindset was the evolution of a largely unregulated parallel banking system performing the functions of banks but without being subject to banking regulations (Krugman, 2008).

Robust responses to Greenspan's arguments have been made by James Galbraith (2010), Paul Krugman (2010) and Robert Solow (2009), among others. They suggest that the securitisation of subprime mortgages through their marketing as a combined financial product was little understood by the market. This, together with complex credit default swaps, as well as several other financial innovations, should be regarded as fraudulent practice that should have been tightly regulated. Krugman (2010) suggests that, had the wide-ranging reforms currently under discussion in the US Congress been in place earlier, 'a handful of lavishly-paid leaders of the financial industry would not have been able to mislead and exploit consumers and investors'.

3.2   World financial imbalances

Apart from the above question of regulatory deficits with respect to the functioning of financial markets, many economists believe that the huge global imbalances in the current accounts of nation-states contribute to financial fragility and crisis. The latter arises because deficits that cannot be financed could result in disorderly and unwanted currency depreciations. Fear of such events may lead to widespread turbulence in financial markets and national economies.

In 2004, the US current account deficit amounted to US$666 billion, comprising 69 per cent of the total deficit of countries running negative current account balances that year (Table 3.2). This compares with a current account deficit of US$413.5 billion in 2000, which accounted for 62.2 per cent of total deficits. In the last quarter of 2005 (using a figure not in Table 3.2) the US deficit was estimated to be around US$700 billion , or 7 per cent of US GDP. Thus before the crisis, an already high US deficit was getting bigger, which, on the face of it, was not a healthy development. Nevertheless, an essential point is that the markets seemed then to have accepted the situation as indicated by the relative stability of exchange rates of the main currencies (see Cooper, 2005 and Summers, 2006).[3] (See below for further discussion on exchange rate stability.)

An RIS (Research and Information System for Developing Countries) 2008 policy brief provides a stark outline of the evolution of the US

Table 3.2   Current account balances (selected economies), 2000–2004

Year		2000	2002	2004	2000	2002	2004
Economies		($ Billion)			(As a percentage of global surplus or deficit)		
Surplus economies	Japan	119.6	112.6	171.8	23.8	21.1	19.3
	Germany	−25.7	43.1	96.4	3.9	8.4	10.0
	China	20.5	35.4	70.0	4.1	6.9	7.9
	Russian Federation	44.6	30.9	59.6	8.9	6.0	6.7
	Saudi Arabia	14.3	11.9	49.3	2.9	2.3	5.5
Deficit Economies	United States	−413.5	−473.9	−665.9	62.2	72.5	69.0
	Spain	−19.4	−15.9	−49.2	2.9	2.4	5.1
	United Kingdom	−36.5	−26.4	−47.0	5.5	4.0	4.9
	Australia	−15.3	−16.6	−39.4	2.3	2.5	4.1
	Italy	−5.8	−6.7	−24.8	0.9	1.0	2.6

Source: Singh (2007). Adapted from IMF, *World Economic Outlook*, April 2005.

international and national financial situation, as follows. In the period 1970–91, the cumulative current account deficit of the US was US$881.5 billion, increasing to US$1,569.3 billion during the period 1992–2000 and in the period 2001–06 it reached US$3,572.5 billion, with a deficit of US$811.5 billion in 2006 alone. In recent years, China's foreign exchange surpluses have financed the growing US current account deficits at low interest rates.[4]

It is important to note, however, that China is not the main, let alone *the* only, economy to run a large current account surplus. In 2004, before the global financial and economic crisis, China's current account surplus of US$70 billion accounted for less than 8 per cent of the total surpluses of countries with a positive current account balance (Table 3.2). Table 3.2 also suggests that in 2004 China's surplus was considerably smaller than that of either Germany or Japan, particularly the latter.

RIS data also indicates that the US has been living 'beyond its means' at both the household and government levels, stretching their respective budget constraints. Household savings that had been about 10 per cent of GDP in 1980 and 7 per cent in 1990 were only 0.4 per cent in 2007. The Federal budget, which had a surplus of US$236.2 billion in 2000, recorded a deficit of US$400 billion in the financial year 2008. Mortgage debt ballooned from US$3.8 trillion in 1980 to US$14.4 trillion in the third quarter of 2007 and consumer credit increased from US$0.35 trillion in 1980 to US$2.5 trillion in 2007. By financing the recurring current account deficits through borrowing from abroad, the US became a net debtor to the outside world, with the net investment position showing a negative balance of US$2.5 trillion in 2006.

The US has been both living beyond its means yet growing faster than other advanced industrial countries such as Germany and Japan who are living within their means. Paradoxically, therefore, the international financial system appears to favour profligacy rather than thrift. Further, capital has been flowing from developing to developed countries (from China to the US, for example), that is, in a direction contrary to that which might be deemed appropriate from a development perspective.

Even those who do not regard global imbalances (particularly those of China and the US) to be the root cause of the crisis acknowledge that re-balancing is required, principally involving the elimination of high long-term deficits (as in the US) and persistent high surpluses (as in China). In policy terms this means achieving a zero current account deficit at the rate of growth of GDP that would achieve full employment.

In the case of the US, over the four-year period 2007–10, the current account deficit declined from 5.2 per cent of GDP in 2007 to 2.2 per cent in 2010 (IMF, 2009a, 2009b). This reduction was the result of the compression of economic activity during the recession and the deficit may well grow again as there is a resumption of economic growth.

China's surplus, on the other hand, has remained more or less constant over the four-year period 2007–10, amounting to 11 per cent of GDP in 2007 and an average of 8 per cent over the next three years (UNDESA, 2010). Its optimal surplus would be that which corresponded to the full employment level of the economy and desired growth of real wages. In the cases of both the US and China, this rebalancing may require a considerable change in the economic structure: in the former this will involve a greater emphasis on exports and a lower level of consumption and imports; in the latter, it will mean a lower level of exports and higher domestic consumption of both imports and domestic goods. Such rebalancing is likely to affect all countries, whether or not they have contributed significantly to the global imbalances.

In order to achieve wider rebalancing of the world economy it is also necessary to consider the cases of Japan and Germany as these are also long-term surplus countries (Akyuz, 2010).

Apart from the trade and current account imbalances, there is another major imbalance in the global economy that requires urgent resolution. This concerns the distribution of both personal and functional income and their implications for aggregate consumption and aggregate demand. Under globalisation, the power of workers in most advanced countries has been sharply reduced while that of capital has increased due largely to the free movement of capital. As a consequence, real wage growth has been lower than productivity growth. This process threatens to result in global under-consumption which, other things being equal, will reduce the levels of both growth and employment.

To conclude, there is a need to redress imbalances between consumption and investment in major economies. However, it must be noted that, despite a long-standing and growing US current account deficit, there has been no crisis in the sense of a disorderly devaluation of the dollar. This leads some to reject the notion of financial imbalances being a major cause of the crisis, pointing to the fact that there was no run on the dollar. Opponents of this view suggest that the crisis that emerged in 2008 was the result of uncontrolled US deficits. They further allege that the US took advantage of the US dollar being the world's only reserve currency such that its current account deficits went unchecked.

4   Why has the world economy performed better than expected?

As Christina Romer (Romer 2009) argues, the shocks that hit the US economy in the autumn of 2008 were at least as large as those experienced in 1929. A salient shock in both crises was the fall in household wealth: this fell by 17 per cent between December 2007 and December 2008 in the US. This was more than five times the decrease in 1929.

An important negative feature of the current crisis compared with that of the 1930s is the role and nature of banks and the collapse of interbank relations and that of trade credit for big and small businesses. Banks have refused to lend to other banks or to non-bank financial institutions. Similarly asset price volatility in the US has been greater in the current crisis than in the past, and there is evidence that this is so in other advanced countries. A great deal of research indicates that such volatility has an adverse effect on the level of investment. Notwithstanding these negative factors, the actual outcomes during the current crisis have fortunately been more benign so far.

During the Great Depression, starting in the late 1920s, the peak-to-trough decline in GDP in the major economies averaged nearly 12 per cent, ranging from 30 per cent in the US and Canada to somewhat under 10 per cent in Japan, Italy and Britain. The depressed state of the economy continued until the beginning of the Second World War (Llewellyn, 2008).

In the current downturn, falls in GDP in the US, Europe and the world economy have been of a much lower order. Although the numbers of unemployed, underemployed and discouraged workers have increased during the current crisis, the rise has been far less than during the 1930s depression. Further, there are signs that it is unlikely to amount to more than 10 per cent of the labour force, and there is evidence that it is decreasing.[5]

In 2009, for the first time in 50 years, world GDP shrank, but only by 2 per cent, and was expected to return to positive growth in 2010 (UNDESA, 2009). Whether or not this growth is sustained and leads to the resumption of the previous growth path is as yet an open question. The answer will depend on a number of factors, including the debt and solvency crises in Greece, Spain, and Ireland. Although the decline in GDP for individual advanced countries has been greater than that for the world as a whole, none of these have reached the proportions of the 1930s depression. The greatest reduction in GDP growth in 2009 in individual advanced countries has ranged between 2 per cent and 6 per cent. Furthermore, IMF data and projections indicate that most countries will have positive growth in 2010 (IMF, 2009c).

What explains the seeming ability of the world economy to avert a depression as serious as that in the 1930s? Evidence and analysis suggest three main reasons. The first is the outstanding record of India, China and other emerging countries both before and during the crisis. As Wolf (2008) suggests: 'emerging economies had been an engine of growth for the past five years. China accounted for a quarter: Brazil, Russia and India for another quarter, and all emerging and developing countries together for about two thirds. World growth is measured here in PPP exchange rates'. Despite the crisis these countries, particularly India and China, have been able to continue on their fast long-term growth path. They may therefore be expected to remain a long-term positive factor in the evolution of the world economy: fast growth in these countries helps the US and other economies by maintaining high levels of world demand.

The second major factor explaining the relatively good performance of the world economy during the present downturn has been the unexpected and welcome degree of cooperation between countries, symbolised by their adoption of coordinated global measures through the creation of the G20. This grouping includes all leading advanced countries and a number of emerging nations that together constitute about 85 per cent of world production and about two-thirds of the world population. In 2009 the G20 agreed to a huge international stimulus even when many of them already had fiscal deficits. It was also agreed to cut interest rates and to strengthen the IMF and World Bank in order to help developing countries. This high degree of cooperation stands in striking contrast to the lack of cooperation and 'beggar-thy-neighbour' policies that characterised nation-states' behaviour in the 1930s.[6]

As mentioned above, a significant feature of the response to the current crisis has been an aggregate coordinated fiscal stimulus amounting in 2008–09 to an enormous US$2.6 trillion, equivalent to 3.4 per cent of world GDP (see Table 3.3).[7] As a proportion of their GDP, developing countries in general have had a greater stimulus than developed countries.

There is evidence that the stimulus has been successful in the sense that, in general, the greater the stimulus received, the greater was countries' economic growth (US Council of Economic Advisers, 2010). Nevertheless, alongside this positive effect of the stimulus, the stimulus created fiscal difficulties for governments, leading to calls for the

Table 3.3 Fiscal stimulus to address the global financial and economic crisis[a]

	Share of GDP (percentage)	Fiscal stimulus (billions of US dollars)		Share of GDP (percentage)	Fiscal stimulus (billions of US dollars)
Argentina	1.2	3.9	Luxembourg	3.6	2.0
Australia	4.7	47.0	Malaysia	5.5	12.1
Austria	4.5	18.8	Mexico	2.1	22.7
Bangladesh	0.6	0.5	Netherlands	1.0	8.4
Belgium	1.0	4.9	New Zealand	4.2	5.4
Brazil	0.2	3.6	Nigeria	0.7	1.6
Canada	2.8	42.2	Norway	0.6	2.9
Chile	2.4	4.0	Peru	2.6	3.3
China	13.3	585.3	Philippines	4.1	7.0
Czech Republic	1.8	3.9	Poland	2.0	10.6
			Portugal	1.2	3.0
Denmark	2.5	8.7	Russian Federation	1.2	20.0
Egypt	1.7	2.7			
Finland	3.5	9.5	Saudi Arabia	12.5	60.0
France	1.3	36.2	Singapore	5.8	10.6
Georgia	10.3	1.3	Slovenia	1.0	0.5
Germany	2.2	80.5	South Africa	1.5	4.2
Honduras	10.6	1.5	Spain	0.9	15.3
Hong Kong SAR[b]	5.2	11.3	Sri Lanka	0.2	0.1
			Sweden	2.8	13.4
Hungary	10.9	17.0	Switzerland	0.5	2.5
India	3.2	38.4	Taiwan Province of China	3.9	15.3
Indonesia	1.4	7.1			
Israel	1.4	2.8	Thailand	14.3	39.0
Italy	0.7	16.8	Turkey	5.2	38.0
Japan	6.0	297.5	United Kingdom	1.4	38.0
Kazakhstan	13.8	18.2	United Republic of Tanzania	6.4	1.3
Kenya	0.9	0.3			
Korea, Republic of	5.6	53.4	United States	6.8	969.0
			Viet Nam	9.4	8.4
Lithuania	1.9	0.9			
			All 55 economies	4.7	
			World	4.3	2,633

Source: UNDESA various years, based on information from various source. Note that the definition and contents of the policy measures vary from country to country so that the size of the stimulus packages may not be fully comparable across countries.
[a] This list of countries and economies is not exhaustive.
[b] Special Administrative Region of China.

stimulus to be withdrawn or diminished in size. This would, however, be a serious mistake as a premature withdrawal of the stimulus when the world economy has not yet achieved reasonable economic growth (let alone reverted to its long-term growth rate) may push economies further into recession or even into full-scale depression if there are negative effects on expectations. It is therefore all the more important that the cooperation achieved so far in the G20 arrangement should continue and improve so that there is a coordinated and well organised withdrawal of the fiscal stimulus at the appropriate time. The US experience between 1937 and 1940 (Romer, 2009) and that of Japan more recently should be a warning to present-day policymakers in this respect.

The third positive factor that has also helped improve the performance of the world economy in relation to the present crisis can be described as an issue of governance. It so happened that economic leadership in the US in this period was held by an intellectually and politically close group of conventional (US) Keynesian economists who defined the essential problem facing the world economy as being that of a shortage of aggregate demand, in contrast to, for example, the more radical Cambridge Keynesians. Unlike the Chicago economists, they believed that government-induced stimuli could correct the demand deficits and thereby help the real economy.[8] The cohesive economic outlook of this team of economic advisors helped ensure clarity of purpose in the stimulus programme and its implementation.

Not only were these economists well-versed in economic theory, but also, if not more importantly, some of them, including Ben Bernanke (Chairman of the Federal Reserve) and Christina Romer (Chair, US Council of Economic Advisers), were serious students of the history of the Great Depression and were determined not to repeat the serious policy mistakes made during that period.

To sum up, three factors – namely continuing fast growth in India, China and other developing countries, unprecedented cooperation between countries symbolised by the G20 (see further, below) and the creation and governance by like-minded people of a corrective economic policy programme – have been positive factors in the recent evolution of the world economy. Hopefully, these factors will continue to operate in this direction, even if certain other developments present obstacles to widespread resumption of reasonable growth rates. As will become clear in the following sections, currency volatility, fiscal deficits and the premature drawing-down of sovereign debt can have a negative impact on the rate of growth.

5   Financial globalisation and the real economy

The financial system and the conduct of monetary policy prior to the eruption of the financial crisis and the onset of economic recession in 2008 have received thoroughly deserved criticism for allowing the development of the subprime mortgage bubble, the stock market bubble and asset prices bubbles and not puncturing these in time or minimising the damage. There were, however, some evident benefits, albeit unintended, of this regime for the real economy and which have not been adequately recognised (see below). Without a more balanced picture of the merits and demerits of the pre-crisis financial system and policies, future policy decisions may not be the most appropriate.

Table 3.4 provides broad-brush data for selected countries and for the real economy during the last two decades. What is clear is that the world economy performed exceptionally well in real terms during the present decade, achieving arguably its highest ever growth rate. Further, between 2000 and 2007, developing countries grew at almost twice

Table 3.4   Growth of world output and that of selected countries and regions, 1991–2007 (% per annum)

	1991–2001	2001–2007	2002	2003	2004	2005	2006	2007
World	3.1	3.3	1.9	2.7	4.0	3.4	3.9	3.8
Japan	1.1	1.8	0.3	1.4	2.7	1.9	2.4	2.1
US	3.5	2.7	1.6	2.5	3.6	3.1	2.9	2.2
European Union	2.4	2.1	1.2	1.3	2.5	1.8	3.0	2.9
Germany	1.8	1.2	0.0	−0.2	1.2	0.9	2.9	2.5
United Kingdom	2.8	2.6	2.1	2.7	3.3	1.9	2.8	3.0
Russian Federation	–	6.7	4.7	7.3	7.1	6.4	6.7	8.1
Africa	2.9	5.2	3.7	4.9	5.4	5.7	5.6	5.8
Latin American and the Caribbean	3.1	4.0	−0.5	2.2	6.2	4.9	5.6	5.7
East Asia	7.8	8.1	7.4	7.1	8.3	8.0	8.8	9.1
China	10.3	10.4	9.1	10.0	10.1	10.4	11.1	11.4
India	5.9	8.0	3.6	8.3	8.5	8.8	9.2	9.7

Sources: UNCTAD (2008, 2009, 2010); UNDESA (May 2008).

the rate of developed countries. This helped to marginally reduce the disparity between the rich and poor countries. Among developing countries India and China – the two most populous countries where the bulk of the population hitherto lived in absolute poverty – had stellar performances, experiencing historically unprecedented growth that has resulted in substantial poverty reduction.[9]

Among the developed countries, the United States has been the leader in terms of real economic growth. Evidence suggests that in the period 1995–2003 it achieved a one percentage point increase in its long-term trend rate of growth of productivity. This is an impressive achievement bearing in mind that this is not a 'catch-up' economy but one operating at the frontiers of knowledge. Such a productivity increase implies a high degree of technical progress as well as concomitant organisational changes. This achievement would be considered even greater if the benefits of national productivity growth had been spread more widely.

Evidence suggests that the US, India, China and a clutch of other countries – the pre-crisis top performers in terms of growth rates – were overall beneficiaries of international economic integration and financial globalisation. In the case of India and China, this was partly due to the fact that they managed their integration into the global economy so as to avoid the harmful effects of unfettered capital flows in particular. They also pursued a policy of 'strategic integration' in relation to trade and long-term investment (Singh, 2010).

Financial globalisation enabled China to purchase US Treasury bills, thereby helping the US to finance its current account deficit and keep US interest rates low. In addition, globalisation has helped the US to keep domestic inflation in check, not least through imports of cheap consumer and intermediate products from China. (For a fuller discussion of the economic interactions between the US and the Chinese economy, see Singh, 2007. See also IMF, 2008b).

Table 3.5 Explaining the productivity surge in the US

Average annual growth	1973–95	1995–2003	Difference
Labour productivity	1.49	3.06	1.57
O/w capital deepening	0.89	1.75	0.86
Labour quality	0.26	0.17	–0.09
Total factor productivity	0.34	1.14	0.80

Source: Jorgenson, Ho and Stiroh (2007).

Most students of financial systems would agree that the central purpose is to allocate society's savings and investment resources to those households, corporations and jurisdictions that can use them most effectively. It could be argued that the pre-crisis financial system and monetary policies were performing that function, as is evidenced by very fast growth across the world economy during the period 2000–07. However, the implosion resulting from dubious policies and unregulated practices highlight inherent flaws in this system. These rendered it unsustainable. The best that can be said about the pre-crisis financial regime is that it demonstrated that the world economy had a growth potential of at least 5 per cent a year on the supply side.

The purpose of any reform of the financial system should be to allow the world economy to grow at its full potential in a sustainable manner. It would be a travesty of justice from the perspective of the world's poor if any reformed financial system fell short of the sustainable growth objective.

To sum up, it could be argued that the developing world under the recent global regime has taken a giant step forward. A reformed international financial system must underpin and further promote this economic progress.

6   Economic theory and the current crisis

Economists' analyses and conclusions relating to one particular crisis are not necessarily relevant to another. The analytical lessons derived from the Latin American debt crisis of the 1980s do not explain the following crisis that erupted in Asia in the 1990s. Similarly, the lessons of the Asian crisis of the 1990s do not seem to be applicable to the current financial crisis.

The 1980s debt crisis had a devastating impact on Latin America. It is widely agreed that for the continent as a whole it was a 'lost decade' characterised by little or no growth and a fall in per capita income of more than 15 per cent over the decade. In contrast, per capita income in East Asian countries grew by more than 50 per cent during this period. There is sharp contention between orthodox and heterodox economists regarding the reasons for the enormous differences in the performance of these two regions. Orthodox economists argue that the Latin America debt crisis was caused by domestic factors, namely microeconomic inefficiencies, macroeconomic policy errors, and unwise borrowing and spending. In contrast heterodox economists believe that the Latin American debt crisis was due to external factors over which these countries had no control. In particular, they emphasise the changes in US monetary policy in the late 1970s that resulted in an increase in the real world interest rate from 0.5 per cent in the mid-1970s to 7 per cent in the early 1980s – a fourteenfold increase – (the so-called 'Volcker shock'). The impact on the highly indebted Latin American economies was devastating.

Heterodox economists argue that the restrictive changes in US monetary policy had a greater impact on Latin America than on Asia. This was due in part to Latin America's higher initial level of debt and its structure. In addition, Latin America was more strongly affected by adverse changes in the terms of trade than was Asia.[10] Further, as Fishlow (1991) points out, Latin American countries, unlike Asian countries, were subject to capital supply shocks due to contagion. Taken together, as they should be, these shocks were far greater for Latin America than for Asia. Hence Latin American countries became more heavily balance-of-payments constrained and for a much longer period than did the Asian countries. This explains their relatively poor economic performance in the 'lost decade' (Singh, 1993). Thus it is argued that the budget and current account deficits in Latin America were both the cause and consequence of their debt crisis.

The 1997–2000 Asian crisis was of a rather different kind than that which took place in Latin America. By and large, governments in Asia have had a record of managing their macroeconomic policies well. It was the private sector's excessive borrowing in foreign currency and the consequent mismatch between expected inflows and outflows that led to the Asian crisis. It could be said to have been a case of government virtue and private sector profligacy. However, leading US officials, including Alan Greenspan, Larry Summers, and the IMF itself, later put forward a more ideological explanation for the Asian crisis. They argued that, although some micro- or macroeconomic disequilibria (such as the Bangkok property boom) may have been the trigger for the crisis, the root cause was nothing less than the entire 'Asian way of doing business'. This was characterised by close relationships between government, business and finance in the day-to-day microeconomic behaviour of economic agents, what these critics termed 'crony capitalism'. This is alleged to have resulted in serious distortions in the economy and in economic management, leading ultimately to the crisis. (See Glen and Singh (2005) for a fuller discussion of these issues.)

This version of events is highly disputed by heterodox economists. They argue that the root cause of the crisis was the introduction of financial liberalisation before prudential regulation had been instituted. They point out that other countries, including China and India, which did not fully liberalise their financial sectors escaped the crisis, whereas countries that did (Indonesia, Korea, Thailand) were badly affected. In sum, it is suggested here that the Asian crisis was due to financial liberalisation and the absence of prudential regulation; in other words, rather than 'too much government' in this instance it was a case of too little government.

The essential point, however, is to emphasise that each economic and financial crisis has its own particular characteristics. One hallmark of the present crisis has been the credit crunch, whereby banks stopped lending to other banks and businesses, thereby disrupting the system of credit that oils the workings of a modern economy. In response, governments resorted to bailing out banks and other financial institutions that were deemed too big to be allowed to fail, in the sense that their failure would have enormous external diseconomies for other firms and institutions.

Thus, analyses of major financial crises during the past four decades are not directly applicable to the current crisis. Each crisis has been different from the one before. Every major crisis therefore needs to be examined in its own right with a fresh eye, before any firm analytical and policy conclusions can be drawn from that experience.

In addition to analyzing crisis episodes it is essential to examine the role of macroeconomic theory as currently taught in universities and used by policymakers in central banks in explaining and tackling the present crisis. Neither academic macroeconomists nor the best central bank practitioners foresaw the eruption of the 2008 financial crisis. The two main rival schools of thought (the US Keynesian and the Chicago classical) that currently dominate macroeconomic theory have recently found common ground on key aspects of macroeconomic theory. Both sides have accepted the 'rational expectations' basis of the microeconomic theory that underlies the macro construction. In sum, it is assumed that households maximise utility, firms maximise profits and economic agents make decisions on the basis of rational expectations. These ideas have led to sophisticated dynamic stochastic general equilibrium models (DSGE) that are so complex that they cannot be solved analytically. Rather, they require numerical methods and considerable computer power for their solution. Nevertheless, such models have been singularly unhelpful in predicting the current crisis. It is convincingly argued by Ormerod (2010) that these models are based on risk calculations but do not take into account uncertainty. (Risk is predictable in the sense that the probability distribution of future outcomes can be estimated. This is not so at all for uncertainty.) Ormerod (2010) observes: 'in the brave new world of DSGE, the possibility of a systemic collapse, of a cascade of defaults across the system, was never considered'.

Nevertheless, when it came to devising the policy response to the crisis, key policymakers gained greater wisdom from basic Keynesian economic theory and from economic history than from modern macro-economics. US and European economic advisors and policymakers drew on the former and defined the essential problem of the crisis in terms of a shortage of world aggregate demand, and referred to the economic history of the Great Depression to avoid the policy mistakes of that period. It is commonly believed that the failure of several thousand banks in the US in the 1930s contributed to the prolongation of the Great Depression. This explains the priority given to saving the financial system through unprecedented bailouts.[11] Similarly, the success of the giant economic stimulus programmes associated with the New Deal suggested that similar measures should be used once again to a avert a worsening recession.

7 Conclusion: the way forward

The ongoing policy collaboration between countries provides one of the chief grounds for optimism. Nevertheless, there are well-founded criti-cisms regarding the legitimacy of the exclusive G20 group. Many G20 members are disappointed with the process because the G7 have yet to agree on meaningful reform of the IMF Articles of Agreement, including the weighting of voting power (Chin 2010; and Helleiner and Kirshner 2009). Nevertheless, the G20 process remains a promising start to more meaningful international cooperation.

It has been argued that agreement among the G20 has been entirely due to the recent adverse circumstances and that, once the world econ-omy recovers, collective action will cease. However, on a priori grounds, an equally if not more plausible scenario is that the evident success of collective action will encourage nation-states to take further coordi-nated action. Indeed, it can be argued that international cooperation is imperative if global imbalances are to be corrected.

Although the world economy's growth path for the period 2000–07 was ultimately unsustainable, due in part to the rising US current account deficit and in part to the weaknesses of the financial system, such growth certainly took the global economy a long way forward in various respects. The important issue now is which factors will deter-mine the outcome for the real world economy in the next decade or two after the crisis? Will there be a new growth path and will it be more or less satisfactory than the previous one, from an economic, social and environmental point of view? What is required is a growth path that allows the world economy to operate at its full sustainable potential, while reducing the risks of renewed global financial fragility and crisis.

The central message of this contribution is that, for this to be possible, increasing global cooperation is essential in trade and investment and in the related fields of food, environment and energy. Equally importantly, a more equal distribution of income, wealth, and social protection, as well as returns to capital and labour, are needed, not only for their own sake but also to resolve the incipient world under-consumption problem before this becomes a serious obstacle to fast economic growth, and for the sake of world peace.

It is, however, appropriate to ask whether the above is likely to happen. The most optimistic outcome is one in which the worst of the crisis is over: the global financial system has been thoroughly reformed, ensuring stability and contributing to more equitable global development. At the time of writing, the most affected economies are recovering quite satisfactorily. Blanchard (2010), the chief economist of the IMF, reports that the global economy has been recovering better than expected and global growth is expected to reach a rate of 4.2 per cent in 2010 (an upwards revision) and to reach 4.3 per cent in 2011. Global trade and capital flows have been recovering much faster. Even unemployment, which is normally a lagging indicator, has at long last begun to decline, albeit slowly, at least in the US (Chandra, 2010). These recent short-term improvements can be interpreted as suggesting that the evolution of the world economy is pointing in a positive direction. However, Blanchard warns that these 'good numbers hide a more complex reality, namely a tepid recovery in many advanced economies, and a much stronger one in most emerging and developing economies'. While perhaps somewhat disappointing for advanced economics this scenario suggests some progress towards greater balance in the world economy.

One of the biggest global worries concerns the current European sovereign debt situation that has major implications for the world economy. One cannot dismiss the possibility of a cascading financial crisis due initially to contagion in the euro area (starting with a default in Greece and potentially in Portugal, Spain and Italy, and even elsewhere in Europe) and resulting in a speculative attack on the euro currency. The likelihood of such a turn of events may have a small probability, but in view of our limited capacity to predict the future it would be unwise to rule out a major crisis, particularly bearing in mind very recent experience. To avert such an economic, social and political catastrophe, coordinated consultation and action by nations and European and global institutions are required to tame the financial markets.

In any conflict of interest between states and the financial markets, clearly the interests of the former should and can prevail. In view of the dimensions of the European sovereign debt problem, and to avert a run on the currency, a rescue package of €750 billion has already been put in place. If in the worst-case scenario this should prove inadequate, and European nations consider the European Union and the common currency to be vital for European peace and development, they could in principle act in concert and challenge the markets by introducing a financial package several times larger, thereby stopping speculators in their tracks.[12] In this context it should be noted that the €750 billion bailout represents 6 per cent of the European Union's GDP. Putting this in a historical context, it may be recalled that just over 60 years ago the US administration, faced with what they perceived as a communist threat to Western Europe, intervened with the Marshall Plan. The value of this plan over a three-year period amounted to 4 per cent of US GDP (Glyn et al. 1991).[13]

To sum up, the current challenge to policymakers around the world is, first and foremost, to avoid long-term stagnation resulting from injudicious policies. This would suggest, inter alia, resisting a premature drawing down of government debt in rich countries. The associated reduction in state expenditure and increases in taxation are likely to prolong recession and unemployment, with consequent ripple effects that result in continued long-term stagnation throughout the global economy.

In addition, concerted action is required to introduce national and international supervision and regulation of financial markets, while measures are also needed to achieve a rebalancing of the global economy such that it reaches its full potential, while also achieving an improvement in inter-country distribution of growth and development. In short, markets should serve the people rather than determining their socio-economic destiny.[14]

Notes

1. The causes (both short- and longer-term) of the current global economic and financial crisis have been discussed in a number of contributions (see, for example, Aiginger (2009), IMF (2008a, 2009b, 2009a, 2009b, 2009c, 2010a, 2010b), Krugman (2008, 2010), Ormerod (2010), Solow (2009), UNCTAD (2008, 2009, 2010), UNDESA (2008, 2009, 2010), the US Council of Economic Advisers (2010).

2. These numbers illustrate the orders of magnitude involved in the stock market contagion at that time. In fact in the first six months share prices fell sharply and then rose slowly over the next six months.

3. Another related manifestation of global imbalances before the crisis was the huge and growing foreign currency reserves of the Chinese Central Bank. In the second quarter of 2010 the total value of these reserves was estimated to be around US$2.4 trillion (Chin, 2010).

4. There is a 'blame game' with respect to who bears responsibility for the current large imbalances – the profligate US consumer causing the country's current account deficit, or the Asian peoples' high propensity to save, resulting in current account surpluses. Such a construction of events can be interpreted negatively as suggesting that the US attracts savings from the world's poorer nations thereby depriving the latter of much-needed capital. However, Larry Summers (2006) suggested that such arguments are based on presumptions that do not tally with the broader facts. Specifically, he observed that during the past decade the world has been awash with savings and liquidity. Had the US been extracting savings from the rest of the world at the expense of investment elsewhere, the likely result would have been rising global real interest rates rather than the low rates actually experienced.

5. The only OECD country to reach the unemployment level experienced by the US in the 1930s is Spain, with a current unemployment rate of 19 per cent (Economist, Economic and Financial Indicators, 1 May 2010).

6. However, it can be argued that the G20 is far from an ideal vehicle for international cooperation as it excludes more than 150 countries. Nevertheless, some argue that a group bigger than the G20 may not be a practical device for agreeing and implementing decisive measures to cope with the crisis.

7. The source of these figures is UNDESA (2010, Table 4, page 20).

8. Most 'American Keynesian' economists, following Paul Samuelson, believe in 'the Grand Synthesis', that is, that suitable monetary and fiscal policy can restore and maintain full employment and that, in a fully employed economy, neoclassical economics comes into its own. In contrast, 'Cambridge Keynesian' economists reject neoclassical economics altogether, but rather believe that monetary and fiscal policy alone will not bring about full employment. In their view, only a 'planned' economy in the sense that the government takes a major role in influencing investment decisions (that is indicative planning) can lead to continuous full employment. On the other hand 'Chicago' economists believe in the pre-Keynesian classical model whose central distinguishing feature is that it denies the existence of 'involuntary' unemployment in the modern economy. These ideas find resonance in modern macroeconomics referred to in section 6.

9. There is scholarly dispute over the Indian figures for poverty reduction. However, the Indian government's view and that of many scholars is that gains in poverty reduction due to fast growth have been significant. See further Planning Commission of India (2009).

10. For a detailed analysis of the debt crisis of the 1980s see Singh 1993; Fishlow 1991.

11. Lessons also need to be drawn from the recent history of Japan, whose average annual growth rate for the first decade of the 2000s fell to a mere

1 per cent. Greater research efforts devoted to understanding the Japanese case are likely to be more rewarding than further developing DSGE models.

12. The effectiveness of this measure was demonstrated by the Hong Kong Central Bank's punitive action against speculators during the 1997–99 Asian crisis.

13. An even more pessimistic scenario would, as noted above, involve contagion beyond Europe and wider sovereign debt default. In the absence of coordinated policies and action, such a development would result in widespread financial chaos, economic disruption, unemployment and lower standards of living for many people worldwide.

14. It will be argued by some that reduced long-term economic growth may be positive by effecting a reduction in global warming and conserving natural resources. However, important issues such climate change and redistribution of income are beyond the scope of this short paper.

References

Aiginger, K. (2009) 'The Current Economic Crisis: Causes, Cures and Consequences', *WIFO Working Papers No. 431*, August, Osterreichisches Institut für Wirtshaftschung.

Akyuz, Y. (2010) 'Global Economic Prospects: The Recession May Be Over But Where Next?', *Research Papers 26*. Geneva: South Centre.

Andrews, Edmund L. (2008) 'Greenspan Concedes Error on Regulation', *New York Times*, 23 October.

Blanchard, Oliver (2010) 'World Faces Serious New Economic Challenges', *IMF Blog*, posted on 21 April, 2010 by IMF direct. http://blog-imfdirect.imf.org/ referenced 17 May 2010.

Chandra, Shobhana (2010) 'Productivity in U.S. Rises More Than Forecast, Labor Costs Drop', Bloomberg.com, 13 May. Accessed at http://.bloomberg.com/ apps/news?pid=email_en&sid=an2SOt.

Chin, Gregory T. (2010) 'Remaking the Architecture: The Emerging Powers, Self-insuring and Regional Insulation', *International Affairs*, 86(3), 693–715.

Cooper, R. (2005) *Living with Global Imbalances: A Contrarian View*. Policy Brief, November. Washington, DC: Institute for International Economics.

Economist (2010) *Economic and Financial Indicators*, 1 May.

Fishlow, Albert (1991) 'Some Reflections on Comparative Latin American Economic Performance and Policy', in Tariq Banuri (ed.), *Economic Liberalization: No Panacea*. Oxford: Oxford University Press.

Galbraith, James (2010) 'In Defense of Deficits', *The Nation*, 4 March.

Glyn, Andrew, Hughes, Alan, Lipietz, Alain and Singh, Ajit (1991) 'The Rise and Fall of the Golden Age', in Stephen A. Marglin and Juliet B. Shaw (eds), *The Golden Age of Capitalism*. Oxford: Clarendon Press.

Glen J. and Singh, Ajit (2005) 'Corporate Governance and Finance: Re-thinking Lessons from the Asian Crisis', First published as *Cambridge University Business School Working Paper 288*, June. 2004. Subsequently published in the *Eastern Economic Journal*, 31(2), 219–42.

Greenspan, Alan (2005) 'Consumer Finance'. Speech given at the Federal Reserve System's Fourth Annual Community Affairs Research Conference, 8 April. Washington, DC: Federal Reserve Board.

Greenspan, Alan (2010) Evidence given to the U.S. Congress Financial Crisis Inquiry Committee (established to investigate the sub-prime mortgage crisis). Washington, DC: US Government.

Helleiner, Eric and Jonathan Kirshner (eds) (2009) *The Future of the Dollar.* Ithaca, NY: Cornell University Press.

IMF (International Monetary Fund) (2008a) *World Economic Outlook. Housing and the Business Cycle,* February. Washington, DC: IMF.

IMF (2008b) *World Economic Outlook – Financial Stress, Downturns and Recovery,* October. Washington, DC: IMF.

IMF (2009a) *World Economic Outlook Update. Contractionary Forces Receding But Weak Recovery Ahead,* 8 July. Washington, DC: IMF.

IMF (2009b) *World Economic Outlook – Crisis and Recovery,* April. Washington, DC: IMF.

IMF (2009c) *World Economic Outlook. Sustaining the Recovery,* 15 October. Washington, DC: IMF.

IMF (2010a) *World Economic Outlook. A Policy-Driven, Multispeed Recovery,* 26 January. Washington, DC: IMF.

IMF (2010b) *World Economic Outlook, Rebalancing Growth,* 21 April. Washington, DC: IMF.

Jorgenson, Dale W., Ho, Mun S. and Stiroh, Kevin J. (2007) 'A Retrospective Look at the U.S. Productivity Growth Resurgence', FRB of New York Staff Report 277. Available at SSRN: http://ssrn.com/abstract=970660

Krugman, P. (2008) 'The Big Meltdown', *New York Times,* 2 March.

Krugman, P. (2010) 'Goldman Sachs, Salaried Looters', *The Indian Express, Chandigarh,* 24 April.

Llewellyn, John (2008) 'The Shock of the New', *Prospect,* November.

Ormerod, Paul (2010) 'The Current Crisis and the Culpability of Macroeconomic Theory', *21st Century Society, Journal of the Academy of Social Sciences,* 5(1), 5–18.

Planning Commission, Government of India (2009) *The Tendulkar Commission Report on Poverty Estimates.* Planning Commission, New Delhi.

Romer, Christina (2009) *Back from the Brink.* Address given on 24 September at the Federal Reserve Bank of Chicago, Chicago, Illinois.

Singh, Ajit (1993) 'Asian Economic Success and Latin American Failure in the 1980s: New Analyses and Future Policy Implications', *International Review of Applied Economics,* 7(3), 267–89.

Singh, Ajit (2007) 'Globalisation, Industrial Revolutions in India and China and Labour Markets in Advanced Countries: Implications for National and International Economic Policy', *Working Paper 81, Policy Integration Department.* Geneva: International Labour Office.

Singh, Ajit (2010) 'Globalization, Openness and Economic Nationalism'. Cambridge University Centre for Business Research, *Working Paper No. 404,* June.

Solow, R. (2009) 'How to Understand the Disaster', *The New York Review of Books,* 14 May.

Summers, Lawrence H. (2006) 'Reflections on Global Account Imbalances and Emerging Markets Reserve Accumulation', L.K. Jha Memorial Lecture, Reserve Bank of India, Mumbai, India.

UNCTAD (2008, 2009, 2010) *Handbook of Statistics.* Geneva: United Nations.

UNDESA (United Nations Department of Economic and Social Affairs) (2008) *Global Economic Outlook,* May. New York: United Nations.

UNDESA (United Nations Department of Economic and Social Affairs) (2009) *Global Economic Outlook*, May. New York: United Nations.

UNDESA (United Nations Department of Economic and Social Affairs) (2010) *Global Economic Outlook*, May. New York: United Nations.

US Council of Economic Advisers (2010) *Annual Report of the Council of Economic Advisers*. Washington, DC: US Government Printing Office.

Wolf, Martin (2008) 'The World Wakes from the Wish-dream of Decoupling', *Financial Times*, 22 October.

4
Crises and the Bretton Woods Institutions and the Crises of the Bretton Woods Institutions[1]

Howard Stein

Today, the only crisis faced by the IMF is a crisis of identity. Countries rescued in the 1990s have mostly repaid their debts. With a shrunken loan portfolio, the institution that lectures others about finances has lost operating income and is running a deficit. It faces cuts in its staff and salaries and is even considering the sale of its gold bullion reserves. 'What might be at stake today is the very existence of the IMF... I' (Dominique Strauss-Kahn quoted in Steven Wiseman, 'IMF Faces a Question of Identity', *New York Times*, 28 September 2007)

Today is the proof that the IMF is back. (Dominique Strauss-Kahn, Director, IMF following the completion of the G20 meeting quoted in Landler and Sanger, *New York Times*, 2 April 2009)

Strauss-Kahn says the days of 'one size fits all' policies have changed and that the institution has learned from its mistakes and criticisms. He says his IMF teams are far more adapting and flexible to the peculiarities of each country. (Interview with CNN reporter Robyn Curnow, 3 March 2010)

1 Introduction

The daily focus in the media on the financial crisis in the United States and Europe has overshadowed discussions of the impact of the crisis on the poorest regions of the world where millions of people live on the edge of an abyss that threatens their very survival. Moreover, in the wake of the crisis, and as a result of recent G20 meetings, there has been an unprecedented expansion in the resources and authority of the Bretton Woods Institutions with barely a whisper about their role in promoting an agenda which has been largely antithetical to the development process. Countries that had sworn they would not deal with the Fund have reversed course and are back at the door of the IMF now heavily supported by the G20. This paper will focus on recent lending patterns of the Bank and Fund, the impact of the new crisis on Bank and Fund policy, and the role of the G20. The paper will argue that reforms in the governance and policy structures of the Fund and Bank have been wholly inadequate in view of the miserable track record of these institutions. There are dangers in continuing with the past trajectory of the Bank and Fund whose strategies have left poor countries structurally enfeebled and susceptible to feeling the full effects of the vicissitudes of the global economy. We will begin with a brief background with a focus on recent Bank and Fund lending patterns.

2 Background

The lending from the World Bank's two main groups, the IBRD (the International Bank for Reconstruction and Development) and IDA (the International Development Association – poor lending arm of the Bank), grew rapidly in the 1980s and peaked in fiscal year 1999 at $29.996 billion. The trend is illustrated in Figure 4.1. Table 4.1 follows up the data in the figure with year-by-year lending patterns through 2009.

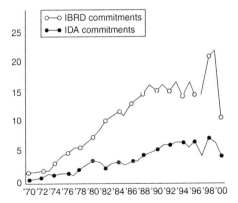

Figure 4.1 IBRD and IDA lending trends, fiscal 1970–2000 (billions of dollars)
Source: World Bank (2000).

Table 4.1 IBRD and IDA lending, 1998–2009 (US$ million)

Year*	1998	1999	2000	2001	2002	2003	2004	2005	2006	2007	2008	2009
IBRD	21,086	22,182.3	10,919	10,487	11,452	11,231	11,045	13,611	14,135	12,829	13,468	32,900
IDA	7,508	6,813	7,282	8,068	6,764	4,358	9,035	8,696	9,506	11,867	11,235	14,000
Total	28,594	28,996	18,201	18,555	18,216	15,589	20,080	22,307	23,641	24,696	24,703	48,900

Sources: World Bank (2000, 2004, 2008, 2009a).
*Fiscal Year ending in June.

In the wake of the Asian crisis in 1997, IBRD lending in 1998 and 1999 increased dramatically by roughly a third and then fell off as countries, especially those in the middle range of incomes, repaid their loans after the economic recovery. Lending through 2008 by the IBRD never returned to the levels of the pre-crisis period 1992 to 1997 as richer developing countries got access to alternative financial sources without the baggage of neoliberal conditionality. This option was not available for poorer countries. IDA loans as a portion of lending increased from around 29 per cent of the total in the 1992 to 1997 period to 47 per cent in 2007–8. Increasingly, it was the poorest of the poor that received the lion's share of World Bank money. For example, the share of IDA lending to sub-Saharan Africa went from 36 per cent in 1997–99 to 50 per cent in 2008 (World Bank, 2000, 2009a).

A similar phenomenon has occurred with IMF lending as seen in Table 4.2.

Between 1992 and 1997, concessional lending (to low-income countries) as a proportion of total outstanding credit averaged 13.6 per cent. By 2007 the average grew to 39 per cent of the total. After 2003 the peak

Table 4.2 IMF resources, disbursements, repayments, income and outstanding credit (billions SDRs), 1998–2010

Time	General resource account				PRGF-ESF				Income
	Useable Res.	Disburs.	Repay.	Out. Crd	Useable Res.	Disb	Repay	Out Crd.	
1998	53.6	20.6	6.7	60.5	9.5	.9	.6	6.3	2.52
1999	94.9	10.0	19.4	51.1	10.3	.7	.6	6.4	2.61
2000	109.7	7.2	15.2	43.0	11.4	.5	.6	6.3	2.41
2001	102.5	23.8	13.3	53.5	14.5	.9	.8	6.4	2.20
2002	100.2	25.2	15.1	63.6	15.8	1.3	.9	6.9	2.29
2003	100.7	20.3	18.9	65.0	15.8	.8	.8	6.9	2.40
2004	111.4	4.2	13.8	55.4	15.8	.8	.9	6.8	2.34
2005	145.2	2.3	29.2	28.4	15.8	.4	.9	6.3	2.23
2006	161.2	2.4	21.0	9.8	15.8	.5	2.9	3.8	1.14
2007	165.4	1.0	4.7	6.0	15.8	.3	.4	3.8	.48
2008	152.4	13.4	1.9	17.5	15.8	.6	.5	4.0	.62
2009	290.2	20.5	.7	37.2	16.8	1.6	.5	5.1	.53
2010*	308.8**	4.2	0	41.4	17.5	.2	.1	5.1	.18

Sources: IMF (various years, 2009d, and 2010a).
*Figures on income are through 31 January 2010. All others are through 22 April 2010.
**Includes borrowing agreements with Japan (US$100 billion), Canada (US$10 billion), Norges Bank (SDR 3 billion), the United Kingdom (SDR 9.92 billion), Deutsche Bundesbank (EUR 15 billion), De Nederlandsche Bank NV (EUR 5.31 billion); and note purchase agreement with People's Bank of China (SDR 32 billion).

year for outstanding GRA (general resource account) levels, countries rapidly repurchased their GRA balances and did their best to avoid any additional loans. Again, poor countries did not have the exit option.[2] After, 2005 reductions in outstanding concessional loans were through the MDRI (Multilateral Debt Relief Initiative) mechanism for HIPC completion point countries, which contained all the usual neoliberal baggage.

Outstanding GRA credit, which went principally to middle-income countries, fell by an unprecedented 91 per cent by 2007 from SDR 65 billion to a mere SDR 6 billion – a level not seen since the 1970s. This revolt began in 2005 when Argentina and Brazil denounced the neoliberal agenda of the Fund and began repaying nearly $25 billion in loans. This was followed by repayments from large debtors, including Indonesia, Philippines, Serbia and Turkey. The unprecedented decline in the use of IMF resources through the GRA, the major source of income for the Fund, led to the threat of large losses and the announcement of $100 million cost reduction plan at the Fund in April, 2008 (IMF, 2008a).

The economic crisis has now remarkably improved the fortunes of the Bank and Fund and re-empowered these agencies. Table 4.1 shows the World Bank has been resurrected with a substantial increase of IBRD lending from US$13.5 billion in fiscal year 2008 to US$32.9 billion in fiscal year 2009 – a rise of US$19.4 billion. The largest increase went to Latin American and Caribbean countries which took on an additional US$9.5 billion in IBRD loans (World Bank, 2009a).

Between September 2008 and February 2010, the Fund approved loans of SDR114 billion to 26 middle-income countries (IMF, 2010a).[3] As we can see in the table above, disbursements from the GRA grew from merely SDR1 billion in 2007 to a total of SDR20.5 billion in 2009.

Some countries have continued to resist, including Turkey. On 26 January 2009 the IMF proudly announced in a press release that 'The mission and the authorities made significant progress in a number of key areas" and that further focus would be on "the medium-term structural and fiscal reform agenda' (IMF, 2009c). In November 2008, despite financial problems, they were openly resisting a return to the IMF to avoid 'the awkward prospect of being forced to accept stringent fiscal conditions' (Thomas, 2008). The previous decade of relations with the IMF created structural weaknesses. As the Turkish economist Erinc Yeldan argued in June 2008, the high interest rates encouraged by the IMF post-crisis programme attracted short-term capital flows. The appreciated exchange rate facilitated a large increase in private consumption and imports leading to an expansion in the current account deficit to 7.5 per cent by 2008 and rising unemployment rates into double digits. The IMF-imposed austerity of the past had reduced government expenditures and led to a serious shrinkage in education and health infrastructure.

In many ways Turkey's predicament is similar to that of many other countries:

> Turkey's post-crisis adjustment under the AKP administration traces the steps of many developing countries which are dependent upon foreign capital and conditioned to adopt or maintain contractionary policies in order to secure 'investor confidence' and 'international creditworthiness'. They are restricted to a balanced budget, entrenched fiscal expenditures, and a relatively contractionary monetary policy with an ex ante commitment to high real interest rates. (Yeldan, 2008)

Given the fragility of the economy and darkening external environment Yeldan predicted Turkey's future stability will be 'more costly and difficult'.

3   Bank and Fund policies and their impact

Yeldan's depiction of typical IMF policies is quite accurate and duly admitted by the Fund. From the IMF factsheet on 'Crisis and IMF Lending' from November 2008 (IMF, 2008b), it is argued that 'the domestic sources' of economic crises can only come from 'excessive monetary creation, unsustainable fiscal deficits, an overvalued domestic currency, political instability, and natural disasters'. Nothing is mentioned about the behavior of any domestic private sector actors.

The focus on these domestic causes of crises occurs largely because of the theoretical underpinnings of the IMF approach which is based on the Polak model (Polak, 1957). The approach relies on a monetarist formulation that ties credit growth to the balance of payments and comes out of the fixed exchange world of the Bretton Woods era. Like the monetarists, it assumes the full employment of resources. There are two key parts to the model: money supply and a fixed exchange rate. Money supply is defined as the domestic credit to the private and public sector plus a country's monetary reserves. Changes in reserves are tied to the country's balance of trade on goods and services and non-traded related currency flows. According to the model, money demand occurs only for use in transactions and not for other reasons. Since the supply and demand for money are assumed to be in equilibrium, any increase in government borrowing would lead to an increase in prices and nominal income, which in turn would increase the demand for imports. This would occur since government borrowing is essentially an increase in the money supply, which must be met with an increase in money demand if equilibrium is to be maintained.

The nominal rise in income would lead to an increase in imports because the level of the domestic production of goods would not have changed. Imports would cause the terms of trade to worsen since the country would now move closer to a trade deficit. Likewise, reserves would also fall, as the country's central bank would have to use its reserves to buy extra domestic currency in order to maintain the fixed exchange rate. The subsequent lowering of reserves would eventually offset the rise in the money supply. However, a country in this situation would be left with higher prices, a worsening balance of payments, and lowered reserves. The lower reserves would encourage speculation against the currency and thereby threaten the stability of the fixed exchange rate of the country.

In exchange for accessing IMF loans, countries were expected to reach financial targets aimed at improving the balance of payments, lowering prices, raising reserves, and thus ultimately maintaining the integrity of the fixed exchange system. Whether the causes of the crises were domestic or external, the model dictated austerity through domestic expenditure contractions, which would be achieved by fiscal retrenchment and credit reductions.

The real world of developing countries is, of course, replete with large-scale unemployment. Employing such a model, which takes as given that all resources, including labour, are fully utilised, is to put it mildly problematic. There is an extensive literature examining the consequences of IMF loans and associated conditionality on social, political and economic indicators. There seems to be considerable evidence that reforms increase unemployment and poverty rates, exacerbate income equality and reduce social services (Kurtz, 2004; Stallings and Peres, 2000; Crisp and Kelly 1999; Garuda, 2000; and Vreeland 2003). The impact on political stability and democracy is also important. Brown (2009) examines the impact of IMF loans in 23 Latin America countries between 1998 and 2003 on democratic variables like political freedom and civil liberties and finds that democracy levels decline with time and the number and types of conditionality. Arguably, the main focus of the IMF is on improving a narrow set of economic indicators. How has the IMF done?

Bird (2001) summarises the empirical work from 1978 to 2000 on the economic dimensions (using a variety of methodologies), including the impact on balance of payments, current account, inflation and economic growth. He finds a mixed picture on the balance of payments and current account, neutral or exacerbation of inflation and a mixed picture on economic growth. In some cases, for example Killick (1995), the results are rather surprising in view of data indicating a clear decline in investment levels. Overall, he suggests that one explanation for the differentiated results might be that countries do not fully implement the programmes. However, other authors have tested whether full compliance and implementation make a difference. Dreher (2006) uses panel data from 98 countries in the period 1978–2000 to examine the impact of IMF programmes on economic growth. He finds that economic growth declines by about 1.7 per cent per year within the first five years of a programme. There is little difference with full compliance with average declines of around 1.6 per cent per year. More recent empirical studies have illustrated the negative impact of IMF conditionality on economic growth (Przeworski and Vreeland, 2000; Barro and Lee, 2002; and Vreeland 2003).[4]

In the case of the Asia crisis the imposition of austerity on governments with largely balanced budgets and tight control of the money supply helped turn a panic from a private sector speculation into a disaster. In a recent interview with the *Chinese Daily* Wing Thye Woo of the Brookings Institute summed up the feelings in East Asia:

> Asian countries, especially those in East Asia, have a deep distrust for the Fund, given its 'poor track record' during the 1997 Asian financial crisis and 'no proof' that it has improved its competence over the years… at the moment no Malaysian, Indonesian and South Korean government could go to the IMF and expect to survive. (*China Daily*, 3 December 2008)

South Korea, for example, which desperately wanted to avoid going to the IMF was bailed out in October 2008 with a $30 billion swap arrangement with the US Fed. Other close allies, including Singapore, Brazil and Mexico, received the same arrangement (Merco Press, 2008).

What of the World Bank? In recent decades, the Bank has had a mix of project and programme aid. The latter became more important after the Bank committed to an agenda focused on neoliberalism as it worked more closely with the IMF in the 1980s. The Bank expanded its programmes over time to incorporate a host of new conditions related to their programmes including governance. Stein (2008) reviews an extensive literature testing the impact of structural adjustment loans on Africa using a variety of different techniques. It finds little consistent evidence that economies have improved from World Bank lending and considerable evidence that the region has done poorly in the adjustment era.[5]

What of the impact on governance which became increasingly central in World Bank loans from the middle of the 1990s? In the late 1990s, the World Bank Institute and the Research Department of the World Bank initiated a research programme on governance indicators and their economic impact. The effort was aimed at illustrating *ex post* the positive impact of governance on economic growth. In other words, improvements in governance indicators have a positive impact on economic growth. The enterprise was on the surface a bit strange since governance had already been operationalised for a number of years. However, this is not unusual in the history of the Bank which often used empirics as an exercise in verification rather than as a mechanism of policy formulation (Stein, 2008). The World Governance Indicators (WGI) have gone through numerous permutations which it is beyond the scope of this paper to review.[6] Even with all the variations over time, the causal link between better governance and economic growth has not been established.

Generally WGI measures use a variety of surveys from multiple counties along six lines:

1. *Voice and Accountability* – measuring political, civil and human rights.
2. *Political Instability and Violence* – measuring the likelihood of violent threats to, or changes in,government, including terrorism.
3. *Government Effectiveness* – measuring the competence of the bureaucracy and the quality of public service delivery.
4. *Regulatory Burden* – measuring the incidence of market-unfriendly policies.
5. *Rule of Law* – measuring the quality of contract enforcement, the police, and the courts, as well as the likelihood of crime and violence.
6. *Control of Corruption* – measuring the exercise of public power for private gain, including both petty and grand corruption and state capture. (Khan, 2007)

The data include more than 300 individual variables provided by more than 30 organisations. Each of those organisations has its own methodology and scale. For comparability, Kaufman et al. (2005) normalise these scores into a 0–1 scale and then use them to produce normally distributed indicators. The estimates for each indicator are then the result of a maximum likelihood function. As such, 99 per cent of the values are between –2.5 and 2.5 with higher scores corresponding to better outcomes.

The literature, to put it mildly, has been very critical of the way the indicators are constructed since they combine radically different and largely subjective surveys using different methodologies into single indicators (Apaza, 2009). It is hard to know what is being measured objectively. For example, the corruption index is a composite of the views of corruption in public officials, accountability, transparency and corruption in rural areas and a political risk index measuring things such as perceptions of nationalism, corruption and nepotism. It arises from information from the Economist Intelligence Unit, IFAD (the International Fund for Agricultural Development) rural sector performance assessments and business environment risk intelligence (BERI) published by Business Risk Service. They all use radically different methods. One person's bribe is another person's way of doing business. There is no way of disaggregating what is important and what is trivial. Moreover, the indicators are overwhelmed by business perceptions. Businesses will likely see governments in a more positive light if there are fewer regulations and lower taxes. In contrast, citizens who are poorly represented in these surveys might see the opposite. So what is governance?

In addition, there is strong evidence that countries that are doing well economically are perceived as having better governance. In other words, rich countries get better scores precisely because they *are* rich. In fact, a study by Kurtz and Shrank (2007) find a strong link in their econometric testing between previous high levels of economic growth and government effectiveness. This raises the entire question of direction of causation.

Kaufmann et al. (2005) have found positive relationships between their governance indicators and economic growth. Khan (2007) questions the results which, he argues, are significant but weak. Using a standard scatter diagram he shows clearly that a positive relationship is overwhelming among developed countries and argues that if you remove the developed countries the relationship disappears. It also shows the likely opposite direction of causation – that is, higher growth and income leads to better governance. Moreover for developing countries, nations with similar governance indicators are divided equally between those with above-average (convergence countries) and those with below-average (divergent countries) indicators, suggesting that the cause of economic growth is something different than governance.

4   G20 and the 'resurrection' of the IMF and World Bank

The G20 meetings in April and September 2009 anointed the IMF to unprecedented heights. Among other things, the Fund received authority to triple its lending capacity to $750 billion and to expand its SDR allocation by an additional $250 billion. The expansion would be done through the New Arrangements to Borrow (NAB) in which the funds would come from the G20 countries without any change in the existing voting structure of the Fund. This is rather contrary to the joint statement of financed ministers of Brazil, Russia, China and India at the mid-March G20 finance minister's meeting that the borrowing arrangement was to 'be a temporary bridge to a permanent quota increase' which would mean the reduction of the dominant voting share of the wealthier countries. SDRs would be allocated on the current quota system meaning that two-thirds of the total would go to the rich countries of the world. By the September meeting the G20 announced it had fulfilled its obligations of $500 billion in new funds under the NAB (G20, 2009). As of April 2010, Japan had allocated $100 billion, European Union $178 billion, Norway $4.5 billion, Canada $10 billion, Switzerland, $10 billion, US $100 billion, Korea $10 billion, Australia $5.7 billion, Russia $10 billion, China $50 billion, Brazil $10 billion, India $10 billion, Singapore $1.5 billion and Chile $1.6 billion (IMF, 2010g).

The expansion of the SDRs comes in the wake of the call by China and others to create a new global reserve currency free of the encumbrances of a single national currency and its baggage of domestic political and economic influence. Zhou's March speech makes an explicit case for SDRs to fulfill that role. It would go beyond its current accounting role inside the Fund to become a widely accepted means of payment in international trade and other types of financial transactions (Zhou, 2009). Yet there is no recognition of the problems of this approach given the current governance of the IMF, the hegemonic role of the US inside the Fund with its veto power nor the very problematic policy model of the Fund which would be sustained and expanded by this powerful new role.

The September G20 meeting also gave unprecedented power to the IMF to advise when to reverse fiscal expansion, to analyse how the financial sector can contribute to the burden of intervening in the financial systems, to monitor the global economy and to report on the efforts to coordinate country economic activity in the new Framework for Strong, Sustainable, and Balanced Growth. The latter includes an assessment of individual G20 countries to assess consistency with a balanced trajectory for the global economy.

The World Bank has also attempted to use the G20 process to tap new resources and expand its sphere and importance. The G20 also asked the Bank to increase lending limits to large countries and to make more funds available to low-income countries at market rates, but to only those with 'sustainable debt positions and sound policies'. Funding for its new vulnerability funds will occur not through the G20 process but through individual bilateral sources (G20, 2009).

Following the September G20 recommendations, at the April 2010 spring meeting of the Bank and Fund, the World Bank's IBRD capital base was dramatically expanded for the first time in more than 20 years by $86 billion in line with a shift of 3.13 per cent in the voting power to developing and transitional countries. The IFC was also provided with an additional 200 million dollars. The largest recipients of the IBRD voting shift were members of the G20, including China (1.64), South Korea (.58), Turkey (.55), and Mexico (.5). Most of the loss of voting is from countries like Japan, the UK and France. Unsurprisingly there is no challenge to the veto power of the US which remains well above the 15 per cent threshold (15.85 per cent) (World Bank, 2010a,b).[7] While the World Bank now claims that the developed countries' share has fallen to only 53 per cent of the vote of the IBRD this has been achieved using a rather suspect classification system. The real total is still close to 61 per cent using the 'high income' category of the IMF (Bretton Woods Project, 2010).

The World Bank claims that as part of its post-crisis reform mandate it will be 'sharpening its strategic focus' emphasizing: (1) Targeting the poor and vulnerable... (2) Creating opportunities for growth with a special focus on agriculture and infrastructure; (3) Promoting global collective action on issues from climate change and trade to agriculture, food security, energy, water and health; (4) Strengthening governance and anti-corruption efforts; and (5) Preparing for crises' (World Bank, 2010a). In essence, the Bank intends to expand its purview in some areas while continuing to focus on many of the same issues, with no discussion of changing the strategies which it has pursued in recent years with such problematic results. What of the IMF?

5 Pro- vs counter-cyclical policies

Increasingly, the Fund has been arguing it has taken a new direction and will now support an increase in fiscal expenditures to deal with the current crisis. This is quite explicit in a now widely quoted IMF paper by Antonio Spilimbergo, Steve Symansky, Olivier Blanchard, and Carlo Cottarelli.

They argue that the economic downturn is being driven by both a financial crisis and the collapse in aggregate demand. The latter is frequently ignored by the Fund for the theoretical reasons I have already discussed above. Moreover, they indicate the usual options for addressing aggregate demand through devaluations and to stimulate exports through monetary policy, are not available. The former because it is a global phenomena and will only lead to competitive devaluations and the latter because it has already been fully utilised in many countries or because the financial sectors have become too dysfunctional for it to work. The authors then state that in these circumstances, the Managing Director of the IMF has called for a sizable fiscal response at the global level. Its precise magnitude should depend on the extent of the expected decline in private sector demand and should therefore be reviewed in light of developments... (Splimbergo et al., 2008, p. 3)

However, the authors add an important caveat:

> while a fiscal response across many countries may be needed, *not all countries have sufficient fiscal space to implement it since expansionary fiscal actions may threaten the sustainability of fiscal finances. In particular, many low income and emerging market countries...* face additional constraints such as volatile capital flows, high public and foreign indebtedness, and large risk premia. (author's emphasis)

The qualifications are made even clearer in an interview with Blanchard and Cottarelli in the *IMF Survey* magazine on 29 December 2008 following the release of the paper:

> In normal times, the Fund would indeed be recommending to many countries that they reduce their budget deficit and their public debt. But these are not normal times, and the balance of risks today is very different... That said, it is critical that this fiscal stimulus isn't seen by markets as undermining medium-term fiscal sustainability. That would be counterproductive, including in its effects on demand today. *Indeed, we've said that not all countries can afford a fiscal expansion.* (IMF, 2008c; author's emphasis)

On the surface the statement would seem to justify the double standard whereby governments in advanced developed countries can intervene to deal with unemployment and the threats to the standard of living of the population while developing countries are forced to focus on austerity and macrostabilization so that they 'live within their means' which is often ever-shrinking once the Fund officials have disembarked in their capitals from their first class seats.

Moreover, the timing of this pronouncement had a strongly political smell. Even as recently as October 2008, the IMF position in a study published in their *World Economic Outlook* took a much more lukewarm position, indicating that fiscal policy might have a 'moderately positive effect on output growth in advanced economies' but 'increases in interest rate risk premiums... render fiscal multipliers negative suggesting that fiscal policy does more harm than good' when applied to emerging markets (IMF, 2008d, p. 158). The arrival of new handlers in the election of Obama and the strong commitment to fiscal stimulus within his economic team provides strong incentives for the Fund to be more firm in their commitment.

At the same time as the IMF was pointing to its flexibility, the *New York Times* ran articles on the 'draconian measures' being imposed on countries like Latvia. The conditionality included a massive 25 per cent cut in public sector wages in 2009, and a huge front-loaded reduction in the lower than expected deficit from 12 per cent to 5 per cent of GDP, one-third from tax increases (regressive VAT and excise taxes)) and two-thirds from across the board massive 25 per cent cut in real government spending. Interbank spreads compared to the European Interbank market rate rose from below zero in October 2008 to over 12 per cent in December 2008 having a depressing impact on investment levels which fell in 2008 by 10 per cent (IMF, 2009a).

Through the end of 2009, the situation had deteriorated further with a 25.5 per cent decline in GDP, second only to the Great Depression of the US in economic collapses. Unemployment has risen to 22 per cent. The situation is exacerbated by the high level of foreign currency loans (estimated at 89 per cent of the total) with worries that if the country tries to stimulate its economy with a devaluation it will lead a massive increase in bankruptcies.[8] As a result, the IMF emphasis is to try to encourage international competitiveness through domestic deflationary pressures and leading to a terrible collapse in living standards (Weisbrot and Ray, 2010).

There have also been claims by the IMF that it has adjusted its austerity stance towards poor African countries. In the IMF's 'Report on Fiscal Policy in SSA' published in May 2009 (IMF, 2009e), they argued:

Countries will need to weigh their options for fiscal policy responses. Countries with output gaps and sustainable debt and financing options have scope to implement expansionary policies, by letting automatic stabilizers work, accommodating declines in commodity-related revenues, and in some cases implementing discretionary fiscal stimulus... In all cases, countries should give priority to expanding social safety nets as needed to cushion the impact of the crisis on the poor... SSA countries, particularly those where inflation has recently been on a declining path, have some room for a more countercyclical monetary policy.

What is the reality? In September 2008, the IMF approved an Exogenous Shock Facility (ESF) for low-income countries to cope with the economic crisis. Between December 2008 and August 2009 six were approved – Malawi, the Kyrgyz Republic, Senegal, Mozambique, Tanzania and Ethiopia. In December 2008 the IMF approved its first Shock Facility loan to Malawi. The Memorandum of Economic and Financial Policies lays out the usual standard array of adjustments, including the contraction of monetary expansion to levels below an increase in nominal GDP, fiscal constraints, a movement towards unified and floating exchange rates, a reduction of inflation to levels below 5 per cent, improvements in governance, including the upgrading of the invasive public finance and economic management system which allow donors to monitor expenditures and large increases in interest rates (IMF, 2009b). To quote from the Memorandum:

> The authorities are committed to a framework that will maintain macroeconomic stability... To this end, they have been tightening monetary policy which has led to a significant increase in interest rates... The authorities are determined to maintain their prudent fiscal policy... A tight budget for the fiscal year 2008/09 has been approved despite significant political hurdles. Targeted domestic debt repayment in 2008/09 is 0.1 percent of GDP, compared with borrowing of 1.3 percent of GDP in 2007/08. (IMF, 2009b)

The ESF for Ethiopia issued 29 August 2009 is little different and also imposes the same largely pro-cyclical policies used with problematic consequences. To quote from the Ministry of Finance and Planning and Governor of the central bank letter to the IMF dated 7 August 2009:

> Our program focuses on entrenching low inflation and building international reserves through appropriately tight fiscal and monetary policies supported by the necessary exchange rate flexibility. We also

intend to enhance monitoring and control of borrowings by the public enterprise sector, develop the central bank's liquidity forecasting and control capacity, and flesh out, with IMF technical assistance, a comprehensive time-bound tax reform strategy to improve domestic revenue mobilization. (IMF, 2009f)

The targets arising from the ESF are also fairly draconian in a time of global crisis. Federal government and public enterprise borrowing is expected to be kept below 3 per cent in 2009–10 from 7.1 per cent in 2007–08. Government revenue is actually expected to rise to 12.2 per cent of the GDP from an estimated 11.7 per cent in 2008–09 by eliminating the temporary reduction of VAT on food products (contrary to the rhetoric of protecting the poor!) and the delayed impact of high inflation on income tax. Inflation is to be reduced to below 10 per cent and is expected to reach a ridiculously low 5.1 per cent in 2009–10 from 25.3 per cent in 2007–08 and an estimated 36.4 per cent in 2008–09. This will be achieved by aggressive open market operations aimed at reducing the expansion of the money supply compared to previous years. The operations are bound to increase interest rates at a time of a severe downturn in investment (IMF, 2009f).

More systematically, Waeyenberge et al. (2010) review IMF programmes in 13 poor countries signed between 2007 and 2009. They find that six have fiscal tightening and seven very moderate increases averaging 2.5 per cent of GDP in 2009. Overall, while there was an initial projection of a rise of deficits of 1.5 per cent of GDP in 2007 to 3.7 per cent in 2009, the latest figures show a rise of only 1.5 per cent in 2009. By 2010 almost all countries are expected to tighten their deficits with an anticipated average decline of .5 per cent of GDP. They conclude that the 'endorsed increase has not only been moderate, but also restricted to the short term'. Moreover, all 13 countries are expected to reduce inflation significantly between 2008 and 2010. Although the run-up in prices in 2008 was largely the result of rising food and commodity prices, the focus in these countries is on restricting aggregate demand through wage freezes, monetary contraction and rising interest rates which is likely to greatly exacerbate recessionary trends and living conditions for the poor.

Weisbrot et al. (2009) review an even larger sample of 41 IMF agreements signed in the wake of the economic downturn and find 31 of them to have clear pro-cyclical fiscal (increasing surpluses or lowering deficits) and/or monetary policies (increasing interest rates). Only one of the 41 cases had both anti-cyclical fiscal and monetary policy (Tanzania), five others had either anti-cyclical fiscal or monetary policy alone (Mozambique, São Tomé and Príncipe, Guatemala, Zambia and Niger) and the other four had neither. However, a closer reading of the IMF agreements indicates that even this interpretation can be considered generous.

Take the case of Tanzania which received an ESF of SDR 210 million in May 2009 and was allowed to embark on a policy of monetary and fiscal expansion. The IMF claims in a press relief that 'expansionary fiscal and monetary policies in the current situation are appropriate to cushion the effects of the crisis' (IMF, 2009g). This would provide the impression that they are in full support of the expansionary policies necessary to deal with the economic downturn. However, a deeper examination indicates a less than robust intervention and the existence of embedded targets that are rather contrary to expansionary fiscal and monetary policy. Among other things, Tanzania is expected to reduce inflation to 5 per cent in 2009–10 compared to 11 per cent in 2008–09, government revenue is expected to rise to 16.8 per cent of GDP in 2010–11 compared to 15.8 per cent in 2008–09, and credit is supposed to diminish by roughly 10 per cent in 2009–10. All of this would indicate the usual IMF fiscal and monetary austerity.

So where are these expansionary policies? The level of government expenditure is projected to increase to 26.3 per cent of GDP in 2008–09 compared with 24.4 per cent the previous year. In 2009–10 they are projected to rise to 27.2 per cent. This sounds like fiscal expansion, except that in reality it exactly matches the planned level of 2008–09 that fell short. By 2010–11 it is to be reduced to levels below the 2008–09 expenditure plans, so we are back to a position of business as usual. The deficit is allowed to rise to 1.2 per cent of GDP in 2008–09 from the planned zero level and 1.6 per cent in 2009–10 but is then expected to decline in 2010–11 to 1 per cent of GDP. Interest rates on new treasury debt are expected to be 12 per cent in 2009–10 from 13.2 per cent in 2008–09. With the targeted decline in inflation from 11 to 6 per cent this is not a cut in the interest rate but a significant increase in real terms from 2.2 per cent to 6 per cent – hardly expansionary monetary policy as suggested by the review (IMF, 2009h).

For Zambia, Weisbrot et al. argue that the 'IMF allowed monetary policy to ease in 2008 in order to accommodate higher food and oil prices... authorities expect to bring inflation down to 10 percent in 2009, while allowing for positive rates of growth of real broad money and real credit to the private sector'. However, an examination of the third year review of the PRGF of Zambia (IMF, 2010c) indicates that the overriding emphasis here is on the classic preoccupation with inflation rather than monetary expansion to counter the economic downturn. 'Monetary policy is to be geared to bringing inflation firmly to the single digit range by the end of the year 2010'. Growth of credit to the private sector in 2010 is to be less than 2007 and 2008. Recent data indicate that broad money relative to GDP fell in 2009 compared to 2008. The growth rate of broad money has rapidly fallen from 45 per cent in 2006 to only 8 per cent in 2009 which is below the inflation rate and why it has declined relative to GDP (IMF, 2010d). This should not be terribly surprising given that interest rates for loans from commercial banks have been steadily rising throughout the crisis period and averaged 22 per cent in 2009 (IMF, 2010e). This is hardly what one could call counter-cyclical monetary expansion.

For Mozambique Weisbrot et al. argue that the IMF is permitting moderate fiscal expansion because 'The fiscal program is revised to incorporate higher levels of domestic financing, which are increasing by about 1.1 percent of GDP.' Indeed in the executive summary of the June 2009 ESF agreement the IMF claims that 'Fiscal policy has been eased to maintain priority spending in the face of lower domestic revenues.' However, a closer look provides a much more nuanced perspective. The figures for 2008 indicate a decline in the deficit due to rising revenue and falling spending relative to GDP (2010d). In the December 2009 review of the ESF, the IMF admits that the fiscal policy was 'less accommodating than expected'. Despite this the IMF expects that 'The return to a prudent fiscal policy stance will be conducive to preserving Mozambique's low debt indicators and low risk of debt distress.' In the same memo, the government made it clear that the growth of the deficit by about 2 per cent in 2009 was partly due to policies to reverse wage compression in the civil service (which has been a priority of the Bank and Fund[9]) and it was kept low by a 'temporary cut in priority expenditures' and that in 2010 it intended to reduce the deficit. In other words, the slight increase in the deficit in one year was partly driven by need to meet other IMF/World Bank targets rather than counter-cyclical policies. They assured the IMF that 'The Government remains committed to its medium-term fiscal strategy geared toward preserving debt sustainability, containing inflationary pressures, and limiting recourse to domestic financing to make room for sustainable private sector credit growth' (IMF, 2010e).

In sum, pro-cyclical policies are alive and well and continue to be the core focal point of IMF programs. What of other reform efforts?

6   *Ex post* to *ex ante* conditionality: real or chimerical reform?

Recent claims by the Fund of other serious reform are, on close examination, rather suspect. At the centre of the IMF claim of 'modernizing conditionality' are the new Flexible Credit Lines with their move from *ex post* to *ex ante* conditionality. In addition, the Fund will move away from structural performance criteria to program reviews (IMF, 2009j). However, the movement to an *'ex ante'* approach is more chimerical than real. If lending is fairly short-term in nature (FCLs are one year), the distinction between an *ex ante* and *ex post* conditionality rather blurs since if countries slip from their original position the credit arrangement will not be renewed. This is little different from a multi-year lending device with annual reviews and benchmarks.

The FCL agreement in April 2009 places a considerable emphasis upon the 'very strong fundamentals' of Mexico which it lists as low inflation and a strong anti-inflationary bias of the central bank, large reserves, cutbacks in government debt, a balanced budget fiscal policy rule and a flexible exchange rate. Despite the rapidly declining growth rates, the IMF is confident of 'the public debt in Mexico remaining manageable under all scenarios, with public sector gross financing requirements set to continue their trend decline as a share of GDP' (IMF, 2009k, p. 15). Expecting a further decline in the deficit under this scenario is little different from imposing austerity as part of a package of conditionality. If the deficit does the opposite, then this can readily be used to point to Mexican slippage from their strong fundamentals which can then block any extension of the FCL after a year. In March 2010, the IMF was pleased to see Mexico replace falling oil revenues with new tax sources leading to the issuing of a new one-year FCL (IMF, 2010f).

7   Summary and conclusions

A number of the policy strategies in the US and elsewhere that generated the current global crisis (financial liberalisation, deregulation, reductions in state social spending, privatisation, the internationalisation of banking, and so on) are similar to those imposed by the Bank and Fund on the least developed countries for more than a quarter of a century. While developed countries are fearfully focused on the possibility of a depression, the least developed countries have been in a Great Depression for decades as a result of these policies.

Between 1980 and 2002 sub-Saharan Africa per capita income fell by more than 40 per cent (World Bank, 2005). The number of people living under $1.25, the international poverty benchmark, increased from 213 million in 1981 to 390 million people in 2005, constituting more than half the population of the continent (Chen and Ravallion, 2008). While there was an increase in GDP growth after 2002, the boom was largely as a result of a temporary increase in commodity prices, particularly in oil, which has not trickled down to the majority of the population. The region has experienced the full effects of the global downturn. In 2009 SSA GDP growth fell by 4.4 per cent compared to the rates of 2004–08 (IMF, 2010d).

In a manner similar to the crisis of 1997–98, the Bank and Fund have now been re-empowered and resurrected into a more central role in the global economy. At some point in the future middle-income countries will again exit from the tentacles of the Fund and Bank. However, poor developing countries that are caught in a permanent debt trap with few alternative sources of financing will continue to be dependent on the Bretton Woods twins.

Changing the policy strategies will mean a fundamental reconceptualisation of what generates growth and development. Evidence supporting Strauss-Kahn's claims above that the IMF has 'learned from its mistakes' and 'flexible to the peculiarities of each country' seems rather hollow in view of the above evidence. The road to reform is daunting but imperative. Like the depression of the 1930s, we must use this moment to intrepidly challenge entrenched interests and the policies that for far too long have been perpetuated at the expense of the poor and dispossessed.

Notes

1. The paper draws on work presented in seminars and conferences at Columbia University, University of Amsterdam, Luiss University, Rome, Cambridge University and the European Parliament in Brussels in 2009 and 2010. I am grateful for the feedback from the audiences at each of these seminars. I also appreciate the comments of Claudia Kedar and the generosity of KITLV, Leiden, Netherlands where I was a visiting fellow while writing the current version of the paper.
2. Contrast the bold denunciations of the Fund by people like Nestor Kirchner with the comments from President Ortega of Nicaragua mild rebuke 'It is a blessing to be free of the Fund, and for the Fund it will be a relief to rid itself of a government that defends the interests of the poor'. Meanwhile he signed a new PRGF arrangement with the Fund in July 2007 with some vague plans of ending loans after five years (Bretton Woods Project, 2007).

3. The lists includes Armenia, Belarus, Bosnia, Costa Rica, El Salvador, Georgia, Guatemala, Hungary, Iceland, Latvia, Mongolia, Pakistan, Romania, Serbia, Seychelles, Sri Lanka, Ukraine, Columbia, Mexico and Poland (IMF, 2009d, 2010a).
4. Even Williamson (2008) of Washington Consensus fame admits that levels of economic growth have not improved under IMF programmes.
5. For negative trends on income distribution and poverty on the continent and their relationship to World Bank agricultural policies see Stein (2010b).
6. The latest iteration is in 'Governance Matters VIII' released in June 2009. See Kaufmann et al. (2009).
7. Key changes in the operation of the Bank and Fund require a vote exceeding 85 per cent. Since their inception, the US has always maintained a voting power exceeding 15 per cent, providing it with veto power.
8. The foreign currency loan problem is a common one in Eastern and Central Europe due to the increasing dominance of foreign bank ownership pushed heavily by the World Bank. See Stein (2010a) for an analysis and critique.
9. Reversing wage compression has been part of the civil service reform efforts embedded in the poverty reduction support credits of the World Bank in Mozambique (World Bank, 2009b).

References

Apaza, Carmen (2009) 'Measuring Governance and Corruption through the Worldwide Governance Indicators: Critiques, Responses, and Ongoing Scholarly Discussion', *PS: Political Science and Politics*, 42, 139–43.
Barro, Robert and Lee, Jong-wha (2002) 'IMF Lending: Who Is Chosen and What Are the Effects?', *NBER Working Papers Series*, no. 8951.
Bird, Graham (2001) 'Do They Work: Can They Be Made to Work Better?', *World Development*, 29(11), 1849–65.
Bretton Woods Project (2007) 'Just say no Vocal rejection of Bank, Fund Increasing', Update 56, July.
Bretton Woods Project (2010) 'Analysis of World Bank Voting Reforms Governance Remains Illegitimate and Outdated', Briefing, 30 April. http://www.brettonwoodsproject.org/art-566281.
Brown, Chelsea (2009) 'Democracy's Friend or Foe? The Effects of Recent IMF Conditional Lending in Latin America', *International Political Science Review*, 30(4), 431–57.
China Daily (2008) 'Bitter IMF Pills Difficult for Asia to Swallow', 3 December.
Chen, S. and Ravaillion, M (2008) 'The Developing World is Poorer Than We Thought, But no Less Successful in the Fight Against Poverty', *World Bank Policy Research Working Paper No. 4703*, September.
Crisp, B. and Kelly, M. (1999) 'The Socioeconomic Impacts of Structural Adjustment', *International Studies Quarterly*, 43(5), 533–52.
Dreher, Alex (2006) 'IMF and Economic Growth: The Effects of Programs, Loans, and Compliance with Conditionality', *World Development*, 34(5), 769–88.
Garuda, G. (2000) 'The Distributional Effects of IMF Programs: A Cross Country Analysis', *World Development*, 28(6), 1031–51.

G20 (2009) 'Leaders' Statement: The Pittsburgh Summit, Sept. 24–25', http://www.g20.org/Documents/pittsburgh_summit_leaders_statement_250909.pdf.

IMF (various) 'IMF Financial Activities – Update'. Washington, DC: IMF.

IMF (2008a) *Annual Report, 2008*. Washington, DC: IMF.

IMF (2008b) 'Fact Sheet: Crisis and the IMF Lending', http://www.imf.org/external/np/exr/facts/crislend.htm.

IMF (2008c) 'IMF Spells Out Need for Global Fiscal Stimulus – Interview with Olivier Blanchard and Carlo Cottarelli', *IMF Survey Magazine*, 29 December, http://www.imf.org/external/pubs/ft/survey/so/2008/INT122908A.htm.

IMF (2008d) *World Economic Outlook*, October.

IMF (2009a) 'Republic of Latvia: Request for Standby Arrangement', IMF Country Report 09/16, Malawi, January.

IMF (2009b) 'Malawi: Request for a One Year Shock Facility Agreement', IMF Country Report 09/16, Malawi, January.

IMF (2009c) 'Statement by the IMF Mission to Turkey', Press Release No. 09/14, 26 January, http://www.imf.org/external/np/sec/pr/2009/pr0914.htm.

IMF (2009d) 'IMF Financial Activities – Update', 27 August, http://www.imf.org/external/np/tre/activity/2009/082709.htm.

IMF (2009e) 'Fiscal Policy in Sub-Saharan Africa in Response to the Impact of the Global Crisis', IMF Staff Position Note, 14 May, SPN 09/10, http://www.imf.org/external/pubs/ft/spn/2009/spn0910.pdf.

IMF (2009f) 'The Federal Democratic Republic of Ethiopia: Request for a 14-Month Arrangement under the Exogenous Shocks Facility-Staff Report', IMF Country Report 09/26, 23 September, http://www.imf.org/external/country/ETH/index.htm.

IMF (2009g) 'IMF Executive Board Approves US$336 Million Exogenous Shocks Facility Arrangement for Tanzania and Completes Fifth Review Under the Policy Support Instrument', Press Release No. 09/190, 29 May, 2009 http://www.imf.org/external/np/sec/pr/2009/pr09190.htm.

IMF (2009h) 'United Republic of Tanzania', IMF Country Report No. 09/179, June, http://www.imf.org/external/pubs/ft/scr/2009/cr09179.pdf.

IMF (2009i) 'Republic of Mozambique: Fifth Review Under the Policy Support Instrument, First Review Under the Twelve-Month Arrangement Under the Exogenous Shocks Facility', IMF Country Report No. 09/327, December, http://www.imf.org/external/pubs/ft/scr/2009/cr09327.pdf.

IMF (2009j) 'IMF Implements Lending Policy Improvements', http://www.imf.org/external/np/pdr/fac/2009/032409.htm.

IMF (2009k) 'Mexico: Arrangement Under the Flexible Credit Line – Staff Report; Staff Supplement; and Press Release on the Executive Board Discussion', IMF Country Report No. 09/126, April, http://www.imf.org/external/pubs/ft/scr/2009/cr09126.pdf.

IMF (2010a) 'IMF Financial Activities – Update', 22 April, http://www.imf.org/external/np/tre/activity/2010/042210.htm.

IMF (2010b) 'Past IMF Disbursements and Repayments from all Members from May 01, 1984 to March 31, 2010', http://www.imf.org/external/np/fin/tad/extrep1.aspx.

IMF (2010c) 'Zambia: 2009 Article IV Consultation, Third Review Under the Three-Year Arrangement Under the Poverty and Reduction and Growth

Facility', IMF Country Report No. 10/17, January, http://www.imf.org/external/pubs/ft/scr/2010/cr1017.pdf.

IMF (2010d) 'Regional Economic Outlook Sub-Saharan Africa: Back to High Growth?', *World Economic and Financial Outlooks*, April. Washington, DC: IMF.

IMF (2010e) 'International Financial Statistics', online.

IMF (2010f) 'Mexico: Arrangement Under the Flexible Credit Line', IMF Country Report No. 10/81, http://www.imf.org/external/pubs/ft/scr/2010/cr1081.pdf.

IMF (2010g) 'Bolstering the IMF's Lending Capacity', April, http://www.imf.org/external/np/exr/faq/contribution.htm.

Kaufmann, Daniel, Kraay, Aart and Mastruzzi, Massimo (2005). *Governance Matters IV: Governance Indicators for 1996–2004*. Available http: http://www.worldbank.org/wbi/governance/pubs/govmatters4.html.

Kaufmann, Daniel, Kraay, Aart and Mastruzzi, Massimo (2009) 'Governance Matters VIII: Aggregate and Individual Governance Indicators, 1996–2008', *World Bank Policy Research Working Paper Series*. WPS 4978. June.

Khan, Mushtaq (2007) 'Governance, Economic Growth and Development Since the 1960s', *DESA Working Paper Series*. No. 54, August.

Killick, Tony (1995) *IMF Programmes in Developing Countries: Design and Impact.* London: Routledge.

Kurtz, Marcus, and Shrank, Andrew (2007) 'Growth and Governance: Models, Measures, and Mechanism', *The Journal of Politics*, 69(2), 538–54.

Kurtz, M.J. (2004) 'The Dilemma of Democracy in the Open Economy', *World Politics*, 56(2), 262–302.

Merco Press (2008) 'Fed Swap Lines with Brazil, Mexico, South Korea and Singapore', 12 October, http://en.mercopress.com/2008/10/30/fed-swap-lines-with-brazil-mexico-south-korea-and-singapore.

Polak, Jaacques (1957) 'Monetary Analysis of Income Formation and Payments Problems', *IMF Staff Papers*, 6: 1–50.

Przeworski, Adam and Vreeland, James Raymond (2000) 'The Effect of IMF Program on Economic Growth', *Journal of Development Economics*, 62, 385–421.

Splimbergo, Antonio, Symansky, Steve, Blanchard, Oliver and Cottarelli, Carlo (2008) 'IMF Staff Position Note: Fiscal Policy for the Crisis', SPN/08/01, December.

Stallings, B. and Peres, W. (2000). *Growth, Employment, and Equity: The Impact of the Economic Reforms in Latin America and the Caribbean*. Washington, DC: Brookings Institution Press.

Stein, Howard (2008) *Beyond the World Bank Agenda: An Institutional Approach to Development.* Chicago and London: University of Chicago Press.

Stein, Howard (2010a) 'Financial Liberalization, Institutional Transformation and Credit Allocation in Developing Countries: The World Bank and the Internationalization of Banking', *Cambridge Journal of Economics*, 34(2).

Stein, Howard (2010b) 'World Bank Agricultural Policies, Poverty and Income Inequality in Sub-Saharan Africa', *Cambridge Journal of Regions, Economy and Society* (available online, August).

Thomas, Landon (2008) 'Turkey Tries to Resist Aid From IMF', *New York Times*, 7 November.

UNCTAD (2008) 'On-Line Statistics'.

Vreeland, James Vernon (2003) *The IMF and Economic Development*. Cambridge: Cambridge University Press.

Waeyenberge, Elsa, Bargawi, Hannah and McKinley, Terry (2010) 'Standing in the Way of Development: A Critical Survey of the IMF's Crisis Response to Low-Income Countries' Eurodad and Third World Network Report', April http://www.boell.org/downloads/Standing_in_the_way_of_development.pdf.

Weisbrot, Mark, Ray, Rebecca, Johnston, Jake, Cordero, Jose Antonio and Montecino, Juan Antonio (2009) 'IMF-Supported Macroeconomic Policies and the World Recession: A Look at Forty-One Borrowing Countries', Center for Economic Policy Research, October.

Weisbrot, Mark and Ray, Rebecca (2010) 'Latvia's Recession: The Cost of Adjustment with an "Internal Devaluation"', Center for Economic Policy Research, February.

Williamson, J. (2008) 'A Short History of the Washington Consensus', in N. Serra and J. Stiglitz (eds), *The Washington Consensus Reconsidered*. New York: Oxford University Press.

World Bank (2000) *Annual Report, 2000*. Washington, DC: World Bank.

World Bank (2002) *Annual Report, 2002*. Washington, DC: World Bank.

World Bank (2004) *Annual Report, 2004*. Washington, DC: World Bank.

World Bank (2005) *African Development Indicators*. Washington, DC: World Bank.

World Bank (2008) *Annual Report, 2008*. Washington, DC: World Bank.

World Bank (2009a) *Annual Report, 2009*. Washington, DC: World Bank.

World Bank (2009b) 'IDA Program Document For A Proposed Credit in the Amount OF SDR 69,500,000 to the Republic of Mozambique for a Sixth Poverty Reduction Support Credit Operation', October. Report N. 5092 1 –MZ http://www-wds.worldbank.org/external/default/WDSContentServer/WDSP/IB/2009/10/22/000333037_20091022001920/Rendered/PDF/509210PGD0P117101Official0use0only1.pdf.

World Bank (2010a) 'World Bank Reforms Voting Power, Gets $86 Billion Boost', Press Release, http://web.worldbank.org/WBSITE/EXTERNAL/NEWS/0, content MDK:22556045~pagePK:34370~piPK:34424~theSitePK:4607,00.html.

World Bank (2010b) 'IBRD 2010 Voting Power Realignment', http://siteresources.worldbank.org/NEWS/Resources/IBRD2010VotingPowerRealignmentFINAL.pdf.

Yeldan, A. Erinç (2008) 'Turkey and the Long Decade with the IMF', Bretton Woods Project Update 61, April, http://www.brettonwoodsproject.org/art-561814.

Zhou, Xiaochuan (2009) 'Reform the International Monetary System', Speech, 23 March. Available at People's Bank of China website.

5
Crisis in the Euro Zone

Jonathan Perraton

1 Introduction

At the outbreak of the current financial crisis many European commen-tators and politicians took it to be an essentially Anglo-Saxon affair. The euro zone was taken to be, in effect, a victim of 'collateral damage' from the fallout of a crisis manufactured elsewhere. The financial systems of core euro-zone countries were held to be fundamentally different from Anglo-Saxon ones and thereby less vulnerable to systemic risks, although there had been a shift towards more capital market-based financial systems amongst European economies. The core euro-zone countries had not seen house price booms on US or UK levels and asso-ciated consumption growth; with greater provision of social housing there was not the same expansion of subprime lending. Nor had European countries run major external deficits – overall the euro zone was in approximate balance, with Germany running a clear surplus, and most of the member countries' trade was conducted with each other. Indeed, the European Commission (2009, p. 48) recently asserted that 'Overall, the role of the euro area in global imbalances was negligible until the crisis broke', rather overlooking the role of Germany's large current account surplus.

Any hopes that the euro area might be insulated from the worst of the crisis have been dashed. Since the crisis first emerged in the US and UK financial markets it has come to engulf the whole of the euro area, and not just those economies that had seen asset price bubbles. The crisis has deepened in the euro zone with recession across the zone and particularly strong falls in previously successful economies such as Ireland. The sharp falls in world trade have hit the euro zone, even though external trade beyond the zone is relatively small. Bank lending has dropped sharply, particularly to the more peripheral economies, as banks consolidate their positions. Consumer and business confidence has plummeted. The derogatory acronym PIGS has come to refer to those countries where speculation over their continued membership of EMU has led to widening interest rate differentials between euro-area countries. This, in turn, has raised questions over the sustainability of the whole zone in its current form, and resulting speculation against the euro. Growth in core economies had been sluggish even before the crisis but as Table 5.1 shows it has now turned to sharp falls in activity with only anaemic recoveries predicted for most countries.

In addition to the effects of emergency monetary and fiscal measures, the IMF (2010) forecasts that any recovery will be largely driven by net exports, with the euro having fallen against other major currencies, and inventory effects as firm stocks dwindle; neither are likely to provide the basis for sustained growth. Unemployment levels were high in many euro-area countries, but they had been falling in most countries, in some cases down to levels not seen in twenty years; most of these gains were wiped out rapidly by the crisis. As Table 5.2 shows, this has now been sharply reversed with predictions that unemployment will persist even with a recovery in output. However, soaring unemployment in the US has meant that the long-standing US–EU unemployment gap has now been eliminated. As discussed further below, there is no simple

Table 5.1   Real GDP growth in the euro area

	2000–07	2008	2009	2010[f]	2011[f]
Austria	2.3	2.0	–3.6	1.3	1.7
Belgium	2.2	1.0	–3.1	1.2	1.3
Finland	3.5	1.2	–7.8	1.2	2.2
France	2.1	0.4	–2.2	1.5	1.8
Germany	1.5	1.3	–5.0	1.2	1.7
Greece	4.2	2.0	–2.0	–2.0	–1.1
Ireland	6.0	–3.0	–7.5	–1.5	1.9
Italy	1.5	–1.3	–5.0	0.8	1.2
Netherlands	2.2	2.0	–4.0	1.3	1.3
Portugal	1.5	0.0	–2.7	0.3	0.7
Slovakia	5.6	6.2	–4.7	4.1	4.5
Slovenia	4.4	3.5	–7.8	1.1	2.0
Spain	3.6	0.9	–3.6	–0.4	0.9
Euro area	*2.1*	*0.6*	*–4.1*	*1.0*	*1.5*

f: forecast.
Source: Eurostat; forecasts – IMF (2010).

Table 5.2   Unemployment rates in the euro area

	2000–07	2008	2009	2010[f]	2011[f]
Austria	4.4	3.8	5.0	5.4	5.5
Belgium	7.7	7.0	7.9	9.3	9.4
Finland	8.6	6.4	8.2	9.8	9.6
France	8.9	7.8	9.4	10.0	9.9
Germany	8.9	7.3	7.5	8.6	9.3
Greece	9.9	7.7	9.5	12.0	13.0
Ireland	4.5	6.0	11.8	13.5	13.0
Italy	8.1	6.7	9.1	8.7	8.6
Netherlands	3.5	2.8	3.4	4.9	4.7
Portugal	6.2	7.7	9.6	11.0	10.3
Slovakia	16.7	9.5	11.9	11.6	10.7
Slovenia	6.2	4.4	6.0	7.4	6.8
Spain	10.0	11.3	18.0	19.4	18.7
Euro area	*8.3*	*7.5*	*9.4*	*10.5*	*10.5*

f: forecast.
Sources: Eurostat; forecasts – IMF (2010).

relationship between output losses and unemployment rises across
euro-area countries.

As the first major test of the euro zone, the crisis has raised questions
not just over the issue of adjustment to asymmetric developments in
the absence of standard mechanisms (notably a centralised budget or
labour mobility), but also long-standing concerns over the ECB's policy
stance and co-ordination within the zone: between national fiscal
authorities, between these authorities and the European Central Bank
(ECB) and between national regulatory authorities in the absence of
a clear regulatory role for the ECB. Space prevents a detailed analysis
of the role of euro-zone financial regulation, but it had implications
for the other issues here – for example, Ireland's financial regulation
regime was relatively weak (cf. Connor et al., 2010). In September 2008
the Irish government moved to guarantee debts and deposits with the
largest financial institutions. Although this drew critical responses from
French and German politicians similar moves followed as a consequence, including the German government signing loans and guarantees
to support the Dublin-based Depfa bank, a subsidiary of Munich property
investor Hypo Real Estate, which reportedly has cost the German
authorities more than €102 billion.

This chapter argues that the euro zone is anything but an 'innocent
bystander' in the current crisis, although there are key differences in the

origin and nature of the crisis from that in the US. Major imbalances emerged in the zone over the years before the crisis and these have exacerbated the impact of the crisis in the euro zone. Germany apart, many euro-zone economies saw the emergence of similar imbalances to those seen in the US and UK. These imbalances were not addressed by the ECB which continued to insist that its policy regime was entirely appropriate, a line it largely persists with to this day. The chapter proceeds as follows: section 2 discusses the emergence of the crisis in terms of the policy regime of the ECB, section 3 analyses the emergence of imbalances within the euro zone in the decade before the crisis and section 4 examines the impact of the crisis and responses to it by national governments and the ECB. Section 5 concludes.

2   The emergence of the crisis in the euro zone

The policy regime for the euro zone is well-known. As Arestis and Sawyer (2004, ch. 10; 2006) set out, the ECB has been founded on the principles of the 'new consensus macroeconomics': monetary policy should be controlled by an independent central bank and essentially directed at controlling inflation alone (a principle effectively enshrined in the Maastricht Treaty). Strictly speaking the ECB does not operate inflation targeting *per se*, and uses its 'two-pillar' approach of a reference value for the growth of the money supply (€M3) – on the assumption of a stable relationship between this aggregate and inflation rates – and a broad-based analysis of price developments. Fiscal policy is intended to be passive, confined largely to the operation of automatic stabilisers within the limits set by the Stability and Growth Pact (SGP), i.e. that budget deficits should not exceed 3 per cent of GDP and should be balanced or in surplus over the business cycle.[1] Output growth and employment are assumed to be determined by supply-side factors so that national authorities can most effectively boost these through the liberalisation of product, financial and (perhaps especially) labour markets. These points have been reiterated through numerous official ECB communications and in more detailed official accounts of the ECB's policy regime (e.g. Issing, 2002). As Arestis and Sawyer (2004: ch. 10; 2006) empha-sise, this entails not simply the assumption that the economy is stable around the natural rate of unemployment but also the further assump-tion that the sectoral balance from this will be consistent with the SGP budgetary rules. Co-ordination of macroeconomic policy between national fiscal authorities, and between these authorities and the ECB is seen as unnecessary and potentially even counter-productive (cf. Issing, 2002).

ECB policy in the run-up to the crisis can at least be readily understood in these terms.

Although the onset of international financial market turmoil is conventionally dated at August 2007 and the Federal Reserve and Bank of England began cutting interest rates at the end of that year, at that stage the ECB's overriding concern was with possible inflationary pressures. As Figure 5.1 shows, the ECB had steadily raised its main refinancing rate over 2006 and 2007 in response to perceived inflationary pressures. This was despite clear signs of falling house prices in euro-area countries, following trends in the US and UK, and increased concerns over the exposure of European banks to global developments. In July 2008 the Governing Council of the ECB raised interest rates by 25 basis points, citing fears of wage–price spirals from energy and food price rises and concerns over growth of monetary aggregates, although core inflation had remained low.[2] Their overall assessment then was virtually identical to previous 2008 ECB *Monthly Bulletins*, asserting that the risks to the economy were to the upside and that economic activity would remain strong:

> While moderating, growth in the world economy is expected to remain resilient, benefiting in particular from continued robust growth in emerging economies. This should support euro area external demand. As regards domestic developments, the fundamentals of the euro area economy remain sound and the euro area does not suffer from major imbalances. In this context, investment growth in the euro area should continue to support economic activity,

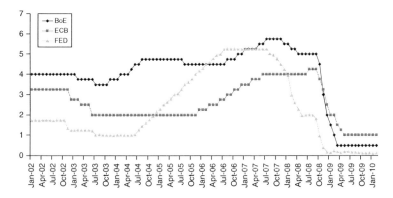

Figure 5.1   Headline interest rates
Sources: Bank of England; ECB; Federal Reserve.

as rates of capacity utilisation remain elevated and profitability in the non-financial corporate sector has been sustained. (ECB, *Monthly Bulletin*, July 2008, p. 5)

The August 2008 assessment, whilst acknowledging that growth was slowing, asserted that recent data had supported the previous month's decision to raise rates. In September 2008 the growth of monetary aggregates was still being cited as pointing to inflationary dangers. A belief that the crisis would have only limited effects on the euro area was also shared by major European governments who declined to take part in a joint bank bailout operation with the US authorities then, although it had been evident from August 2007 that European banks were facing liquidity difficulties too. German banks, in particular, had significant exposure to now 'toxic' financial assets issued in the US. Only on 8 October 2008 were interest rates cut by 50 basis points as part of a co-ordinated international response with the Federal Reserve, the Bank of England and other central banks to the financial crisis. Nevertheless, as Figure 5.1 shows, the ECB cut interest rates later and by a smaller amount than other major central banks. The ECB also shifted from its previous approach of auctioning a fixed quantity of short-term loans to essentially agreeing to replace the market for liquidity where necessary by supplying an unlimited quantity of one-week fixed-rate loans to the European lending markets. The ECB also expanded the range of its longer-term refinancing facilities on 15 October 2008; accordingly, unlimited liquidity could be obtained at a fixed rate of interest (unencumbered by the huge demand for liquidity that would usually drive up interest rates) for maturities of up to six months. The availability of long-term finance was further expanded on 7 May 2009 when the ECB announced that it would extend its October 2008 changes to include 12-month maturities available at the main refinancing rate. To an even greater degree than the Bank of England or the Fed, the ECB has significantly eased its collateral requirements to include a wide range of assets including private securities and commercial paper. As Lapavitsas et al. (2010, p. 7) point out:

> To rescue banks, the ECB engaged in extensive liquidity provision, accepting many and debatable types of paper as collateral for secure debt. ECB actions allowed banks to begin to adjust their balance sheet, engaging in deleveraging. By late 2008 banks were already reducing their lending, including to the periphery. Banks also stopped buying long-term securities preferring to hold short-term

instruments – backed by the ECB – with a view to improving liquidity. The result was credit shortage and accelerated recession across the eurozone, including the periphery.

Nevertheless, the ECB has continued to emphasise inflationary risks from possible wage-price responses to commodity prices rises and from growth of monetary aggregates. Similarly, views on the role of fiscal policy were strongly re-asserted:

> it is essential that governments abide by the rules of the Stability and Growth Pact and ensure the sustainability of public finances. Maintaining sound public finances will enable governments to let automatic stabilisers operate freely and thus contribute to smoothing the economic cycle and to supporting private sector confidence. (ECB, *Monthly Bulletin*, October 2008, p. 7)

This was followed by a reiteration of earlier calls for restraint in wage costs and for labour market reforms as the key means of fostering growth and employment over the long term. To understand the emergence and impact of the crisis it is necessary to examine the emergence of imbalances within the euro area since the formation of EMU.

3 Pre-crisis imbalances and divergence

As noted above, the years before the current crisis were marked by slow growth and relatively high unemployment amongst the core economies of the euro area. The US (and UK) crisis has been seen in terms of rising inequality fuelled by globalisation leading to low or even negative growth in real incomes for average and below-average households; with rising property prices households responded by borrowing and moving into negative net savings (cf. Turner, 2008). Although the growth in wage inequality amongst euro-zone economies has been much less pronounced than in the US (Ireland apart), euro-zone countries had seen a clear shift in income shares from wages and profits with wage increases thus not keeping pace with productivity (IMF, 2007: ch. 5).[3] Private consumption expenditure grew sluggishly as incomes stagnated or declined with falls in real wages (OECD, 2009: 25). Austria and Germany apart, euro-zone countries saw house price rises at similar rates to those in the US over the five years preceding the crisis, with France, Ireland and Spain recording double-digit annual house price rises over 1999–2007; Germany apart, in euro-zone countries the majority of households were owner-occupiers by 2007 (ECB, 2009: 13; European Commission, 2009: 12; OECD, 2009: 25–6). However, this had less impact on consumption in most euro-zone countries compared to the US or UK, with lower household borrowing against property.

Within this picture there was, of course, considerable variation with several more peripheral economies, notably Ireland and Spain, experiencing more rapid growth. However, the three largest economies – Germany, France and Italy – all saw below-average growth over this period. It is the performance of Germany in particular that led to particular imbalances and a deflationary bias within the euro zone. German wage bargaining faced strong downward pressure from institutional changes and globalisation, with the increased use of outsourcing by German companies. Wage settlements consistently lagged behind productivity growth with episodes of negative wage drift (Hein et al., 2006; OECD, 2008a, p. 28). As German households did not experience house price booms and their savings rates remained stable there was sluggish growth in consumer private demand, whilst non-financial corporations became net savers during this decade despite the shift to profits, in part due to the consolidation of earlier corporate debts (Deutsche Bundesbank, 2009; OECD, 2010). Thus, there was no investment boom in response to shift to profits and real interest rates falling to levels below those in the previous two decades. The corollary of these developments was a current account surplus as savings exceeded investment (and the investment itself was concentrated in the export sector); during this period net exports provided the main (at points virtually the sole) source of growth for the German economy. Overseas investment by German companies rose as some of the counterpart to the current account surplus. The key development here is the emergence of payments imbalances with other euro-area economies – by 2007, around 60 per cent of Germany's current account surplus was with other euro-area economies and 80 per cent with EU-27 countries (OECD, 2010: 29). Germany gained strongly in competitiveness over this period whilst Italy, Portugal, Spain and Ireland all lost competitiveness. There are two possible qualifiers to this: that this is largely an adjustment by Germany to earlier 1990s losses of competitiveness in the aftermath of unification and/or that higher inflation elsewhere in Europe was an equilibrium effect from growth (i.e. a Balassa–Samuelson effect). However, neither of these claims receives clear empirical support (Fischer, 2007); on some estimates Germany had already restored price competitiveness relative to euro-zone countries by around 2000 (OECD, 2008a, p. 25).

These developments imparted a deflationary bias to the euro-zone economy (cf. Hein et al., 2006): German core inflation rates fell to low levels, risking deflation, whilst the growing surpluses with other euro-zone economies contribute to stagnation elsewhere in the zone. Further, these developments put downward pressure on wage settlements, thereby also contributing to deflationary pressures. Nor is this a case of being wise after the event. Earlier simulations indicated that although small countries pursuing competitive wage strategies would not have significant negative effects on the euro-zone economy as a whole if pursued by a large economy like Germany it would have net negative effects on the euro-area economy with any falls in interest rates such a strategy might permit not outweighing the negative demand effects (Fritsche et al., 1999). It certainly can be argued that the ECB pursued an excessively tight and asymmetric monetary policy in the pre-crisis period (cf. Bibow, 2009; Hein et al., 2006). But this is only part of the story and herein lies the significance of fiscal policy: even had interest rates been lower in the euro area during the pre-crisis period this would have been unlikely to have had much effect on either household consumption or firms' investment expenditure. With both households and non-financial corporations as net savers, balance could only have been restored with a fiscal expansion.

The other side of this process of divergence was the effect on countries with expansionary pressures on inflation and asset prices. There was little evidence of real convergence between countries of the euro zone in the period before the crisis and actual divergence on some indicators (e.g. Christodoulakis, 2009; Hein and Truger, 2005). The counterpart foreign investment in more peripheral economies could have strengthened their capacity and longer-term competitiveness if it had flown to the tradable sector; however, available evidence indicates that it much of it flowed to the non-tradable sector, including property (Christodoulakis, 2009). With at most only limited convergence in business cycles, centrally determined monetary policy will periodically be too loose for countries experiencing upswings. With convergence in nominal interest rates inevitably this leads to a process of monetary policy aggravating divergence by producing pro-cyclical real interest rate movements. Estimates of interest rates consistent with a Taylor rule need to be interpreted cautiously – the ECB inflation target is likely to have been too low with negative effects on output (cf. Arestis and Sawyer, 2004: ch. 10; 2006; Hein et al., 2006) and such estimates are dependent upon measures of the output gap that are subject to considerable margins of error. Nevertheless, broad estimates that indicate that the ECB's actual interest rate policy was roughly consistent with a Taylor rule for the euro area as a whole also point to interest rates being too low in expanding economies (Ahrend et al., 2008). For example, for most of the 2000s before the crisis the ECB policy rate was below Irish inflation rates (Connor et al., 2010, p. 12). As Bibow (2006) points out, in practice the problems go beyond this with effectively low real interest rates in expanding economies fuelling growth of credit and asset price booms, and further aggravating payments imbalances within between euro-zone economies. Setzer et al. (2010) find clear evidence of divergence in the growth of broad monetary aggregates between euro-zone economies in the period before the crisis, with money demand significantly related to house prices developments and differences in housing markets and associated financial regimes. Interestingly, this appears to be very much a post-EMU formation phenomenon: countries experiencing house price booms could tap into a much larger and more liquid capital market, attracting capital inflows. Thus, this is not the textbook problem for a monetary union of adjustment to an (external) asymmetric shock, but the result of mechanisms intrinsic to the operation of EMU. Germany engineering a position of current account surplus through wage restraint faced little effective pressure to adjust but created simultaneously for other economies a problem of low effective external demand and excessively loose monetary policy.

These effects can be seen clearly in several more peripheral economies during the pre-crisis period. The Irish economic experience closely resembles that of the US or UK, with in effect Ireland's continued growth becoming increasingly dependent upon 'house price Keynesianism' (Hay et al., 2008). Even here there were key differences, with Irish financial institutions making much less use of subprime lending or derivative instruments (Connor et al., 2010). There was considerable property speculation, fuelled in part by capital inflows, and encouraged by relatively light financial regulation, but much of this was at the higher end of the market, including commercial property. In other respects these cases in particular resemble the US/UK experience. As Figure 5.2 shows, although France and Germany maintained relatively high and stable household savings rates, elsewhere these fell in the pre-crisis period in some cases into negative territory.

The ECB response to such developments was that adjustment to inflation differentials and/or payments imbalances should take place through wage flexibility and fiscal consolidation if the countries were judged to be running structural budget deficits. Indeed, the ECB has

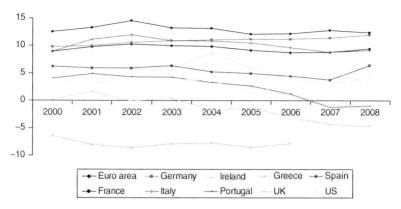

Figure 5.2   Net household savings rates (% disposable income)
Source: AMECO database.

identified inflation differentials as driving the adjustment process within EMU:

> Inflation differentials can be an integral part of the adjustment mechanism resulting from dispersion of economic developments across the participating countries, a mechanism which in turn reflects the impact of various economic shocks as well as the fact that the economic structures in place vary from country to country. Inflation differentials are, then, the product of an equilibrating adjustment process within a monetary union and, as such, are not only unavoidable, but also desirable. (ECB, *Monthly Bulletin*, May 2005, p. 61)

There are several reasons why this has been of limited effectiveness. Earlier simulations indicated that relative price adjustment mechanisms would be very slow and variable in their operation amongst European countries, both in terms of adjustment to asymmetric shocks within the euro area and in terms of different responses to a common external shock (Mazier and Saglio, 2008). In a monetary union, wage and price pressures will be felt most acutely in the tradable sector with inflationary pressures more pronounced in the non-tradable sector and, especially, on asset prices. With generalised wage moderation amongst euro-area economies for much of the 1990s and the current decade, so that real wages have not kept pace with productivity growth, this would place particular burdens of adjustment on households which have, as noted, typically seen sluggish growth in real incomes. Fundamentally, adjustment of this form would only be likely to be expansionary through net export effects external to the euro zone. A shift from wages to profits would not necessarily be associated with falls in demand if it induced an investment response but the German trends towards low investment and consolidation by the corporate sector were common across Europe in this decade. Nor would an increase in net borrowing by the corporate sector necessarily solve external payments imbalances. An increase in external competitiveness relative to countries outside the euro zone would tend to raise net exports and thereby maintain activity, but this was a limited option for euro-zone countries who conduct most of their trade with each other and during a period when the euro tended to appreciate relative to other major currencies.

Instead these developments are strikingly consistent with the flow-of-funds model developed by Godley and Lavoie (2007), models of this form having had a good track record of predicting the current crisis.[4] Instead of automatic mechanisms of adjustment operating between a rich and poor region of a monetary union, a surplus in the former and a deficit in the latter can persist as an equilibrium so long as bonds issued by the poor region are held willingly at the common interest rate. The account here is not an exact fit with developments in the euro zone – in particular, the countries running trade deficits saw these largely covered by private capital flows and did not have counterpart fiscal deficits before the crisis (Christodoulakis, 2009). Nevertheless, the key point remains that deficits between the two regions are not automatically self-correcting. If assets issued by the poor region are no longer willingly held at a common interest rate then there are limited adjustment possibilities: a rise in interest rates on the poor region's assets simply leads to explosive debt–GDP ratios as the cost of servicing debt rises. A stationary state could be achieved if the deficit area were to respond by reducing expenditure to eliminate budget and trade deficits, but this adjustment would act to lower demand and output within the monetary union. Clearly this is the form of adjustment mandated by the SGP as and when countries operate fiscal imbalances. The alternative mechanism of adjustment, expansion by the rich surplus region would also produce a stationary state but this is clearly a form of adjustment not mandated by SGP rules. Adjustment to reduce inflation and/or payments imbalances by domestic deflationary policies risks producing 'beggar-my-neighbour' deflation throughout the euro area. These dangers were magnified once the euro economy moved into the present crisis conditions.

4   The current crisis in the euro area

Standard explanations for the current crisis in the US typically locate it either in lax regulation combined with loose monetary policy, or in terms of deeper structural changes in the global economy – surplus funds generated in emerging market economies sought 'safe haven' investments primarily in the US (relatively sluggish European performance making it unattractive to these investors) leading to falling interest rates and fuelling (ultimately unsustainable) asset price booms (Caballero et al., 2008; Jagannathan et al., 2009).

At one level there are clear differences between the US (and UK) experience and the euro zone in the genesis of the crisis. With greater provision of social housing there was much less subprime lending – even in Ireland the property price bubble was increasingly fuelled by higher-end speculation, including in commercial property, rather than problems with subprime mortgages (Connor et al., 2010). European financial institutions had generally been much less involved in the issuance of CDOs and similar derivative instruments. Monetary policy had been less expansionary, and although similar house price booms had been seen outside Austria and Germany, the associated growth in consumer expenditure had been less marked. As a bloc, the euro zone had not seen high capital inflows and as a bloc it did not have an external payments deficit; as detailed above, though, several euro-zone countries had experienced both house prices booms and current account deficits.

Germany apart, though, the contrast between the euro zone and the US and UK can easily be overstated. Household savings fell in most euro-zone countries and household debt relative to disposable income had risen to almost 100 per cent by 2007, up from 75 per cent a decade earlier, although this remained some way below US and UK levels (Be Duc and Le Breton, 2009; ECB, 2009: 67). Amongst the non-financial corporations, net borrowing had fallen back from peaks in the 1998–2001 period (Be Duc and Le Breton, 2009), in part reflecting the consolidation of earlier debts. Significant current account imbalances had emerged in several countries. European banks may have been less involved in the issuance of CDOs and similar assets than their American and British counterparts, but German banks in particular had made extensive acquisitions of overseas bonds in search of favourable returns (German banks intermediating growing funds from domestic savers). Thus, euro-zone countries had experienced developments that often differed in degree, rather than kind, from Anglo-Saxon economies.

As house prices began to fall from 2007 those euro-zone countries with house price bubbles – notably Ireland and Spain – experienced similar crises. Further, Holland et al. (2009) find a negative association between imbalances in the housing market and the cumulative budget position thus far over the crisis period: the fallout from the end of house price booms has been costly in terms of both falls in output and public rescue packages for the financial system. The second key channel for crisis generation was through the collapse in global trade – Holland et al. (2009) find a negative association between net trade relative to GDP in 2007 and change in output over the crisis amongst European economies, i.e. those countries with the strongest trade orientation have in general seen the greatest falls in output through exposure to the global downturn.

Conversely, there has been a positive association between the size of government expenditure and changes in output (Holland et al., 2009), indicating that fiscal policy stabilisers have operated as expected. Of course, this has resulted in sharp rises in budget deficits and projected debt–GDP ratios relative to SGP provisions so that at the time of writing the European Commission has issued deficit warnings to 13 of the euro-zone member countries and Germany has introduced a new constitutional deficit rule limiting the structural deficit at the Federal level to 0.35 per cent of GDP. It is difficult to disentangle the active component of the fiscal stimulus from the operation of automatic stabilisers. In 2007 the euro zone as a whole exhibited approximate budget balance. An October 2008 extraordinary euro-area Heads of Government summit agreed the principles of a European Action Plan to bolster the financial system, followed in November by a European Economic Recovery Plan for counter-cyclical fiscal policy. Thus, there has been some fiscal co-ordination between euro-zone national governments, albeit of a somewhat ad hoc nature. Riet (2010) estimates that the active stimulus package amounts to around 2 per cent of euro-zone GDP across 2009–10. Germany launched a fiscal expansionary of the order of 3 per cent of GDP, with a similar-sized package in Spain and around 1 per cent of GDP in France but Italy has hardly changed its active fiscal stance. Early estimates indicate that these fiscal policy responses and the monetary policy response of the ECB added about 0.5 percentage points each to euro-zone GDP (Barrell et al., 2009). This is in the context of circumstances where fiscal policy would be likely to be most effective with interest rates close to the zero bound but credit growth has plummeted. The EU-wide budget is too small and inflexible to play a stabilising role, although there have been some proposals for increased capital expenditure. When EMU was first seriously proposed in the 1970s the MacDougall Report recommended an area-wide budget of around 7 per cent of GDP to play a stabilising role and variants of this have been proposed since.[5] Nevertheless, there are two important qualifiers here. First, there is little immediate prospect of the necessary political union to create an EMU-wide fiscal authority. Second, such a budget would not necessarily have ameliorated the imbalances that emerged within the euro zone over this decade: there was no clear relationship between current account positions and fiscal positions. The centralised budget is typically proposed as a solution to the classic textbook problem of an external asymmetric shock to a monetary union inducing current account and budget deficits in the country experiencing a negative external shock (and hence an economic downturn) and the reverse in a country experiencing a positive shock. The developments in EMU over this decade before the crisis did not arise from external shocks, but from developments within the euro zone, and did not give rise to this pattern of imbalances; hence, there would no reason to presume that funds would have flowed from Germany to the countries with which it had a payments surplus.

The full fiscal costs of the financial stability packages, the level of contingent liabilities incurred by euro-area governments as a result of policies to support national financial institutions, remain unclear. Past experience with financial crises – not least amongst Scandinavian economies in the early 1990s – indicates that the fiscal cost of bank rescue policies can be considerable. Riet (2010) reports an estimate of contingent liabilities ceiling of around 20 per cent of GDP across the euro zone, with an astonishing 172 per cent of GDP in the case of Ireland.

The ECB has mounted a robust defence of its own response. Although, as noted above, it has held interest rates at slightly higher levels than the Bank of England and the Fed it has defended its policy stance in terms of the use of 'non-standard' measures of expanding liquidity. It is too early to make any clear judgements, but Milas and Naraidoo (2009) find evidence of a policy shift by the ECB in response to the crisis so that whereas in effect the ECB had been operating an inflation targeting policy before the onset of the crisis, since then it has effectively switched to operating an output-stabilising policy and has moved from an asymmetric response to inflationary conditions to a more symmetric stance. It remains too early to tell whether this is indicative of a regime shift: the ECB itself has insisted that the 'non-standard' measures are simply designed to improve the operation of the monetary transmission mechanism and do not affect the stance of monetary policy and hence specific operations will be sterilised. The growth of nominal broad monetary aggregates has been falling rather than rising for most of the period since the initiation of 'non-standard' measures and latterly turned negative.

The impact of the crisis and national policy responses has produced diverse results in terms of output and unemployment. Figure 5.3 shows the cumulative percentage declines in output thus far since the onset of the current crisis across euro-zone countries and comparator economies.

However, as Figure 5.4 shows there is no simple relationship between these output losses and the percentage point rises in unemployment since the start of the downturn.

Several trends stand out here, notably the actual fall in German unemployment and the small rise in Italian unemployment despite strong recessionary falls in output. Ireland and Spain have similar sharp rises in unemployment even though Spain's fall in output was only around half that of Ireland's. As noted above, the US has seen a particularly sharp rise in unemployment so that the US unemployment rate has now risen to the same level as that of the EU15. Overall, the rise in the unemployment rate is below what would have been expected in Okun's law terms from the output decline in Finland, Austria, the Netherlands and Germany (Arpaia and Curci, 2010; IMF, 2010, ch. 3). The experience of the Scandinavian countries is striking here: Finland has experienced the largest output fall amongst industrial countries since the crisis began, whilst non-EMU members Denmark and Sweden

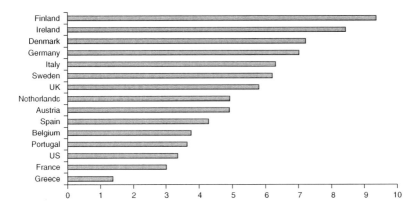

Figure 5.3 Peak-to-trough decline in output
Source: IMF (2010).

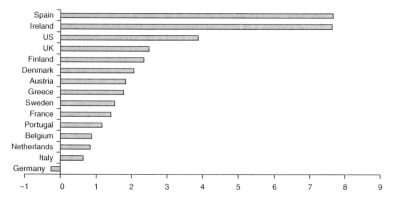

Figure 5.4   Peak-to-trough changes in unemployment
Source: IMF (2010).

have also seen large output falls, but these countries have seen only modest rises in unemployment. There are important differences between the more successful cases here: Germany and Italy have seen relatively small job losses but a strong incidence of short-time working and other measures, whilst the Scandinavian countries have maintained relatively dynamic labour markets and have seen relatively strong out-flows from unemployment – in these countries those people who have become unemployed have managed to find new jobs relatively quickly and at similar rates to those before the crisis.

The positive aspect of these developments, for the relatively success-ful economies, is that it indicates that even within a monetary union national authorities retain some autonomy to influence unemploy-ment rates through fiscal policy and active labour market policies, whilst national wage bargaining systems can still deliver relatively low unemployment. So far labour force participation rates have held up well in Europe, so that people are either employed or seeking work and have not dropped out of the labour force altogether. However, the incipient recovery in Europe remains fragile. In reviewing recent per-formance amongst European economies even the IMF has warned that: 'The downside risks could become more pronounced if policy support in the advanced economies is withdrawn too early, if political pressures delay financial sector reforms, or if policy co-ordination falters' (IMF, 2009, p. 78), and whilst acknowledging concerns over fiscal sustainability warns that 'discretionary fiscal stimulus should not be withdrawn too early' (ibid.: 79) particularly as experience of previous crises indicates that recovery in private consumption and investment expenditure is likely to be sluggish. Stimulus measures apart, net exports currently provide the main positive contribution to demand in Europe with a weakening euro – with growth weak in the rest of the world this is unlikely to sustain any recovery. Deflationary trends and damaging payments imbalances emerged within the euro area even before the crisis; if these were to persist they would endanger both the recovery and potentially the unity of the euro area itself. Past experience indicates that crises are especially severe, and their effects on unemployment particularly long-lasting, when they result from property price crashes or financial crises more generally. Property price crashes lead to consolidation by households and worsen the balance sheets of firms and banks. Financial crises disrupt the workings of credit – firms with short-term cash-flow problems that may be viable long-term nevertheless go under; even as the economy recovers firms with growth potential are unable to borrow in order to invest and expand employment. Although the non-financial corporate sector in euro-zone countries was mostly only a small net borrower, and in some countries was a net saver, before the crisis began this partly reflected consolidation of earlier debts. The limited an investment boom even before the crisis, despite relatively high profitability and low real interest rates, indicates the significant expansion in capacity with an upturn is unlikely. Persistent effects on output and a jobless recovery in output appear likely.

The most acute problems have been felt in Portugal, Ireland, Greece and Spain – the so-called PIGS group[6] – where there has been active speculation over their continued participation in EMU. Speculation has been concentrated on these countries with relatively high projected debt levels and anticipated costs of bank rescue packages, but also reflects increased risk-aversion by some investors (Riet, 2010: 40–71); these countries are also notable as peripheral EMU economies where imbalances had developed and economy cycles were most out of synchronisation with core euro-zone economies. This speculation has resulted in sharply widening differentials on government debt within the euro zone, with consequently increased cost of debt servicing. By May 2008 a €100 bn loans package being agreed for Greece between the European Commission, the ECB and the IMF.[7] The policy package agreed by the Greek government entails unprecedented austerity measures in terms of tax rises and public expenditure cuts. The involvement of the IMF, initially resisted, suggests limits to the ability of the euro zone to regulate itself. Lapavitsas et al. (2010) point out that a number of features that have made Greece particularly vulnerable to speculation, including revelations about the true state of public finances, a relatively under-developed tax system and the thinness of markets for Greek bonds. Banks in other euro-area countries have considerable exposure to Greek public debt; precise figures are not available but French banks are estimated to hold around a quarter of all foreign bank holdings of Greek government bonds (€27–52 billion) and German banks around 14 per cent (€15–30 billion) with banks in the euro area as a whole estimated to hold over half of the foreign bank holdings of Greek public debt (€62–121 billion).[8] In addition to potential negative spillovers to euro-zone financial institutions outside Greece is the prospect of contagion effects spreading any Greek crisis to other euro-zone economies. One of the key expected gains from EMU was precisely to avoid speculation against national monetary authorities and contagion effects spreading across countries. In practice, speculation on bonds over EMU member-ship appears to have replaced earlier speculation against currency pegs. Similar principles though may apply – speculation leading to rising interest rates could create self-fulfilling crisis conditions for countries with high debt–GDP ratios, at least in the absence of supporting policy coordination by other area members. Estimates for the external position of the PIGS – it is less the debt–GDP ratio than outstanding external debts that appears to be inducing vulnerability – are reported in Table 5.3.

The striking point here is not just that affected economies have high levels of net external debt – both public and private – with much of it held by institutions elsewhere in the euro area. Further, as Cabral (2010) emphasises, these indicators are at similar – or even higher levels – to emerging market countries immediately before major external debt crises. At the time of writing, it remains to be seen whether the EU support

Table 5.3   External position of PIGS, end-2009

	General government gross debt (GGGD) (% GDP)	General government net external debt (% GGGD)	Net international investment position (% GDP)
Portugal	77.2	74.9	–111.7
Ireland	64.5	70.6	–73.1
Greece	113.4	78.9	–82.2
Spain	55.2	47.3	–93.5
Italy	115.1	42.9	–19.0
Germany	72.5	48.5	37.3

Source: Cabral (2010).

packages, and the policy measures agreed to affected countries, will be sufficient to stem speculation and restore domestic balance.

The upshot of these developments is increased pressure to cut budget deficits, primarily through cuts in expenditure. This can be seen most clearly in Ireland which has recently created a National Asset Management Agency to take over toxic debts with some predictions that the notional value of the bad loans book could rise to around half of Ireland's GDP. The government response to the rising costs of the financial crisis has been to enforce the sharpest cuts in public sector pay and social welfare payments of any EU government (at least until the Greek austerity measures take effect). More generally, the pressure towards fiscal consolidation carries the danger of premature withdrawal of stimulus. In the euro zone, in the absence of co-ordination there is a strong danger of continued trends towards 'beggar-my-neighbour' deflation as countries simultaneously attempt to cut their fiscal deficits and rely on net exports to maintain output (cf. Lapavitsas, 2010). Official ECB and European Commission policy continues to emphasise product and labour market liberalisation – as well as fiscal consolidation (e.g. European Commission, 2009). This is intended to reduce hiring cost and boost productivity; however, trends at least since the completion of the Single European Market have been to greater liberalisation without strongly stimulating investment. European Commission (2009) estimates find that wage and price flexibility would act to ameliorate adjustment. Even under relatively stable conditions, though, such flexibility only appears to provide a relatively slow mechanism of adjustment, as is illustrated by the experience of imbalances within the euro zone before the crisis. However, it is far from clear that this would be the case under conditions of substantial private sector outstanding debt commitments. It is precisely under such conditions of nominal debt commitments that deflation with wage and price flexibility may not be stabilising as falling wages and prices cause debtors' cash flows to fall relative to their commitments (Caskey and Fazzari, 2007). The experience of Scandinavian economies following their early 1990s financial crises – which in retrospect appear as forerunners to the current global crisis – indicates that even successful bank rescue packages may be insufficient to avoid sharp losses of output and persistent rises in unemployment.

5   Summary and conclusions

Briefly on the occasion of the tenth anniversary of the launch of EMU there was an air of self-congratulation for the ECB for having overseen a successful project and embedding monetary policy credibility. The crisis has undermined much of this, and as the 'great moderation' has unravelled the role of a combination of fortuitous factors, rather than the policy decisions of central bankers, has increasingly been highlighted in producing the earlier stability. Although some commentators have characterised the post-crisis period in terms of a 'return to Keynesianism' or even the emergence of a new economics, there are only limited signs of a paradigm shift at the ECB or the European Commission. On the contrary, the pre-crisis assumptions on the role of macroeconomic policy in a monetary union, and assertions of the centrality of labour and product market liberalisation to determining economic performance, remain at the core of ECB policy pronouncements. Further evidence will be needed to assess whether there has been an effective shift in the ECB's monetary policy, although there are some indications of a shift towards output stabilisation and an attempt to avoid outright deflation.

The experience of other European countries, such as Iceland and several East European economies, cautions against concluding that crisis-hit euro-zone countries would have been better off outside EMU or that they would gain from either leaving it or trying to suspend their membership. Nevertheless, the analysis here indicates that the operation of EMU led to profound imbalances between member countries which left it vulnerable to, rather than insulated from, the crisis when it started in the US and the UK. In particular, the overdependence of the German economy on net exports left it vulnerable to external demand conditions. Imbalances elsewhere in the euro zone led to asset price bubbles, which collapsed with the crisis. The crisis emerged in euro-zone countries through similar processes as occurred in the US and the UK. House price booms and associated declines in household savings emerged in most euro-zone countries outside Germany. There were differences in levels of household indebtedness and the precise mechanisms for crisis generation, but these were differences of degree rather than kind from the experiences of the US and the UK. The euro zone lacks effective mechanisms for co-ordinated recovery and the attempts at fiscal consolidation risk producing 'beggar-my-neighbour' deflation and endangering the slight recovery amongst euro-zone economies. Fiscal policy coordination thus far has been only ad hoc in character. The emergence of the crisis points to still unresolved issues concerning the regulatory operation of the ECB and national financial authorities.

Notes

1. Indeed, analysis for the European Commission suggested that even automatic stabiliser effects of fiscal policy were likely to be limited with negligible gains from output stabilisation once public expenditure exceeded 40 per cent of GDP (Debrun et al., 2008). The role of fiscal policy in counteracting the current crisis raises doubts over their conclusion, but it may be indicative of official thinking before the crisis.
2. Other official assessments were similarly sanguine. For example, an April 2008 OECD report on Ireland – the euro-zone economy that most closely resembled the US or the UK – confidently predicted that 'Despite the slowdown, growth could remain above the euro area average' and asserted that 'Economic fundamentals remain sound... Financial system risks have been contained... The Irish banks are highly profitable and well-capitalised, so they should have considerable shock-absorption capacity' (OECD, 2008b, pp. 11 and 13).
3. The more limited wage inequality effects may have affected consumption patterns and thereby the crisis; Zezza (2008) finds a relative income effect on consumption operating for the US so that households tried to maintain consumption levels of those in quintiles above them; household consumption patterns display much less of this behaviour in the euro zone.
4. On this point see Bezemer (2009).
5. See the discussion in Arestis and Sawyer (2006).
6. Italy has sometimes also been included in this group, with its high outstanding debt levels, but thus far has largely escaped these pressures with relatively low foreign holdings of Italian government debt.
7. This has not been, as some commentators have asserted, a breach of the no-bailout rule enshrined in the Maastricht Treaty, although arguably it does breach the spirit of the rule. It does not directly involve the ECB. Under the no-bailout clause the European Union is not liable for the debts of any member governments. However, this does not preclude governments of EU nations voluntarily deciding to provide financial assistance to other member states, with Article 100, section 2[1] expressly allowing for this.
8. Figures from 'Greece's Sovereign Debt Crisis', *The Economist*, 15 April 2010.

References

Ahrend, R., Cournède, B. and Price, R. (2008) 'Monetary Policy, Market Excesses and Financial Turmoil', *OECD Economics Department Working Paper No. 597*.
Arpaia, A. and Curci, N. (2010) 'EU Labour Market Behaviour During the Great Recession', *European Economy Economic Papers No. 405*.
Arestis, P. and Sawyer, M. (2004) *Re-examining Monetary and Fiscal Policy for the 21st Century*. Cheltenham: Edward Elgar.
Arestis, P. and Sawyer, M. (2006) 'Macroeconomic Policy and the European Constitution', in P. Arestis and M. Sawyer (eds), *Alternative Perspectives on Economic Policies in the European Union*. Basingstoke: Palgrave Macmillan.
Barrell, R., Fic, T. and Holland, D. (2009) 'Evaluating policy reactions to the financial crisis', *National Institute Economic Review*, 207, 39–42.

Be Duc, L. and Le Breton, G. (2009) 'Flow-of-Funds Analysis at the ECB – Framework and Applications', *European Central Bank Occasional Paper No. 105.*

Bezemer, D. (2009) '"No One Saw This Coming": Understanding Financial Crisis Through Accounting Models'. Available at http://mpra.ub.uni-muenchen.de/15892/1/MPRA_paper_15892.pdf.

Bibow, J. (2006) 'How the Maastricht Regime Fosters Divergence as Well as Fragility', *The Levy Economics Institute Working Paper No. 460.*

Bibow, J. (2009) 'The Euro and its Guardian of Stability: The Fiction and Reality of the 10th Anniversary Blast', *The Levy Economics Institute Working Paper No. 583.*

Caballero, R., Farhi, E. and Gourinchas, P. (2008) 'Financial Crash, Commodity Prices, and Global Imbalances', *Brookings Papers on Economic Activity*, 2, 1–55.

Cabral, R. (2010) 'The PIGS' External Debt Problem' , VoxEU.org, 8 May. Available at http://www.voxeu.org/index.php?q=node/5008.

Caskey, J. and Fazzari, S. (2007) 'Aggregate Demand Contractions with Nominal Debt Commitments: Is Wage Flexibility Stabilizing?', *Economic Inquiry*, 25(4), 583–97.

Christodoulakis, N. (2009) 'Ten Years of EMU: Convergence, Divergence and New Policy Priorities', *National Institute Economic Review*, 208, 86–100.

Connor, G., Flavin, T. and O'Kelly, B. (2010) 'The U.S. and Irish Credit Crises: Their Distinctive Differences and Common Features', *Irish Economy Note No. 10.* Available at http://www.irisheconomy.ie/Notes/IrishEconomyNote10.pdf.

Debrun, X., Pisani-Ferry, J. and Sapir, A. (2008) 'Government Size and Output Volatility: Should We Forsake Automatic Stabilization?', *European Economy Economic Papers No. 316.*

Deutsche Bundesbank (2009) *Financial Accounts for Germany 1991 to 2008.* Special Statistical Publication No. 4.

ECB (2009) 'Housing Finance in the Euro Area', *European Central Bank Occasional Paper No. 101.*

European Commission (2009) 'Economic Crisis in Europe: Causes, Consequences and Responses', *European Economy 7.*

European Commission (2010) *Quarterly Report on the Euro Area,* Special issue: the impact of the global crisis on competitiveness and current account divergences in the euro area, vol. 9(1), March.

Fischer, C. (2007) 'An Assessment of the Trends in International Price Competitiveness among EMU Countries', *Deutsche Bundesbank Economic Studies Discussion Paper No. 8.*

Fritsche, U. et al. (1999) 'Is There a Need for a Co-ordinated European Wage and Labour Market Policy?', in G. Huemer, M. Mesch and F. Traxler (eds), *The Role of Employer Associations and Labour Unions in the EMU.* Aldershot: Ashgate.

Godley, W. and Lavoie, M. (2007) 'A Simple Model of Three Economies with Two Currencies: the Eurozone and the USA', *Cambridge Journal of Economics*, 31(1), 1–23.

Hay, C. et al. (2008) 'Ireland: The Outlier Inside', in K. Dyson (ed.), *The Euro at 10.* Oxford: Oxford University Press.

Hein, E., Schulten, T. and Truger, A. (2006) 'Deflation Risks in Germany and the EMU: The Role of Wages and Wage Bargaining', in E. Hein, A. Heise and A. Truger (eds), *Wages, Employment, Distribution and Growth.* Basingstoke: Palgrave Macmillan.

Hein, E. and Truger, A. (2005) 'European Monetary Union: Nominal Convergence, Real Divergence and Slow Growth?', *Structural Change and Economic Dynamics*, 16(1), 7–33.

Holland, D., Barrell, R., Fic, T., Hurst, I. Liadze, I., Orazgani, A. and Whitworth, R. (2009) 'The World Economy: Prospects for Fiscal Consolidation in Europe', *National Institute Economic Review*, 210, 25–35.

IMF (2007) *World Economic Outlook: Spillovers and Cycles in the Global Economy.* Washington, DC: International Monetary Fund.

IMF (2009) *World Economic Outlook: Sustaining the Recovery.* Washington DC: International Monetary Fund.

IMF (2010) *World Economic Outlook: Rebalancing Growth.* Washington DC: International Monetary Fund.

Issing, O. (2002) 'On Macroeconomic Policy Co-ordination in EMU', *Journal of Common Market Studies*, 40(2).

Jagannathan, R., Kapoor, M. and Schaumburg, E. (2009) 'Why are We in a Recession? The Financial Crisis is the Symptom not the Disease!', *NBER Working Paper No. 15404.*

Lapavitsas, C., Kaltenbrunner, A., Lindo, D., Michell, J. Painceira, J.P., Pires, E., Powell, J., Stenfors, A. and Teles, N. (2010) *Eurozone Crisis: Beggar Thyself and Thy Neighbour.* RMF Occasional Report. Available at www.researchonmoney andfinance.org.

Mazier, J. and Saglio, S. (2008) 'Interdependency and Adjustments in the European Union', *International Review of Applied Economics*, 22(1), 17–44.

Milas, C. and Naraidoo, R. (2009) 'Financial Market Conditions, Real Time, Nonlinearity and European Central Bank Monetary Policy', *Rimini Centre for Economic Analysis Working Paper 42-09.*

OECD (2008a) *Economic Survey: Germany.* Paris: Organisation for Economic Co-operation and Development.

OECD (2008b) *Economic Survey: Ireland.* Paris: Organisation for Economic Co-operation and Development.

OECD (2009) *Economic Survey: Euro Area.* Paris: Organisation for Economic Co-operation and Development.

OECD (2010) *Economic Survey: Germany.* Paris: Organisation for Economic Co-operation and Development.

Riet, A. van (ed.) (2010) 'Euro Area Fiscal Policies and the Crisis', *European Central Bank Occasional Paper No. 109.*

Setzer, R, van den Noord, P. and Wolff, G.B. (2010) 'Heterogeneity in Money Holdings Across Euro Area Countries: The Housing Channel', *European Economy – Economic Papers 407*, European Commission.

Turner, G. (2008) *The Credit Crunch: Housing Bubbles, Globalisation and the Worldwide Economic Crisis.* London: Pluto Press.

Zezza, G. (2008) 'U.S. Growth, the Housing Market, and the Distribution of Income', *Journal of Post Keynesian Economics*, 30(3), 375–401.

6
The Impact of the Current Crisis on Emerging Market and Developing Countries

Jesus Ferreiro and Felipe Serrano

1 Introduction

When analysing the relations between developed economies and emerging market and developing economies, it is easy to see how the latter have been traditionally dependent and influenced by the cyclical behaviour of the former and by the turmoils generated in them. Expansions in advanced economies implied a positive development framework for developing countries, which benefited from higher export flows and from a suitable financial environment in the shape of higher capital inflows. By contrast, recessions in developed economies dragged developing economies with them due to the negative impact generated on exports and net capital inflows. Even more, the economic deterioration in developing economies was aggravated by episodes of currency and banking crisis and by the inability of these countries the application of anti-cyclical policies. In fact, the need to restore some sound macroeconomic foundations, mainly to reduce fiscal unbalances and ensure capital inflows, forced to apply restrictive demand-side policies, which, in turn, damaged the economic situation. The final result was a strong convergence and synchrony of the economic cycle of developed and developing economies, but where the cycle volatility was bigger for the latter.

Taking this traditional pattern as a basis, we would expect that the present economic crisis, generated in advanced countries, would have affected emerging market and developing economies with higher intensity, and that the economic deterioration of these economies, given its magnitude, would have been the most serious since the Great Depression, especially if we consider that the record figures of foreign trade and capital flows of these economies, in principle, imply an increased relevance of the traditional transmission channels of economic activity of advanced countries over the rest of the world economy and, consequently, a greater importance of the global factors in the determination of the developing countries economic performance.

However, in practice this has not occurred. As a whole, the present crisis has curbed, quite significantly, emerging and developing economies. But this growth deceleration does not seem to give an answer to the patterns of previous crises. Actually, as we will explain later, short-term and medium-term economic prospects still make reference to very high growth rates, higher than those reached in the 1980s and 1990s although lower than the ones recorded before the crisis.

The existence of a series of structural transformations in the economic, institutional and policy spheres have not only allowed emerging and developing economies (if not all at least a significant number of them) to accelerate their growth paths in recent decades, but have also made them less dependent on advanced economies – a phenomenon some authors describe as the 'decoupling' thesis. This lower dependence would have permitted this group of economies, with some exceptions in Central and East European countries, to be less affected than what we would otherwise expect due to the present economic crisis.

This chapter is structured as follows. In the second section we analyse the evolving relation of interdependence between the economic cycles in advanced and emerging markets and developing economies, based on the past and current economic performances in both groups of countries. The next two sections analyse the current relevance of the traditional transmission channels of the shocks generated in developed economies to emerging and developing countries, namely the trade and financial channels. The final section summarises and concludes.

2 Economic crisis and emerging market economies decoupling

One of the essential characteristics of the world economy behaviour is the synchrony of economic cycles between developed and developing economies. As is shown in Figure 6.1,[1] with a small delay, economic cycles of both countries are virtually identical, with a few provisos, such as the 1991–93 crisis, centred on developed countries, fundamentally European countries as a result of the crisis of the European Monetary System, and the 1997–99 crisis, focused on developing economies, mainly in South East Asian countries.

Figure 6.2 shows another performance pattern directly connected to the previous one. Figure 6.1 showed how, regardless of the cycle,

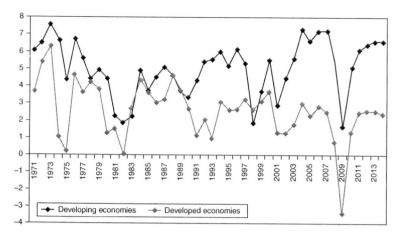

Figure 6.1 Annual rates of real economic growth (%)
Source: UNCTAD Handbook of Statistics Online and International Monetary Fund World Economic Outlook Database October 2009.

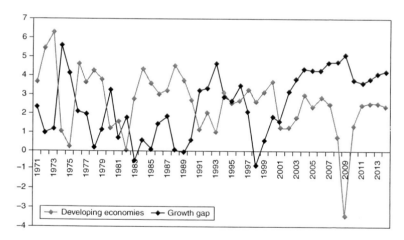

Figure 6.2 Growth rate in developed economies and difference between economic growth of developing economies with regard to developed economies
Source: UNCTAD Handbook of Statistics Online and International Monetary Fund World Economic Outlook Database October 2009.

developing economies have had higher growth rates than developed countries in recent decades. Figure 6.2 compares the growth in developed economies with the growth difference between both groups of countries. In addition to showing the existing delay between the economic cycles of both groups of economies, Figure 6.2 clearly shows how the growth difference also has a marked cyclical performance pattern in such a way that the growth differential of developing economies with regard to developed economies is closely connected with the economic perform-ance of advanced countries. Thus, when developed economies enter a phase of economic deceleration, the growth differential tends to decrease drastically. In other words, crises arisen in advanced economies were trans-mitted to developing economies but with a wider extension. Developing economies were highly dependent on advanced economies. Through commercial and financial channels, crises in advanced economies became global, thereby affecting both developed and developing economies.

Despite what we have mentioned, the data of both graphics also show that from the beginning of the new millennium there is a clear change in behaviour in terms of the performance dynamic of both groups of economies. Thus, Figure 6.1 shows how, since 2001, growth rates recorded in developing economies are the highest of the whole analyzed period, whereas, by contrast, the growth of developed economies has been significantly lower. In addition, and most importantly, the growth differential of developing economies with regard to developed ones has maintained unprecedented levels (Figure 6.2). In fact, although the recession in the 2008–09 biennium has negatively affected the growth of the world economy, something obvious since it is a global crisis, the impact on developing economies has been smaller, clearly smaller than expected, thus reducing by scarcely one percentage point its growth differential with advanced economies. The result is that, in contrast to previous occasions, a large crisis beginning in developed economies has not been transmitted to developing economies, where the crisis has resulted in comparatively small falls in their growth rate, except in the year 2009.[2] As Levy-Yeyati states (2009): 'If, in the 1990s, whenever the world caught a cold, emerging markets got pneumonia, crises have immunised emerging markets so that, if anything, when in 2008 the G7 economies got pneumonia, emerging economies just got a cold.'

This behaviour has led us to propose a new hypothesis: the decoupling of developing economies from developed economies, especially in the case of emerging market economies. A bigger economic and financial integration of developing economies would not have made them more dependent on the economic cycle and on real financial tensions built in developed countries, but less dependent on the latter, altering the impor-tance of traditional transmission mechanisms of economic disturbances, whose direction was usually from developed economies to developing economies (Kose, Otrok and Prasad, 2008a, 2008b). This decoupling

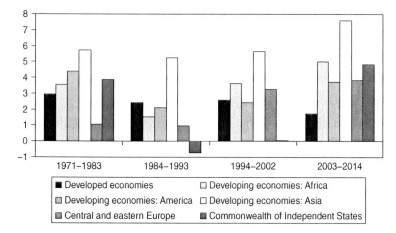

Figure 6.3   Economic growth rate (%)
Source: UNCTAD Handbook of Statistics Online and International Monetary Fund World
Economic Outlook Database, October 2009.

not imply a reduced influence of the global factors on emerging economies
but a greater integration between these economies – in particular, an
increased dependence or sensitivity with regard to the Chinese economy
(Levy-Yeyati, 2009). This process explains not only the bigger growth
differential of developing economies but the fact that, unlike previous
crises, the present one, which arose in the most advanced economies,
has not had the anticipated effect on developing countries.

Figures 6.3 and 6.4 support the decoupling hypothesis. Figure 6.3
shows the average growth rates of developed economies and developing and emerging economies grouped into geographical regions. It can
be seen how variations in the growth of developed economies are
transmitted, with different degrees of intensity, to the different developing economies. However, since 2003, the deceleration in the growth
of developed economies has been accompanied by an increase in the
economic growth of all developing economies, with the result that
these have registered (will register) the highest growth rates of the last
five decades, with the only exception being Latin America.

Figure 6.4 more clearly shows this change in the structural performance of emerging and developing economies and in their relation with
advanced economies. Such a figure reflects the differences between
the growth rates of the different developing economies and advanced
economies. Until the beginning of the new millennium, all developing

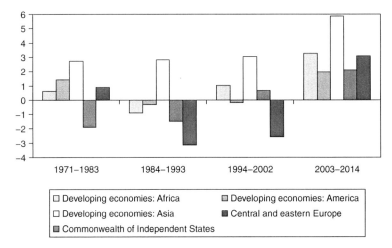

Figure 6.4 Growth gap between developing economies and developed economies
Source: UNCTAD Handbook of Statistics Online and International Monetary Fund World
Economic Outlook Database October 2009.

economies, except for those in Asia, had witnessed how their pace of
economic growth fluctuated around developed economies, growing above
or below in different stages without being able to make them all grow
above advanced economies. However, in the recent period, all regions,
without exception, have achieved growth rates above those in developed
economies, enjoying an unprecedented growth differential. The deep crisis
suffered by advanced economies has not been transmitted to developing
and emerging economies with the same intensity as in previous crises.

Figure 6.5 shows the figures for economic growth in the period
2003–10. It can be seen clearly how the direct impact of the crisis was
much more intense for Central and East European economies and the
CIS (International Monetary Fund, 2009b and 2010b; World Bank, 2010),
whereas the impact is smaller in Africa and America and, particularly in
Asia, where the crisis has led to a slight slowdown of economic growth
(Goldstein and Xie, 2009).

In this respect, Kose et al. (2008b) point out how the globalisation
process has meant the emergence of group-specific cycles for emerging Asian and American economies, that is, a 'concomitant divergence
or decoupling of business cycles' (Kose et al., 2008b, p. 27) between
industrial countries and emerging market economies, explaining in
this way the lesser impact of the present economic crisis in the latter
economies.

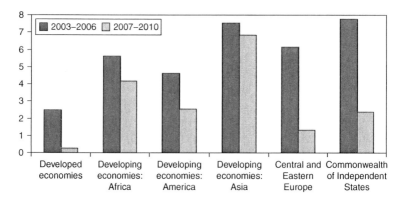

Figure 6.5   Economic growth rates (%) in the period 2003–2010
Source: UNCTAD Handbook of Statistics Online and International Monetary Fund World
Economic Outlook Database, October 2009.

Data show, in short, that the financial and real crisis of advanced economies has not been transmitted as would have been expected from past experiences to emerging and developing economies. This implies that transmission channels of the financial turmoil generated in advanced economies towards emerging market economies – foreign trade links, international capital flows, exchange market pressures and currency mismatches, banking and financial sector fragilities, and the scope for taking counter-cyclical monetary and fiscal policy actions (Goldstein and Xie, 2009) – are not working as expected.

This result contradicts the opinions of several authors, including Frank and Hesse (2009) and Bui and Bayoumi (2010), for whom the financial problems of developed economies have been transmitted to the financial sector of emerging economies and from there to the real economies. It is clear that the global economic crisis has affected developing economies and that all regions, without exception, have witnessed a fall in their development rates. However, the most relevant point is that the behaviour of emerging market economies has been significantly better than advanced economies[3] (International Monetary Fund, 2009b).

Two new facts mark the difference of the performance of developing economies during the present crisis. The first is that with some exceptions, such as Central and Eastern Europe (World Bank, 2010), the international credit crunch has not led to a generalised sudden stop, as did occur in previous crises (Canales-Kriljenko et al., 2010), putting a halt to the financial turmoil. The second is that the slowdown in the economic activity of advanced economies has not had a negative effect on export flows in developing economies or in their trade balances.

Certainly, as most analyses reflect, a great deal of the positive economic results of emerging economies is explained by the application of intense packages of fiscal and monetary stimuli (International Monetary Fund, 2009b, 2010a and 2010b; World Bank, 2009). The existence of stronger macroeconomic policy frameworks, principally robust fiscal positions at the onset of the crises (Berkmen et al., 2009 and 2010), promoted resilience and allowed timely policy responses to support economic activity. These impulses were significantly important in Africa, East Asia, and Latin America.

The novelty in this case is not that emerging and developing economies have applied demand-side stimuli measures (and support measures to financial and banking sectors) quantitatively and qualitatively different to those applied by advanced economies. The novelty is in the fact that it has been possible to apply this kind of measures for the first time, avoiding the application of pro-cyclical measures which in the past deepened the effects of the economic crisis. For the first time emerging economies have been in a condition to apply fiscal and monetary stimuli to correct the effects of a crisis that had not been generated in their countries. These stimuli are possible, as we will see later, thanks to the cushion of mass holdings of international reserves, to the lesser external dependence to finance the internal capital demand (rising from the demand for investment and fiscal unbalances) due to the higher levels of domestic savings, and the recovery of capital inflows in these economies registered since 2009.[4]

In spite of its obvious importance, this point is not the main issue of this chapter. In the following sections, we will focus, on the contrary, on the transmission channels related to trade flows, on the one hand, and financial flows, on the other.

3   The trade channel

As can be seen in Figure 6.6, the current account balance has been closely connected to the economic cycle of developed economies. Traditionally expansions of the latter have been transformed into surpluses on the current accounts of developing economies in such a way that international trade behaved as the engine of these countries. Conversely, recessions in advanced economies implied a deterioration of the current account balance of developing countries, negatively affecting their growth.

According to this transmission channel, expansions in developed economies caused an increase in the import demand from developing

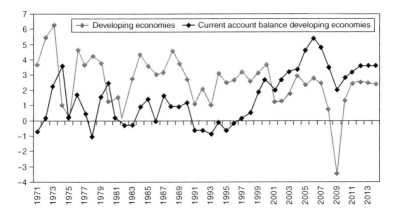

Figure 6.6 Annual growth rates (%) of developed economies and current account balance of developing economies (in %GDP)
Source: UNCTAD Handbook of Statistics Online and International Monetary Fund World Economic Outlook Database October 2009.

economies, consequently the improvement in net exports of the latter accelerated their economic growth. Obviously, economic decelerations in advanced economies generated the opposite effect in developing economies.

However, during the past decade this performance pattern has broken down. The whole group of developing economies begins to register continuous and increasing surpluses in their commercial flows. Even though the evolution of these balances remains closely linked to the economic cycle of advanced economies, developing economies maintain a high and growing surplus, avoiding the negative impact which comes from the decrease in the demand of advanced economies. Thus, both during the 2001–03 crisis and during the present recession, developing economies are still generating substantial surpluses in their current account balance, above 2 per cent of their GDP.

This structural change in the behaviour of the current account balance of developing economies has been accompanied by a smaller dependence of trade flows of developing economies on advanced economies. Tables 6.1 and 6.2 show the geographical distribution of trade goods flows (exports and imports) in the period 1980–2008. Data show that, whereas the geographical pattern of trade flows in developed economies has been virtually constant over the past three decades, the spatial distribution of foreign trade of developing economies has changed radically. Foreign trade of developing economies, whether exports or

Table 6.1 Distribution of goods exports depending on the destination (% total exports)

	Developing economies	Economies in transition	Developed economies
World			
1980	24.8	3.1	69.6
1984	24.1	2.9	70.5
1988	21.9	2.6	73.7
1992	25.9	0.8	71.8
1996	28.5	2.1	67.8
2000	27.8	1.4	69.7
2004	29.5	2.2	67.1
2008	33.3	3.6	61.7
Developing economies			
1980	25.6	1.5	68.2
1984	27.7	1.5	65.4
1988	30.8	1.4	63.4
1992	37.7	0.6	58.8
1996	41.1	1.0	54.7
2000	39.7	0.6	57.5
2004	44.7	1.1	52.3
2008	48.5	2.0	47.2
Economies in transition			
1980	18.4	28.4	53.2
1984	10.7	9.2	79.8
1988	11.6	6.4	81.9
1992	16.2	8.3	75.4
1996	15.6	27.4	55.3
2000	15.7	20.1	62.3
2004	20.0	17.9	61.3
2008	19.7	20.3	58.8
Developing economies: Africa			
1980	9.1	1.5	72.6
1984	9.0	1.4	75.2
1988	10.8	1.7	70.7
1992	17.8	0.9	72.4
1996	25.5	1.0	69.5
2000	26.8	0.4	67.9
2004	29.4	0.5	68.2
2008	31.6	0.8	65.9
Developing economies: America			
1980	26.7	2.5	68.3
1984	20.3	1.7	73.0
1988	22.5	1.6	72.1
1992	25.2	0.1	72.1

(Continued)

Table 6.1   Continued

	Developing economies	Economies in transition	Developed economies
1996	27.2	0.7	67.3
2000	23.4	0.4	72.8
2004	28.0	0.7	68.2
2008	34.7	1.1	60.3
Developing economies: Asia			
1980	29.9	1.2	66.9
1984	35.0	1.5	60.3
1988	36.0	1.3	60.0
1992	43.1	0.7	54.2
1996	46.0	1.1	50.2
2000	45.0	0.7	52.7
2004	49.6	1.2	47.6
2008	53.2	2.3	42.5
Developed economies			
1980	24.6	3.6	70.3
1984	23.3	3.2	72.1
1988	19.4	2.8	76.7
1992	21.8	0.8	76.3
1996	23.6	1.7	73.9
2000	22.4	1.2	75.8
2004	21.9	2.1	75.3
2008	23.9	3.5	71.9

Source: UNCTAD Handbook of Statistics Online.

imports, takes place mainly among developing economies themselves. Thus, in 2008, good exports to developed countries accounted for barely 47.2 per cent of the total exports of developing countries, 21 percentage points less than in 1980; on the other hand, imports from developed countries were just 40.3 per cent of the total exports of developing countries, 25 percentage points lower than in 1980. Since the 1990s the drop in the weight of trade relations between developing and developed economies is very sharp for the whole group of developing economies. Especially significant is the case of Asian economies, where the weight of their exports to developed economies is reduced by 24.4 percentage points, whereas the weight of imports from developed economies falls 27.1 percentage points.

The lessening dependence of developing economies on advanced economies means that there has been less impact on their patterns of international trade and economic activity than would have occurred in previous crises as a result of the economic turmoil that originated

Table 6.2 Distribution of the imports of goods by destination (% total imports)

	Developing economies	Economies in transition	Developed economies
World			
1980	30.5	2.9	65.4
1984	27.6	2.9	68.4
1988	23.0	2.5	73.3
1992	25.6	1.0	72.0
1996	28.5	2.4	67.8
2000	32.0	2.4	64.5
2004	34.7	3.0	60.9
2008	39.2	4.4	54.7
Developing economies			
1980	30.5	1.1	65.3
1984	30.9	1.3	65.3
1988	30.6	1.5	65.2
1992	35.0	0.8	61.9
1996	38.1	1.4	58.2
2000	41.9	1.5	54.1
2004	47.5	2.3	46.9
2008	53.3	2.7	40.3
Economies in transition			
1980	17.6	18.2	64.1
1984	15.3	8.8	75.7
1988	13.0	5.8	81.2
1992	15.6	8.9	75.2
1996	10.3	39.5	49.7
2000	11.1	39.3	49.1
2004	14.7	31.0	53.7
2008	23.2	26.1	50.1
Developing economies: Africa			
1980	14.2	1.3	74.3
1984	14.9	2.0	76.2
1988	15.3	1.7	75.8
1992	24.7	0.9	69.4
1996	31.5	1.2	62.9
2000	35.1	2.0	60.2
2004	40.2	2.4	53.8
2008	45.5	2.5	48.4
Developing economies: America			
1980	33.9	0.1	63.3
1984	37.7	0.6	59.2
1988	26.4	0.5	71.8
1992	24.3	0.1	74.1
1996	27.0	0.6	68.3

(Continued)

Table 6.2   Continued

	Developing economies	Economies in transition	Developed economies
2000	26.2	0.5	69.9
2004	36.2	0.8	60.3
2008	44.8	1.3	52.7
Developing economies: Asia			
1980	33.8	1.5	63.5
1984	33.4	1.3	64.0
1988	34.4	1.7	61.9
1992	39.0	1.0	57.9
1996	41.6	1.6	55.1
2000	47.3	1.8	48.6
2004	50.7	2.6	43.2
2008	56.3	3.1	36.4
Developed economies			
1980	30.6	3.2	65.5
1984	27.0	3.3	69.1
1988	21.2	2.7	75.3
1992	22.3	0.8	75.6
1996	24.8	1.8	72.4
2000	28.3	2.1	69.0
2004	29.3	2.6	67.5
2008	31.8	4.2	63.6

Source: UNCTAD Handbook of Statistics Online.

in developed countries. This helps to explain why the trade surplus discussed above has remained stable during the present crisis.

Anyway, even when the smaller economic activity in industrial economies may have affected trade flows with developing and emerging economies and, by extension, the respective current account balances, this does not necessarily imply a strong negative impact on the growth of these economies. The size of this impact will depend upon how economic growth is explained by the existence of a high positive trade net balance. In other words, the contribution of foreign trade to the growth of an economy does not depend upon the size or the growth of export and import flows but on the net export balance.

Contrary to what is usually expected, the engine of emerging economies growth is not so much the foreign demand as the domestic demand. Although these economies have witnessed how their exports have increased significantly, these bigger exports have implied a parallel increase of their imports, thus the contribution of their trade balances to economic growth has not been very high. For example, for Asian economies, Prasad (2009) shows how the contribution of net exports to the economic growth of the region during the period 2000–08 is very small, lower than the contribution of public or private consumption or investment, hardly 0.4 percentage points for an average economic growth rate of 5.2 per cent. In the particular case of China, net exports would only explain 10.8 per cent of the economic growth registered in that period (compared with 27.5 per cent of private consumption, 12.7 per cent of public consumption or 49 per cent of investment).

Finally, it is important to underline that the change in the productive structure of emerging and developing economies and in their integration in the international productive chain turns the volume of trade flows (and their balance) with industrial economies into a structural factor, relatively independent from the economic situation of advanced economies and from external factors. This behaviour is reflected in the existing disconnection between the size and evolution of trade balances and the exchange rates evolution between advanced and emerging economies.

In this sense, Figures 6.7 and 6.8 show the performance of the balance on goods and services in United States and the euro zone with China, together with the evolution of the renminbi exchange rate against the euro and the dollar. In the case of the US economy, we can see how the rapid deterioration of the trade balance with China is taking place at a stable nominal exchange rate. In fact, the renminbi valuation against the dollar in 2005 did not coincide with an increase in the North

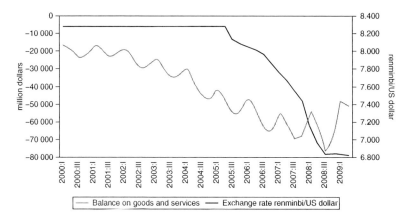

Figure 6.7   Balance on goods and services US–China and nominal exchange rate of renminbi
Source: Federal Reserve System.

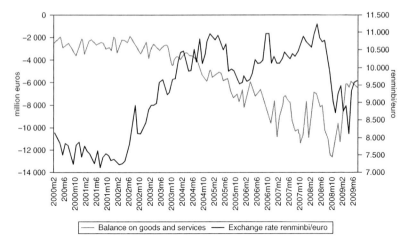

Figure 6.8 Balance on goods and services USA–Euro zone and nominal exchange rate of renminbi
Source: European Central Bank.

American deficit with China, rather than the anticipated fall. In this sense, for the World Bank (2009) a flexibility of the exchange rate will not eliminate China's tendency to generate large trade surpluses. The reduction of these surpluses would only be possible if they produce structural changes which modify the present saving and investment rates. Moreover, we cannot reject the possibility that an appreciation of the exchange rate of the Chinese renminbi increases even more the already huge Chinese trade surpluses. The final effect of a variation in the exchange rate on the value of exports and imports flows, and, consequently, on the value and sign of the net trade balance, depends on the price-elasticity of the exports and imports demands. An inelastic demand for exports and imports would mean that an appreciation of the Chinese renmimbi with respect, for instance, to the US dollar, would mean that the value of Chinese imports from the US economy would fall, while at the same time the value of Chinese exports to the US would increase. The final result would be an increased Chinese trade surplus with the USA. This possible scenario[5] means that the usual recommendations made to the Chinese economic authorities – to flexibilise the exchange rate of the renminbi as a necessary and, even, sufficient measure to correct the huge imbalances of the Chinese and US balances of payments[6] – may well generate opposite consequences to those anticipated by their proponents.

In the case of the euro-zone economy, there is once again a clear lack of any stable correspondence between the performance of the renminbi/euro exchange rate and the balance on goods and services with China. Thus, the very strong valuation of the euro (in nominal terms) with regard to the renminbi between 2002 and 2004 did not lead to a deterioration of the trade balance with China. Likewise, the renminbi valuation in 2005 and 2008 did not imply an improvement in the balance on goods and services with China but rather increased the deficit. Only the period 2006–07 saw the expected effect of the renminbi depreciation against the euro in the shape of a bigger trade deficit in the euro zone with China.

In any case, an assumption implicit in the view that the Chinese external surplus (and the mirror US external deficit) can be corrected with a proper flexibility (and the consequent appreciation) of the Chinese renminbi is that there is an equilibrium exchange rate that leads the trade balance to an equilibrium, that is, to a zero net exports. In other words, that the exchange rate is determined by the size and sign of a country's trade balance, and thus, that the only function of foreign financial flows is to finance the trade surplus or deficit. However, if the exchange rate is mainly determined by the capital account, then the level and evolution of the exchange rates stops to be related and determined by the evolution of the goods and services balance. In this scenario, a Chinese flexible exchange rate would not necessarily correct the trade Chinese and US trade imbalances. As Turner argues, the greater integration of emerging market economies with international capital markets has the implication that 'the exchange rate was becoming more responsive to international shifts in asset preferences, which could increase exchange rate volatility' (Turner, 2008, p. 4). If capital flows are the main determinant of the exchange rate, if we assume that the exchange rate can influence trade (exports and imports) flows and balances, then to correct trade imbalances, we must implement measures to 'control' capital flows. This, obviously, involves an opposite causality between trade flows, exchange rate and capital flows than the usual one appearing in simplistic textbooks.

4 The financial channel

In the last quarter of the year 2008, capital flows addressed towards emerging economies began to experience a rapid deceleration. Although the crisis has not had its origin in these countries, the evolution of these flows has been similar to that observed in the previous crisis. The search for low-risk positions by institutional investors as well as the recomposition of bank balances in developed countries affected by the crisis led to an asset sale and to a slowdown in the credit granted to those economies. The first effects of the crisis appeared in stock markets and in debt markets (both short-term and long-term) and in flows of bank credit. Nevertheless, before presenting these data it would be appropriate, in order to have a better understanding of the effects of the crisis upon emerging economies, to offer a brief explanation of the growth process of these flows, which started in the first years of the past decade, as well as the growth of capital flows from emerging economies towards the capital markets of developed economies.

4.2.1 Expansion process of capital flows towards emerging economies

The increase in net private capital flows towards emerging economies started in 2002.[7] These capital inflows reached their highest point, about 16 per cent of the GDP of emerging economies, in 2007, which is a historic record. In the years before the financial crisis of Southeast Asia these flows were about 9 per cent of their GDP.

South East Asian economies are the main recipient of these flows (47 per cent of the total), which represented 15 per cent of their GDP in 2007. Latin American countries received 12 per cent of these capital flows in the same year, which represented 6 per cent of their GDP. The countries of Central and Eastern Europe received 26 percent of the flows (amounting to 20 per cent of their GDP).

The composition of capitals, on the other hand, reflects a greater balance than the one existing in previous times. The foreign direct investment flows shows a downward tendency during the whole decade, representing 30 per cent of the total net private flows in 2007. Portfolio investments (debt and equity) accounted for 32 per cemt of these flows (14 per cent in debt and 18 per cent in equity) and 'other investment inflows' another 32 per cent.

The growth of these flows was the result of different factors. Firstly, it was due to the exceptional world liquidity conditions which had existed in the years before the crisis.[8] The expansion in liquidity was caused by an increase in the world net savings rate, which rose from 21.5 per cent of world GDP in 2001 to 24.5 per cent in 2007. This increase was fuelled by a rise in the savings of emerging economies, which rose from 26.6 per ¬t of their GDP in 2001 to 35.4 per cent in 2007. Developed economies, ·vhole, kept their saving rates stable, although with some significant ·l changes. Thus, Germany and Japan increased their saving rates, respectively, from 19.5 per cent and 26.9 per cent of their GDP in 2001, to 25.8 per cent and 28.9 per cent in 2007. Over the same period the United States, by contrast, decreased its saving rate from 16.4 per cent to 1.2 per cent. On the other hand, the expansion in the level of global liquidity was also caused by the long-standing falls in interest rates which took place in developed economies in the years before the crisis. The real interest rate of the American federal funds remained below 1 per cent from the middle of 2001 to the end of 2005. The European Central Bank kept its short-term real interest rates below 1 per cent throughout the entire period. These short-term rates, together with the glut of world savings, put downwards pressure on long-term real interest rates, which fell from 4 per cent in 2000 to 2 per cent in 2007 (Bank for International Settlements, 2009b), creating the necessary conditions for a credit expansion and for a search for new and more profitable assets towards which the excess of saving and liquidity could be channelled.

The second factor which would explain the growth of flows is the new credit channels opened by the intense process of financial innovation. The development of derivative markets is very likely to have contributed to channelling a part of the world liquidity excess towards emerging economies. The increase in bank credit to these economies, for example, could have been positively influenced by the facilities offered by the derivative from transferring the risk of these credits, thus contributing to an increase in the number of potential countries opting for these resources. The development of this kind of financial instruments allowed, on the other hand, as the World Bank stated, a greater implication of institutional investors in the financing of these economies: 'the proliferation of securitised and derivative products enabled pension funds and insurance companies, many of which face regulatory restrictions on the kinds of investments they can make, to take *indirect positions* in developing country loans by purchasing the more highly-rated tranches of securitized loans' (World Bank, 2010, chapter 2, p. 9, emphasis added).

Finally, the third factor behind growth was the boost given to financial intermediation in some emerging economies through the development of local financial markets (Bank for International Settlements, 2009a). This is usually considered to be a necessary condition so that those countries which liberalise their capital account can obtain positive benefits from such a process[9] (Kose et al, 2006). Furthermore, the development of such markets improves the capacity of economies to react before financial convulsions, which can cause sudden capital stops and reversals. There is a two-way connection between capital flows and the development of local financial markets. On the one hand, the diversification of local financial markets contributes to raising external resources and, on the other, the external capital can contribute positively to a more intensive development of those markets.

4.2.2   Gross private capital outflows from emerging market economies

One of the most significant characteristics of the last phase of financial globalisation has been the impulse observed in capital exports by emerging market economies, with capital flowing uphill from poor to rich countries (Lucas, 1990; Alfaro, Kalemli-Ozcan and Volosovych, 2005).[10] Between 1990 and 1997 these exports, in average values, rose to US$76 billion; by contrast, in 2002–06 they were US$327 billion. Then in 2007 they had risen to US$830 billion – of which South East Asian countries, mainly China, accumulated 60 per cent of these flows. The composition of these capitals, in contrast to what happened to inflows, was focused on portfolio investments (48 per cent in 2007) and, more particularly, on bonds (40 per cent in 2007). The foreign direct investment flows represented 22 per cent of these investments, while 'other investments' accumulated the rest: 30 per cent.

These capital exports reflect a saving excess above the investment needs of emerging economies, which had not been seen in previous years.[11] For the whole group of emerging economies this excess was equivalent to 5 points of GDP in 2007. Again, South East Asian economies, and above all the Chinese economy, showed the highest gaps, at 5 and 11 points of their GDP, respectively.

This impulse to capital exports was caused by the confluence in time of a massive capital inflow with positive balances of the current account balance, with the exception of emerging economies in Europe, which generated an important accumulation of external reserves by these economies. In April 2009 the reserve stock rose to US$3,886 billion. China alone accumulated 45 per cent of the total amount of these reserves and the rest of emerging economies of South East Asia had 30 per cent.

4.2.3   The effects of the crisis

The starting situation of emerging economies, therefore, did not reflect the same weaknesses as those observed in other recent crises, whether these were originated in advanced or in developing economies. Its insertion in the global financial process had intensified though they had protected their position by means of the reserve accumulation, the attainment of trade surplus[12] and the development of local and regional financial markets.

The financial crisis could be clearly felt in these economies at the end of 2008. The 'Emerging Markets Financial Stress Index' elaborated by the International Monetary Fund (2009a) reveals that the intensity of the crisis in these countries was deeper than in previous times.[13] This index also reflects the fact that the crisis was first transmitted through the banking system, it was then felt in the exchange market and, later, it increased the debt spreads and the volatility of the stock market. The flows of foreign direct investments kept the growing trend of previous years, although noticeably in slow motion.

The concatenation of events followed the same logic as in previous crises. The recomposition of the securities portfolio towards safer assets as well as the rearrangement of banking balances caused, on the one hand, the withdrawal of funds from emerging economies. This was particularly noticeable in the stock markets, where prices started to fall parallel to what was happening in developed economies. This process brought about pressures from exchange rates, which began to depreciate against dollar.

On the other hand, there was a contraction in credit to emerging economies. Capital inflows towards stock markets dropped. Yield differentials of international bonds increased, in some cases (for example, Russia, Turkey and South Africa) up to 800 average basic points. In the economies of Latin America and Central Europe the increase was lower, though the level was between 400 and 600 basic points. Local bond yields increased in emerging economies[14] with an increased dependence on foreign capital. Debt issuing ceased and the negotiation of the securities of these countries in the secondary market decreased. In addition, banks in developed countries reduced their cross-border loans in, approximately, 1 per cent of the GDP of emerging economies (Bank for International Settlements, 2009b).

Nevertheless, the effects were not symmetrical in the different emerging economies. Some of them could minimise these effects by using the reserves they had accumulated during previous years (Frankel, 2009). By doing so, they were able to, on the one hand, cope with pressures on exchange rates and, on the other, provide internal liquidity in order to offset the negative effects of the international credit crunch. In some countries the development of local debt markets, although they were also subject to pressures as we had already pointed out, permitted a partial compensation for the necessities of domestic financing   ·‚ ·¹ 2009; Bank for International Settlements 2009c).

The biggest differences among countries, though, com different composition of capital flows they received before

An interesting paper (Tong and Wei, 2009, p. 19) stated that 'Liquidity shocks are more severe for emerging economies that have a higher pre-crisis exposure to foreign portfolio investments and foreign loans, but less severe for countries that have a higher pre-crisis exposure to foreign direct investments.' As we have previously mentioned, the foreign direct investment flows decreased throughout the past decade at the same time as there was an increase in portfolio investment and cross-border bank credits. The relative situation of each country with relation to these flows, though, is not similar. Therefore, the intensity of the crisis has been different according to the exposure level of these more volatile flows. From the group of emerging economies, the countries in Central and Eastern Europe are the ones showing more severe economic problems and greater financial tensions.[16] The main reason lies in their extreme dependence on cross-border bank credits, fundamentally on those granted by mother European banks to their affiliates in those countries, the main transmission channel of financial tensions between developed and emerging economies during this crisis[17] (International Monetary Fund, 2009a). According to the information provided by the Bank for International Settlements about the external positions of BIS reporting Banks vis-à-vis emerging market economies, in 2007 bank credit these countries received was equivalent to 32.4 per cent of their GDP, whereas ten years earlier the rate had been 12.1 per cent. The rest of emerging economies, on the contrary, show a clear reduction of their dependence on this kind of capital flow. For the Southern Asia countries, this rate had dropped, by the same date, from 26.6 per cent down to 16.9 per cent. Latin America countries also showed a decrease from 13.9 per cent down to 11.1 per cent.

4.2.4   Recovery signs

One of the most outstanding features of this crisis, in the case of emerging economies, is that its negative effects upon the finances of these countries do not seem to linger, as had happened in previous financial crises. During the year 2009 some recovery signs started to be detected in capital flows addressed to these economies, although with some variation from region to region.

The economic recovery symptoms in Asia and Latin America could be noticed in a recovery of external capital flows in the first months of the year. It was a gradual process in all of the segments, beginning with the share markets. Debt spreads began to fall until they reached levels similar to those existing before the crisis. This recovery also took place in emerging European economies, although with a lower level of intensity (World Bank, 2010; International Monetary Fund, 2009b).

During the second and third quarters of 2009 there was also a clear increase in the cross-border bank assets with regard to emerging economies, especially in Asia-Pacific and Latin America and the Caribbean. However, the exposure was reduced in respect of emerging economies in Europe. This increase in exposure is more striking if we bear in mind that during the whole year the total gross international assets of the banks reporting the Bank for International Settlements was reduced in US$360,000 million (Avdjiev et al., 2010).

It is not easy to forecast the scope of this recovery of external capital flows. Economic growth of emerging economies has been strongly influenced by the economic stimulus policies implemented in these countries. In the case of developed economies, we still do not know what will happen to economic growth when these stimuli start to be withdrawn and what effect this will have on international capital flows.

5   Summary and conclusions

The current economic crisis has been global in nature, which explains why no single country or region has escaped unscathed. Even though the core of the crisis was in the North American financial sector, commercial and financial transmission channels ensured that it would spread to both the rest of advanced economies and the emerging and developing economies, significantly reducing their growth rates, and in some cases bringing about economic shrinkage.

From the point of view of developing economies, the performance and reaction of these economies facing the crisis has been substantially different from that registered at similar moments in the past. Thus, developing countries and, above all, emerging market economies, are recovering before advanced economies. The most recent data show an outstanding recovery in their activity levels, in their trade flows and in their capital inflows. This improved macroeconomic performance can be explained by two main factors. The first is the relative decoupling from developed economies, which has the principal effect of making emerging market economies less dependent on advanced economies, thus reducing the importance of the financial and trade transmission channels of the shocks originating in developed countries. The second factor is that emerging markets have enjoyed an unprecedented policy space to implement fiscal and monetary impulses to support the activity in the domestic economic.

In both cases, they talk of a structural change registered in the emerging and developing economies during the last decade. Both their insertion in the international value chains and their stronger macroeconomic policy positions have promoted resilience to external shocks and allowed timely policy responses, explaining the good – or not so bad – performance of these economies. Actually, those economies that are more highly integrated in trade and financial terms with advanced economies and more dependent on volatile capital inflows to finance their public and private investment and consumption processes, as is the case in the economies of Central and Eastern Europe, have been the ones most severely affected by the crisis in advanced economies and are therefore the ones with the most uncertain economic prospects.

Obviously, this does not mean that the economic activity in emerging and developing economies is not affected, or even determined, by what goes on in advanced economies. What we do mean is that emerging and developing economies are currently less dependent than in the past on developed economies.

Notes

1. In the tables and figures presented throughout this work, except if the contrary is indicated, data corresponding to the period 1970–2008 come from the UNCTAD, particularly the UNCTAD Handbook of Statistics Online, whereas data (corresponding to forecasts) of the period 2009–2013 come from the World Economic Outlook Database of the International Monetary Fund of October 2009.

2. For Coricelli (2010) 'Economists and policymakers are still debating the causes of the global crisis and the prospects for recovery in the world economy... But one point of agreement is that emerging economies have so far have weathered the crisis much better than advanced countries'.

3. The updating carried out by the International Monetary Fund in January 2010 of the prospects of economic growth for the years 2010 and 2011 shows not only the weakness in the recovery of advanced economies and the growth of developing economies but, more importantly, a substantial improvement in the growth prospects in the case of developing countries (International Monetary Fund, 2010a).

4. All of these factors would help to explain the bigger impact of the crisis in the emerging European economies.

5. Giavazzi (2009) argues that to correct the Chinese and the US foreign imbalances a change in the US (decline) and China (rise) consumption is not enough. These changes in the patterns of consumption must come with a change in the composition of world demand, that is, a change in the type of goods demanded.

6. In this sense, see, for instance, Blanchard (2009) or Eichengreen (2010).

7. Data provided on flows, both inflows and outflows, have been taken from Mihaljek (2008) and Bank for International Settlements (2009a).

8. The global imbalance phenomenon is directly connected to this first factor (Ferreiro and Serrano, 2009). This phenomenon is usually attributed to the

combination of two elements: on the one hand, the increase of saving rates of emerging and developing economies as well as of some advanced economies affected by ageing processes, the one known as the 'global savings glut' (Bernanke, 2005); and, on the other, the massive liquidity injections and the reductions of interest rates generated by the expansionary monetary policy applied from 2001 (Bibow, 2008–9; Blinder, 2009).

9. This view connects with the argument that not all of the developing economies have the conditions required to reap the potential benefits generated by the capital account liberalisation and that only a small number of developing economies, mainly emerging market economies, will benefit from the liberalisation process of capital markets (Arestis, Ferreiro and Gomez, 2006; Chinn and Ito, 2002; Edison et al., 2002; Edwards, 2001; Ferreiro, Correa and Gomez, 2008–9; Klein, 2005; Prasad, Rajan and Subramanian, 2007).

10. Europe would have been an exception with capital flowing downhill, from rich European economies to Central and Eastern Europe countries (see Abiad, Leigh and Mody, 2007).

11. A phenomenon directly related to the surplus on the current account balance mentioned above.

12. In International Monetary Fund (2009a) it is argued that in the presence of strong financial stress in advanced economies, fiscal surplus or balance of payment surplus, as well as the accumulation of reserves, have a small impact in pre-crisis moments although they help mitigate the transmission effect. International investors do not take into account the singularities of countries in the event of a financial shock.

13. Which is unsurprising if we consider that we are going through the biggest global economic and financial crisis since the Great Depression

14. The higher profitability of domestic bonds shows that the development of domestic financial markets does not offer a full protection against external financial turmoils. The reason is that in those markets the participation of foreign capital is also important. However, as far as these markets grow, the level of foreign participation declines. For the whole set of South East Asian countries, in 2001 the share of foreign capital in the domestic debt securities was 7.6 per cent of the outstanding amounts. This share was 6.9 per cent in 2006. In the case of Latin American economies these rates had moved from 22.8 per cent to 15 per cent, and in the Central European economies they have increased from 20.7 per cent to 40.1 per cent. The highest dependence was registered in Russia, with a share of 123.5 per cent in 2006, although this rate had peaked at 288.2 per cent in 2001 (Bank for International Settlements, 2009a).

15. For an analysis of the composition of capital inflows in emerging market and developing economies by types of capital flows, see Ferreiro, Gomez and Rodriguez (2006).

16. In a study of the transmission of turbulences generated in the stock markets in advanced economies to those markets in emerging economies, Beirne et al. show that in the period 2004–08 a significant increase in conditional correlation between mature and emerging stock markets during episodes of turbulence in the former markets was only found in emerging European economies (Beirne et al., 2008). This reflects the higher dependence of emerging European economies on advanced (European) economies than the rest of emerging economies.

17. In their analysis of the regional integration of financial systems in advanced and emerging economies of Europe, Galeshi and Sgherri argue that: 'Greater financial integration and the increasing prevalence of cross-border ownership of assets are found to be associated with better growth opportunities, with the link stronger in countries where integration is faster. At the same time, though, these developments in international financial markets have the potential to further amplify business cycle fluctuations and the impact of asset price movements on real activity by increasing the strength of cross-border financial spillovers. In particular, the sizable cross-border financial linkages across Europe highlight the vulnerabilities arising from reliance on concentrated foreign funding. International banking statistics suggest hat most emerging European economies are heavily exposed to – and dependent on – western banks (either directly or through the local borrowing systems)' (Galeshi and Sgherri, 2009, p. 14).

References

Alfaro, L., Kalemli-Ozcan, S. and Volosovych, V. (2005 [2002]) 'Why Doesn't Capital Flow from Rich to Poor Countries? An Empirical Investigation', *National Bureau of Economic Research Working Paper*, no. 11901.

Abiad, A., Leigh, D. and Mody, A. (2007) 'International Finance and Income Convergence: Europe is Different', *International Monetary Fund Working Paper*, WP/07/64.

Avdjiev, S., Gyntelberg, J. and Upper, C. (2010) 'Highlights of International Banking and Financial Market Activity', *BIS Quarterly Review*, March, 13–24.

Arestis, P., Ferreiro, J. and Gomez, C. (2006) 'Is There a Role for Capital Controls?', in L.P. Rochon and S. Rossi (eds), *Monetary and Exchange Rate Systems: a Global View of Financial Crises*. Cheltenham: Edward Elgar, pp. 140–66.

Bank for International Settlements (2009a) 'Capital Flows and Emerging Market Economies', *CGFS Papers*, No. 33, Committee on the Global Financial System, Bank for International Settlements.

Bank for International Settlements (2009b) *79th Annual Report 1 April 2008–31 March 2009*. Basel: Bank for International Settlements.

Bank for International Settlements (2009c) 'The International Financial Crisis: Timeline, Impact and Policy Responses in Asia and the Pacific', BIS Representative Office for Asia and the Pacific.

Beirne, J., Caporale, G.M., Schulze-Ghattas, M. and Spagnolo, N. (2008) 'Volatility Spillovers and Contagion from Mature to Emerging Stock Markets', *International Monetary Fund Working Paper*, WP/08/286.

Berkmen, P., Gelos, G., Rennhack, R. and Walsh, J.P. (2009) 'The Global Financial Crisis: Explaining Cross-country Differences in the Output Impact', *International Monetary Fund Working Paper*, WP/09/280.

Berkmen, P., Gelos, G., Rennhack, R. and Walsh, J.P. (2010) 'Differential Impact', *Finance and Development*, March, 29–31.

Bernanke, B. (2005) 'The Global Saving Glut and the U.S. Current Account Deficit', Remarks delivered before the Federal Reserve Board, 10 March. Available at www.federalreserve.gov/boarddocs/speeches/2005/200503102/default.htm.

Bibow, J. (2008–09) 'Insuring Against Private Capital Flows. Is it Worth the Premium? What are the Alternatives?', *International Journal of Political Economy*, 37(4), 5–30.

Blanchard, O. (2009) 'Sustaining a Global Recovery', *Finance and Development*, September, pp. 8–12.

Blinder, A. (2009) '6 Bad Moves that led US into Crisis', *International Herald Tribune*, 26 January.

Bui, T. and Bayoumi, T. (2010) 'Their Cup Spilleth Over', *Finance and Development*, March, 32–4.

Canales-Kriljenko, J.I., Coulibaly, B. and Kamil, H. (2010) 'A Tale of Two Regions', *Finance and Development*, March, 335–6.

Chinn, M. D. and Ito, H. (2002) 'Capital Account Liberalization, Institutions and Financial Development: Cross-country Evidence', *National Bureau of Economic Research Working Paper*, No. 8967.

Coricelli, F. (2010) 'The Crisis and the Developing Countries', VoxEU.org, 1 May.

Edwards, S. (2001) 'Capital Mobility and Economic Performance: Are Emerging Economies Different?', *National Bureau of Economic Research Working Paper*, No. 8076.

Edison, H. J., Klein, M., Ricci, L. and Sløk, T. (2002) 'Capital Account Liberalization and Economic Performance: Survey and Synthesis', *International Monetary Fund Working Paper*, WP/02/120.

Eichengreen, B. (2010) *Global Imbalances and the Lessons of Bretton Woods*, The Cairoli Lectures, Universidad Torcuato di Tella. Cambridge, MA: MIT Press.

Ferreiro, J., Correa, E. and Gomez, C. (2008–9) 'Has Capital Account Liberalization in Latin American Countries Led to Higher and More Stable Capital Inflows?', *International Journal of Political Economy*, 37(4), 31–63.

Ferreiro, J., Gomez, C. and Rodriguez, C. (2006) 'The Pattern of Inward FDI Geographical Distribution: Can Developing Countries Base Their Development on Those Flows?', in P. Arestis, J Ferreiro and F. Serrano (eds), *Financial Developments in National and International Markets*. Basingstoke: Palgrave Macmillan, pp. 149–64.

Ferreiro, J. and Serrano, F. (2009) 'El fenomeno de los global imbalances y la crisis financiera actual', *Ekonomiaz*, 72, 180–97.

Frank, N. and Hesse, H. (2009) 'Financial Spillovers to Emerging Markets During the Global Financial Crisis', *International Monetary Fund Working Paper*, WP/09/104.

Frankel, J.A. (2009) 'What's In and Out in Global Money', *Finance and Development*, September, pp. 13–17.

Galeshi, A. and Sgherri, S. (2009) 'Regional Financial Spillovers Across Europe: A Global VAR Analysis', *International Monetary Fund Working Paper*, WP/09/123.

Giavazzi, F. (2009) 'Growth After the Crisis', *Finance and Development*, September, 24–5.

Goldstein, M. and Xie, D. (2009) 'US Credit Crisis and Spillovers to Asia', *Asian Economic Policy Review*, 4, 204–22.

International Monetary Fund (2009a) *World Economic Outlook. Crisis and Recovery*, April. Washington, DC: International Monetary Fund.

International Monetary Fund (2009b) *World Economic Outlook. Sustaining the Recovery*, October. Washington, DC: International Monetary Fund.

International Monetary Fund (2010a) *World Economic Outlook Update*, 26 January. Washington, DC: International Monetary Fund.

International Monetary Fund (2010b) *World Economic Outlook. Rebalancing Growth*, April. Washington, DC: International Monetary Fund.

Jara, A., Moreno, R. and Tovar, C.E. (2009) 'The Global Crisis and Latin America: Financial Impact and Policy Responses', *BIS Quarterly Review*, June, 53–68.

Klein, M.W. (2005) 'Capital Account Liberalization, Institutional Quality and Economic Growth: Theory and Evidence', *National Bureau of Economic Research Working Paper*, no. 11112.

Kose, M.A., Otrok, C. and Prasad, E.S. (2008a) 'How Much Decoupling? How Much Converging?', *Finance and Development*, 45(2), 36–40.

Kose, M.A., Otrok, C. and Prasad, E.S. (2008b) 'Global Business Cycles: Convergence or Decoupling?', *National Bureau of Economic Research Working Paper Series*, October, no. 14292.

Kose, M., Prasad, E., Rogoff, K. and Wei, S. (2006) 'Financial Globalization: a Reappraisal', *International Monetary Fund Working Paper,* WP/06/189.

Levy-Yeyati, E. (2009) 'On Emerging Markets Decoupling and Growth Convergence', VoxEU.org, 7 November.

Lucas, R. (1990) 'Why Doesn't Capital Flow from Rich to Poor Countries?', *American Economic Review*, 80(2), 92–6.

Mihaljek, D. (2008) 'The Financial Stability Implications of Increased Capital Flows for Emerging Market Economies', *BIS Papers, No. 44, Financial Globalization and Emerging Market Capital Flows*, December, 11–44.

Prasad, E.S. (2009) 'Rebalancing Growth in Asia', *National Bureau of Economic Research Working Paper Series*, July, no. 15169.

Prasad, E.S., Rajan, R.G. and Subramanian, A. (2007) 'Foreign Capital and Economic Growth', *National Bureau of Economic Research Working Paper Series*, November, no. 13619.

Tong, H. and Wei S. (2009) 'The Composition Matters: Capital Inflows and Liquidity Crunch During a Global Economic Crisis', *International Monetary Fund Working Paper*, WP/09/164.

Turner, P. (2008) 'Financial Globalisation and Emerging Market Capital Flows', *BIS Papers, No. 44, Financial Globalization and Emerging Market Capital Flows*, December, pp. 1–10.

World Bank (2009) *Global Economic Prospects 2010: Crisis, Finance and Growth in Developing Countries*. Washington, DC: World Bank.

World Bank (2010) *Global Economic Prospects 2010: Crisis, Finance and Growth*. Washington, DC: World Bank.

7
The Crisis in Western and Eastern EU: Does the Policy Reaction Address its Origins?

Özlem Onaran

1 Introduction[1]

We are in a new phase of the global crisis: the struggle to distribute the costs of the crisis. This crisis has been an outcome of a global process of increased exploitation and inequality, since the post-1980s. Neoliberalism tried to solve the crisis of the golden age of capitalism through a major attack on labour. The outcome was a dramatic decline in labour's bargaining power and labour's share in income across the globe in the post-1980s period. However, the decline in the labour share has been the source of a *potential realisation crisis* for the system. The decline in the purchasing power of workers limited their potential to consume. Demand deficiency and financial deregulation reduced investments despite increasing levels of profitability. Thus neoliberalism only replaced the profit squeeze and the over-accumulation problems of the 1970s with the realisation problem. Financial innovations and debt-led consumption seemed to offer a short-term solution to this potential realisation crisis. Since summer 2007 this solution has also collapsed. The crisis was tamed through major banking rescue packages and fiscal stimuli. Now the financial speculators and corporations are relabelling the crisis a 'sovereign debt crisis' and pressurising the governments in a variety of countries ranging from Greece to the UK to cut spending to avoid taxes on their profits and wealth. The governments agreeing to the cuts are acting as if these same speculators were not the beneficiaries of decades of neoliberal policies and the main creators of the crisis. The public spending cuts are being formulated as 'cutting the waste' and are obscuring the fact that public debt would not be there, if it were not for the bank rescue packages, counter-cyclical fiscal stimuli, and the loss of tax revenues due to the crisis. The pressure on wages associated with budget cuts is great news for the corporations! However, the push for a reduction in the level of public debt is the biggest threat to recovery. It is debatable where the recovery will come from, even if the bottom of the recession were reached, once the fiscal stimuli are withdrawn.

The realisation crisis at the origin of the crisis based on wage suppression was connected deeply to global imbalances. The debt-led consumption model generated a current account deficit in countries like the US and the UK. This deficit was financed by the surpluses of developed countries such as Germany and Japan, developing countries like China and South Korea, or the oil-rich Middle Eastern nations. In most cases current account surpluses were made possible by wage suppression.

In the European context, the wage suppression strategy and current account surpluses of Germany in particular created imbalances within Europe in the form of current account deficits, public or private debt on the periphery of the euro zone, in particular in Greece, Portugal, Spain, and Ireland, or in Eastern Europe, in particular in Hungary, the Baltic States, Romania, and Bulgaria. The crisis laid bare the historical divergences within Europe, and led to a European crisis and a new stage in the global crisis. The restrained policy framework, which is based on a strict inflation targeting, and which lacks a common fiscal policy, is the root of the divergences, as it has failed to generate convergence within the EU in the first place. In countries like Greece, where both public debt and the budget deficit to GDP ratio is high and is coupled with a high current account deficit, the attack of the speculators asking dramatically higher yields has brought the country to the edge of a sovereign debt crisis in 2010. Indeed before Greece, in 2009 Hungary, the Baltic States, and Romania were under attack. It looked as if the euro saved Slovakia and Slovenia from the turbulence in the currency markets, but their problem will be a permanent loss of international competitiveness as is unfortunately illustrated by the problems of the periphery of the euro zone. Initially, Eastern Europe was seen the only problem zone in Europe. However, together with Greece, the attention of speculators turned to the public debt and deficits in Portugal, Spain, Ireland, and then towards the core to Italy, Britain and Belgium. Now market pressures are threatening convergence and social cohesion both in the East and the West.

The rest of the paper is structured as follows: Section 2 discusses the crisis in Western Europe. Section 3 presents the evidence about Eastern Europe. Section 4 concludes with an alternative framework for economic policy.

2 Western Europe

Although the crisis originated in the US, it spread quickly to Europe due to the exposure of the European banks to the toxic assets, and the impact has been heavier in Europe. The difference in the depth of the crisis between the US and Europe can be explained by the larger size of the fiscal stimulus plan as well as the faster reaction in the US in terms of both monetary and fiscal policy compared to Europe.

The crisis has also laid bare important divergences within Europe. Britain had a deep recession due to its overdependence on the financial sector, overextended banks and over-indebted private sector, and a housing bubble. The recession in Britain lasted longer than in any other G7 countries, with GDP having contracted by 6.2 per cent between early 2008 and the third quarter of 2009. German and Italian GDP declined by 4.9 per cent and 5.0 per cent respectively in 2009, while French GDP contracted by just 2.6 per cent in 2009. Germany did not have a problem of household debt problem, but it is suffering considerably from the curse of its neo-mercantilist strategy – that is, growth based on export markets via wage dumping – as its export markets are shrinking. In contrast to Germany, in France a better developed system of automatic stabilisers, a larger state sector and a better position in terms of income inequality made the conditions of the crisis more moderate at the onset, since the weakening of demand was less important (Fitoussi and Saraceno, 2010). On the periphery of Europe, Ireland, with its disproportionately large banking sector and the bust of its housing bubble; and Spain, with the collapse of the housing bubble and the consequent contraction in construction, are both expected to be in recession throughout 2010, with only a limited capacity to reverse course. The contraction in Ireland's GDP in 2009 has reached 7.47 per cent Most importantly, the imbalances between the core and periphery of Europe, and the limited fiscal capacity of the periphery to tame the crisis evolved into a sovereign debt crisis in Greece followed by Portugal, Spain, and Ireland at the end of 2009.

In the euro zone in particular, the Stability and Growth Pact and the statute of the ECB restrained discretionary macroeconomic policies during the crisis. The response of monetary policy remained more restrictive in Europe than in the US (Fitoussi and Saraceno, 2010). The creativity in terms of the injection of liquidity into the system through quantitative easing has also been unable to reverse the credit crunch, since the banks hoarded liquidity to improve their balance sheet. The government conditions for support to banks have been weak, which does not punish the liquidity hoarding behaviour of banks.

The ratio of the financial rescue package in 2008 reached 28.6 per cent of GDP in Britain and to an unprecedented level of 235.7 per cent in Ireland (OECD, 2009).[2] Although continental European banks claim to have a more conservative banking and credit policy at home than the Anglo-Saxon banks, they also proved to be prone to significant risks via the purchasing of CDOs of US banks even in Germany or via excessive credit expansion in Eastern Europe as in the case of Austria, Sweden, Italy, and partly Greece. In 2008 Austria had a financial rescue package of 36.9 per centof its GDP and Sweden 50.5 per cent.

Fiscal policy has also been significantly less expansionary in Europe than in the US. Mainstream economists (e.g. OECD, 2009) emphasise that the automatic stabilisers like unemployment insurance benefits in the EU, particularly in the northern EU, are almost three times the fiscal stimulus plans, and that therefore the total size of the fiscal stimuli is adequate. However, the total US fiscal stimulus including automatic and discretionary measures is still above 10 per cent of GDP compared with a mere 6 per cent in Germany in 2008–10 (OECD, 2009).[3] The size of the total fiscal stimulus exceeds that in the US in only four EU countries (Sweden, Luxembourg, Spain and Denmark).

Apart from the size of the fiscal stimuli, one major problem in the EU has been the absence of a coordinated policy reaction. The ECB, who acted as a lender of last resort to the private European banks, did not fulfill the same function in the case of the Eurozone governments until May 2010 when the markets speculated fiercely about a default in Greece. In 2007–10, different from the US or Britain, euro-zone governments had to finance their rescue plans in financial markets, which has raised the costs of the rescue packages. Ironically from the summer of 2007 to October 2008 European banks shifted their lending towards the peripheral countries in the euro zone, assuming that the toxic assets in those countries' banks were limited (Lapavitsas et al., 2010). Government bonds with higher yields in the periphery were also seen as an attractive and safe alternative. The ECB's quantitative easing policy helped the banks to acquire cheap funding for their operations. More ironically, it was the same banks that later fled to the US government bonds, and cut lending to the periphery in 2009 as they became more risk averse. Not only were these same banks bailed out by the ECB, but the macroeconomic environment in which they are operating was also supported by an expansionary fiscal policy in order to prevent the recession turning into a great depression. Eventually the rescue packages, fiscal expansion, and the decline in tax revenues due to the recession led to a significant increase in budget deficit. Now it is again the same banks who are asking for high risk premiums from the governments with high budget deficits and public debt. They are asking for cuts in spending, in particular in public wages and employment, and threatening to cut off lending to the governments who fail to do so. Even when the countries on the periphery faced excessively high interest rates and borrowing hardships, the ECB statute was preserved; thus the function of lender of last resort to the governments was not permitted.

At the root of the problem is the neoliberal model that turned the periphery of Europe into markets for the core countries without any prospect of catching up. The lack of a sufficiently large European budget and significant fiscal transfers targeting productive investments in the periphery led to persistent differentials in productivity. The Stability and Growth Pact as well as EU competition regulations limited the area for manoeuvre for the implementation of national industrial policy. In the absence of industrial policy and productive investments to boost productivity, the strategy of competitiveness was based mainly on wage moderation, and increased deregulation and precariousness in the labour markets, which further eroded labour's bargaining power throughout the EU. Overall labour's share in income declined sharply in that period (see Figure 7.1). However, wage moderation also did not save the periphery of the Eurozone, like Greece, Portugal, Ireland, Spain, who were unable to increase their relative competitiveness by devaluing their currency, since Germany was engaged in a much more aggressive wage and labour market policy.

Between 2000 and 2007 unit labour costs declined by 0.2 per cent a year in Germany while rising by 2 per cent in France, 2.3 per cent in Britain, between 3.2 per cent and 3.7 per cent in Italy, Spain, Ireland, and Greece. In particular, in the periphery nominal labour costs have increased faster than in Germany as the result of a higher rate of inflation. This, however, does not mean that there was no wage moderation in these countries: in the 1990s and 2000s productivity increases exceeded changes in real wages in all western EU countries. In Germany as well as in Italy, Spain, and Portugal real wages even declined in the 2000s, with the gap being largest in Germany (see Table 7.1). The gap between wages and productivity in Germany was to the result of a decline in the level of real wages, and not necessarily high productivity. Indeed, the productivity increase in Germany has been quite modest – that is, it was lower than in Britain, Ireland, Greece, or Portugal in the period 1991–2007. The phenomenal competitive advantage of Germany

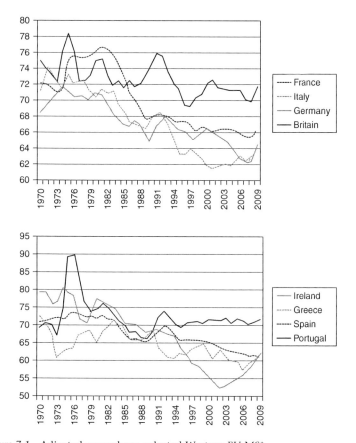

Figure 7.1   Adjusted wage share, selected Western EU MS*

Note: *Compensation per employee as percentage of GDP at factor cost per person employed.

Source: AMECO (Economic and Financial affairs, Annual Macroeconomic Indicators online database), April 2010.

was simply the result of wage suppression rather than an increase in productivity. The low level of investments, despite a high profit share, explain the stagnant productivity and low rates of GDP growth in Germany. Most strikingly, the real wage decline in Germany in the 2000s went along with the worst employment performance in the western EU (see Table 7.1). This proves again that the suppression of wages does not necessarily lead to high investment, employment, and productivity. Moreover with significantly lower wages Eastern Europe was a much

Table 7.1 Average annual growth in GDP, employment, productivity, and real wage, 1991–2009, Selected Western EU MS

	1991–2000				2000–2007			
	GDP	Employment	Productivity	Real wage	GDP	Employment	Productivity	Real wage
Britain	2.98	0.55	2.42	1.70	2.56	0.88	1.66	1.50
Germany	1.75	0.15	1.60	1.39	1.24	0.21	1.03	-0.15
France	2.09	0.56	1.39	0.97	1.83	0.77	1.03	0.90
Italy	1.60	-0.15	1.65	-0.03	1.14	1.38	-0.21	-0.05
Spain	2.83	1.92	1.02	1.50	3.42	3.86	0.09	-0.80
Greece	2.26	1.34	0.91	1.04	4.20	1.41	2.75	2.28
Ireland	7.69	4.01	3.25	1.00	5.53	3.22	2.21	2.33
Portugal*	2.72	0.75	1.96	2.62	1.09	0.41	0.67	-0.11
Euro12**	2.12	0.61	1.50	0.81	1.86	1.16	0.69	0.07

	2008				2009			
	GDP	Employment	Productivity	Real wage	GDP	Employment	Productivity	Real wage
Britain	0.55	0.76	-0.20	-0.59	-4.65	-2.09	-2.61	0.22
Germany	0.97	1.39	-0.42	0.56	-4.90	-0.09	-4.81	-1.62
France	0.32	1.39	-0.22	0.20	-2.30	-0.45	-1.21	0.38
Italy	-1.04	0.83	-1.35	-0.06	-4.80	-0.91	-3.98	-2.06
Spain	0.86	-0.48	1.48	3.35	-3.59	-6.77	2.92	3.57
Greece	2.01	1.10	0.91	0.49	-1.06	-1.19	0.14	3.53
Ireland	-3.02	-0.51	-1.92	5.12	-7.47	-8.18	0.10	1.73
Portugal*	-0.04	0.62	-0.66	0.66	-2.75	-2.40	-0.37	2.86
Euro12**	0.48	1.01	-0.53	0.56	-3.98	-1.60	-2.42	0.19

Notes:
*Real wage data for Portugal starts in 1995.
**Euro12 refers to 12 old Euro area MS.
Employment is total economy. Productivity is Real GDP/Employee. Real wage is labour compensation deflated by private consumption deflator, index 2000 = 100.
Period averages are geometric averages.
Source: OECD Economic Outlook, online database, April 2010.

more attractive location, if there were any investment motives in search for lower wages. The German case is also in striking contrast to France, where real wage growth has more or less kept up with productivity. France did not have Germany's export boom, but domestic demand and employment growth has been much stronger.

With weak domestic demand because of low wage levels, exports were the main source of economic growth in Germany, but this has led to current account surpluses at the expense of the current account deficits on the periphery of the EU. As a core country Italy has also faced the same fate of high current account deficits despite real wage losses because of falling productivity. Indeed, it seems apparent that we should reverse the dominant narrative that the peripheral countries enjoyed low interest rates, since they were members of the euro zone, and thereby avoided fiscal discipline. German firms enjoyed a high level of competitiveness thanks to their low wages and the inability of the countries on the periphery of the euro zone to devalue. This has been detrimental for the exports of the peripheral countries due to both the loss of competitiveness and the contraction of domestic demand in Germany. Indeed Germany can be regarded as the China of Europe with a large current account surplus, high savings and low levels of domestic demand. Thanks to its political power there is much less talk about the competition policies of Germany, albeit there has been a recent rise in complaints from France. This neo-mercantilist policy has also been a model for some other countries such as Austria and the Netherlands, which also have high current account surpluses. In the countries on the periphery consumption led by private debt has filled in the gap that was created by low exports and high imports. A construction boom, real estate bubbles, and private debt have been a typical feature, particularly in the cases of Spain and Ireland. In Greece – and to a lesser extent Portugal – the fiscal deficit also played a compensating role, along with the debt of the households and corporations.

As a result of these diverging experiences, the countries in the core vs the periphery of the EU experienced the crisis as an asymmetric shock. This is the background of the sovereign debt crisis in the periphery, as it was unleashed in Greece in December 2009. Following speculations about Greece's default and exit from the euro, the Eurozone governments' first decision came at the end of March 2010 after months of hesitation and worries about Germany's constitution court, who could rule out any bailout as being against the treaties. As part of a package involving substantial IMF financing and a majority of European financing via coordinated bilateral loans, euro-area member states declared their readiness to support Greece subject to strong conditionality based on an assessment by the European Commission and the ECB and at a penalty interest rate In April 2010, as the IMF and the Eurozone technocrats were bargaining the conditions of the credit, the interest rate of the two-year government bonds increased to 19 per cent; the cost of credit default swaps (CDS) for Greek bonds hiked as speculation about default spread; and Greek bonds were downgraded to junk status. The contagion began to threaten Spain and Portugal, whose bonds were also downgraded slightly; in Ireland the interest rates on bonds increased and eyes turned to the sovereign debt problem in the core countries such as Italy, Belgium, Britain, and even the US. Worries also rose about the solvency of those private banks holding government bonds. Under pressure the initial amount of €30 billion turned out to be the first part of a larger three-year bailout package of €110 billion. EU unveiled in May a further surprise package of €500 billion to be supported by a €250 billion IMF facility to defend all Eurozone countries. The Eurozone governments are indeed protecting their own banks that are holding Greek bonds against a default; the bulk of the Greek bonds are held by German and French banks (The Economist, 2010a).

The ECB's initial response was to announce in March 2010 that it would continue to accept bonds with ratings as low as triple-B-minus as collateral; later it even accepted the Greek bonds after they were downgraded to Junk status.[4] The rating of the private agencies was, of course, still the basis. However, in May under the pressure of banks and the Commission ECB finally made a U-turn and launched a programme of buying up the bonds of the peripheral Eurozone countries.

According to EU politicians, Greece should follow the example of Ireland: Ireland has already smashed public sector wages between 5 and 15 per cent, cut social welfare spending and other spending in order to decrease its budget deficit from 12.5 per cent in 2009 to 10 per cent in 2011 and 2.9 per cent in 2014. This detrimental pro-cyclical fiscal policy has been praised since they have restored market confidence without any assistance from the EU. However, it did not prevent the speculators from asking for higher interest rates on Irish bonds following the crisis in Greece. The other role model celebrated for its self-discipline has been Latvia, which has managed a real devaluation not by abandoning its pegged exchange rate, but by deep cuts in wages and public spending.

Greece is now pushed to cut its budget deficit from 13.6 per cent of GDP in 2009 to 3 per cent in 2013 through a combination of dramatic cuts in spending, public sector wages and pensions, an increase in the retirement age and tax hikes along with a fight against tax evasion.

The bulk of the austerity measures will hurt the wage earners in both the private and the public sectors, as wage cuts in the public sector play a signal role for bargaining. Cuts in public services will also lead to further increases in the cost of living. However, there is a substantial inconsistency in this austerity plan: as the recession becomes deeper, tax revenues will become lower and, despite severe cuts, the budget deficit might not improve as much as planned. High interest rates are also exacerbating the problem of insolvency. If the interest rate on public debt is higher than the growth rate, the stock of government debt will rise as a ratio to GDP unless the government runs a very high primary budget surplus (budget balance excluding interest payments). The Economist (2010b) estimates that the nominal GDP of Greece will be 5 per cent lower by 2014, if it is to reduce its budget deficit to 2.6 per cent of GDP by 2014, which would however still mean a debt to GDP ratio of 153 per cent. Thus it is unclear how the austerity plan will rescue Greece from insolvency.

Portugal and Spain have also committed to austerity packages with higher taxes on consumption and wage cuts.

Outside the euro zone, Britain is another major site of debate in relation to the issue of budget deficits. The election campaign in 2010 has witnessed a race between the Conservatives and the Labour Party over how and when to reduce the budget deficit. Although the deficit is one of the highest in the EU – with a ratio of 11.7 per cent to GDP in 2009 – the heated debate surrounding Britain's public debt is surprising when one considers that average maturity of the debt is 13.7 years, the interest rate is at historically low levels, and the ratio of debt to GDP is 68.6 per cent. Moreover part of the increase in the public debt to GDP ratio is because of a lower GDP in both actual and potential terms due to the decline in the productive capacity of the private sector. At the end of 2009 the recession turned into stagnation; this raises fears that public sector cuts at this stage could turn stagnation into a double-dip recession. Estimates show that the GDP in 2013 will be about 12 per cent lower than would have been the case if the pre-2007 trends had continued (Arestis and Sawyer, 2009). Under these circumstances the talk of fiscal crisis looks more like an excuse on the part of the business lobbies to avoid financing the budget deficit through tax increases, and make wage earners pay the costs of the crisis through cuts in income, jobs, and social services, and to create a situation of 'national emergency' to smash the remaining power of public sector trade unions.

The speculators now worry that these measures do not offer a solution to the problems: first they believe that a Greek default is inevitable given the popular resistance, the size of the debt and the recession. Second, in a schizophrenic fashion, they are also worried that austerity measures will deepen the recession in not only Greece but many other rich countries, create a double dip in the global economy, decrease tax revenues, and make it even harder to pay the debt back.

A long recession seems very likely without the support of strong fiscal stimuli. The uncertainty about the strength of the recovery is making new investments as well as hirings less likely. Declines in income and confidence, job losses, the pressure to pay back debt is restraining household consumption. Both investments and consumption will not return back to normal even when the banks relax credit. The withdrawal of the government from economic activity and liberalisation have not created new investments and jobs in the post-1980s despite an increasing profit share; why should more of the same policy do the job now and solve the imbalances within the EU? The presumed positive effect of reduced budget deficit on private investments is based on the argument that lower government borrowing leads to lower interest rates and a higher private investment and spending. Under the current conditions where consumers and firms are trying to reduce their debt and interest rates are already low, this channel has no relevance. Quite on the contrary public investment could increase the productivity and potential output of the economy, crowd in private investment and therefore offer a long term solution to the problem of debt.

The EU's decision assumes that the problem is one of a lack of fiscal discipline and repeats the old faith in strengthening the surveillance of budget deficits; it does not question the reasons behind the deficits; it ignores all the structural problems in respect of divergences in productivity, and imbalances in current accounts resulting from the 'beggar my neighbour' policies of Germany. The austerity packages throughout the EU are pushing the countries into a model of chronically low internal demand based on low wages. The deflationary consequences of wage cuts may turn the problem of debt into insolvency for both the private and the public sectors. In the past in Germany the low level of domestic demand was substituted by a high demand for exports. But it is not possible to entire the whole euro zone into a German model based on wage suppression and austerity, since without the deficits of the periphery the German export market will also stagnate. As the world's periphery emerges from recession, this demand can help the exporters of Germany for some time, but not every country can be the winner in this game. Particularly in respect of the periphery of Europe the contraction in domestic demand implies a prolonged recession.

Real wages have already declined in 2008–09 compared to 2007 in Britain, Germany, Italy, and Sweden. Ireland, Greece, Portugal and Spain are preparing for severe real wage cuts in 2010. Sharp and long-lasting increases in unemployment are likely to make the wage losses much stronger. The wage share has already declined in 2009 in Spain and Ireland; the counter-cyclical increase in the wage share in other countries is rather a symptom of the decreases in productivity. The case of Japan shows that during the initial phase of a deflationary crisis (or a long-lasting recession), labour's income share either stagnates or increases slightly, but as the recession and deflation persists, even nominal wage declines take place; in Japan the wage share declined by 8.9 per cent between 1992 and in 2007. The decline in the wages in Eastern Europe will also add further international competitive pressures on wages in Western Europe.

Unemployment has already increased in 2009 by 1.9 percentage points in the euro area, and by 2.3 percentage points in the UK. Particularly significant increases took place in Ireland and Spain (6.0 and 6.7 percentage points respectively) as a result of the collapse of the construction and loss of temporary jobs. Unemployment is expected to increase further and displays significant persistence. ILO (2010) estimates that employment rates will not return back to the pre-crisis levels before 2014. In all countries the level of working hours decreased more than employment, and there has been a rise in part-time employment. Some countries, including France, Germany, Austria, and the Netherlands, have introduced short working time arrangements, supported by government subsidies. However, the short working time arrangements may eventually be terminated as the financial markets are increasing the pressure over governments to decrease the levels of public debt. ILO (2010) estimates that five million additional jobs could be lost if these practices were discontinued. This may spread the problem of unemployment from lower-skilled temporary workers to higher-skilled workers. Moreover firms might want to make use of the recession to rationalise a strategy of increasing productivity and start a new wave of firing or introduce a freeze on hiring long after the recovery. If firms increase the working hours and delay hiring, this will worsen the job chances of the unemployed and the young first-time job seekers. The crisis will then lead to an increase in long-term unemployment as well as discouraging workers who drop out of the labour market. There are also structural problems of unemployment in sectors like the automotive industry and construction, where the crisis has only uncovered the already existing bottlenecks. The recovery of the aggregate economy will not necessarily create jobs in these sectors.

3   Eastern Europe

Eastern European member states (MS) are being severely affected by the credit crash and capital outflows, and the possible currency crisis accompanying the banking crisis, although recent problems in the old periphery countries of Europe removed the focus on these countries as Europe's 'subprime'. After the initial transition shock and a decade of restructuring, these countries will once again face the costs of integration to unregulated global markets. The early optimism about the decoupling of the East from the West proved to be wrong. The hopes for a soft landing were replaced by fears of a hard landing in autumn 2008; the conventional wisdom of the markets shifted from optimism to pessimism, and the EU anchor seems to be helping to only a limited extent. The fundamental problem of the region was an excessive dependency on foreign capital flows, and as a typical consequence of this a bust episode following the boom was an unavoidable outcome of reversals in capital flows. Many authors, including myself, were pointing at these risks, and a bust did happen again (Onaran, 2007; Becker, 2007; Goldstein, 2005). If it were not due to the global crisis, this could have been triggered through traditional channels of expectations regarding the sustainability of the overvalued exchange rate and high current account deficits. Ignoring the possibility of capital outflow was gambling in policy making. This behavior is like ignoring a gas leakage in your house, and choosing a 'wait and see' strategy, rather than trying to fix the leak. Markets in the last instance could not prevent the systemic risk, but only postponed it and made it bigger.

The difference between this crisis and the former boom–bust cycles in the periphery is that it is a global rather than a regional crisis. It has originated from the core, but the consequences for the periphery of Europe are heavier. The credit crunch has a global dimension, which makes it unlikely that usual capital inflows will resume after the bust phase. Again due to the global character of the crisis, the export markets have contracted severely, and depreciation, which is a usual outcome of boom–bust cycles, now only have the negative balance sheet effects, and no positive demand effect. The austerity packages in Western Europe are a further threat to recovery. The extent of debt-led growth, and household and private sector debt, particularly in foreign currencies, is also increasing the risks more than the former crises with wider social implications for depreciation.

The slowdown in global demand, the decline in FDI inflows, portfolio investment outflows, the contraction in remittances, and the credit crash are affecting all of the countries in Eastern Europe, but the degree of accumulated imbalances including current account deficits, an appreciation of the exchange rate, a boom in the housing market, and foreign-currency-denominated private debt determine the differences in the depth of the effects among these countries. The Baltic Countries, Hungary, Romania, Bulgaria, are more exposed than Poland, the Czech Republic, Slovenia, and Slovakia. In Hungary the problem of debt affects the public sector, households and firms. But even Poland, the Czech Republic, Slovenia, and Slovakia are suffering from the contagion effects, the slowdown in global demand, and the decline in FDI inflows. An excessive dependence on export markets and a dangerous overspecialisation in the automobile industry as occurred in the case of Slovakia in particular, but also in the Czech Republic and Slovenia, turn out to be major risks. Poland is currently experiencing only stagnation rather than a recession thanks to its more diversified market and large domestic economy with a lower trade volume as a ratio to GDP. However, growth rates in Poland only accelerated in 2006; thus the boom had not been as long-lasting and the economy was not yet so vulnerable. Both Slovakia and Slovenia have escaped turbulences in the currency markets by adopting the euro; however, their problem will be a permanent loss of international competitiveness relative to their Eastern European competitors, whose currencies depreciate. To avoid speculation, Estonia is also willing to opt for the lesser evil, i.e. to adopt the euro.

The myth that these countries would not experience bottlenecks regarding the current account deficits thanks to FDI being a major source of finance of the deficit also proved to be wrong. It is true that FDI is still more robust than the other capital flows, but FDI inflows have also fallen back significantly, reaching the level recorded in 2001–02 (Hunya, 2009). Although the current account deficits are also falling because of a lower level of imports, FDI is now financing a shrinking part of the deficits. Furthermore FDI not only finances but also creates current account deficits; the average repatriation rate of profits in the region has been 70 per cent, and FDI inflows are either only as large as or even less than the repatriated profits in Hungary, Slovakia, and the Czech Republic (Hunya, 2009).

Nine Eastern European economies in the EU have had a recession in 2009, with Poland being the only exception (see Table 7.2). Employment has declined and unemployment increased significantly in all countries, with the sharpest increases taking place in the Baltic Countries. Real wages have fallen in the Czech Republic, Hungary, the Baltic Countries,

Table 7.2 Average annual growth in GDP, employment, productivity, and real wage, 1989–2009 and sub–periods, Eastern EU MS

	1989*–1994				1994–2000				2000–2007			
	GDP	Employment	Productivity	Real wage	GDP	Employment	Productivity	Real wage	GDP	Employment	Productivity	Real wage
Czech Republic	-2.3	-2.0	–	-3.0	2.2	-0.8	3.2	3.2	4.5	0.8	3.8	4.7
Hungary	-3.2	-4.2	3.7	-1.9	3.3	0.5	2.1	-1.9	3.7	1.1	2.0	4.3
Poland	-1.6	-3.6	2.0	-3.5	5.7	-0.2	5.0	4.8	4.1	0.6	2.6	1.1
Slovenia	-2.3	-4.6	3.8	-6.0	4.3	-0.3	4.7	2.9	4.4	0.9	3.3	3.0
Slovakia	-2.4	–	12.6	-5.6	3.8	-0.6	4.8	5.3	6.2	1.0	5.9	3.3
Estonia	-1.6	-4.3	2.7	-17.3	6.0	-2.7	8.9	8.0	8.1	1.7	6.4	8.6
Latvia	-11.2	-5.1	19.0	8.2	4.3	-2.3	2.7	3.4	9.0	2.4	5.7	9.9
Lithuania	-11.5	-2.0	0.0	-19.8	4.5	-1.2	8.3	6.9	8.1	1.3	5.6	8.5
Bulgaria	-5.7	-5.8	8.5	-13.4	-0.2	0.0	0.0	-4.4	5.6	2.0	3.2	4.0
Romania	-4.6	-1.8	1.6	-6.7	0.1	-2.4	5.0	6.5	6.1	-0.8	5.5	9.3

	1989*–2009				2008				2009			
	GDP	Employment	Productivity	Real wage	GDP	Employment	Productivity	Real wage	GDP	Employment	Productivity	Real wage
Czech Republic	1.5	0.1	2.9	2.1	2.5	1.2	1.1	1.3	-4.2	-1.2	-2.3	-1.1
Hungary	1.2	-0.2	1.9	0.2	0.6	-1.3	1.6	0.9	-6.3	-3.6	-3.4	-4.5
Poland	3.0	0.3	3.0	1.1	5.0	3.8	0.5	3.8	1.7	0.4	1.0	1.0
Slovenia	2.0	0.3	3.2	0.6	3.5	2.8	0.5	1.5	-7.8	-2.2	-5.4	4.0
Slovakia	2.7	0.3	5.4	1.5	6.2	2.8	4.1	1.3	-4.7	-2.4	-0.5	3.6
Estonia	4.4	-0.5	5.6	1.4	-3.6	0.2	-5.1	0.6	-14.1	-9.9	-4.2	-2.2
Latvia	0.1	0.0	4.8	5.0	-4.6	0.9	-6.2	-1.0	-18.0	-13.6	-3.7	-14.6
Lithuania	0.3	-0.2	5.0	-1.1	2.8	-0.5	0.7	2.9	-15.0	-6.9	-8.1	-11.5
Bulgaria	0.4	0.6	3.2	-2.9	6.0	3.3	2.3	7.4	-5.0	-2.9	-0.9	6.9
Romania	0.9	-0.8	3.9	4.0	7.3	-0.2	6.7	13.5	-7.1	-1.0	-6.1	-0.1

Notes: The starting date differs with respect to data availability. GDP data is only starting in Estonia in 1993, the employment data starts in Slovakia in 1994, in Hungary in 1992, and in Estonia in 1990, the employee data starts in 1995 in Czech Republic, in 1992 in Hungary and Latvia, in 1993 in Slovakia, Estonia, and Lithuania, in 1990 in Romania and the wage data starts in Latvia 1993 and in Estonia 1990. GDP is in 2000 prices in national currencies. Employment is total economy. Productivity is Real GDP/Employee. Real wage is labour compensation deflated by private consumption deflator, index 2000 = 100.

and Romania. The austerity programmes in Hungary, Romania, and Latvia will further reinforce the pressures of the crisis. The wage share has already fallen in Latvia, Hungary, Poland, and the Czech Republic (see Figure 7.2). Moreover, a long-lasting recession cannot be ruled out, which would certainly have negative effects on the real wage and labour share.

In the Eastern European economies the record of GDP, employment, and real wage growth over the past twenty years has been shocking

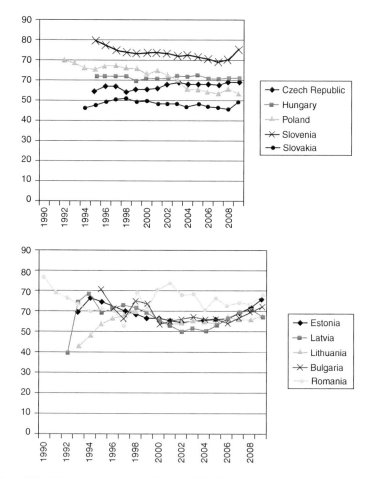

Figure 7.2   Adjusted wage share, Eastern EU MS*
Note: *Compensation per employee as percentage of GDP at factor cost per person employed.
Source: AMECO (Economic and Financial affairs, Annual Macroeconomic Indicators online database), April 2010.

(see Table 7.2): affected first by a transition recession and then by a global crisis, the gains in terms of growth and wages are far from spectacular. Employment has at best stagnated, and in several countries – Romania, Estonia, Lithuania, and Hungary – it has declined compared to 1989. Real wages have stagnated in Hungary and Slovenia, and have even fallen in Lithuania and Bulgaria. Overall, real wage growth has lagged behind productivity growth. The only significant real wage growth has taken place in Romania, but then only equal to improvements in productivity. As a consequence of this moderate wage growth, which lags behind productivity, and low employment, the labour share has been declining in Slovenia, Poland, Bulgaria, and Romania and stagnant in Hungary and Slovakia (Figure 7.2). The only exception to this pattern has been in recent years in the Baltic States and the Czech Republic, when the labour share was back to the levels recorded at the start of the transition; however, data do not allow us to compare their current situation with the pre-transition phase; moreover as mentioned above, this recovery will be reversed during the current crisis. This does not appear to be a politically and socially viable balance sheet of integration.

The current global crisis has created no change in the policy stance in respect of European enlargement. The concerns of the EU for the NMS are shaped by the interests of the MNEs, in particular western banks, and are limited to maintaining the stability of the currency rather than employment and income. The EU did not have the political will to create the institutions and tools for a unified counter-cyclical stimulus plan, but rather delegated the issue of the NMS to the IMF, albeit with some financial support to prevent a big meltdown of the Western European MNEs in the region. The IMF's damaged credibility following the Asian crisis was restored at the G20 via an increase in the available funds to the IMF, but not much has changed in the policy framework, despite the seemingly different discourse. Faced with the pressure of capital outflows, Hungary, Latvia, and Romania have resorted to the IMF. The EU connection thanks to the interests of the MNEs, in particular West European banks in the region, has determined the size of the packages rather than the genuine content. As it was in the case of the former crises in the developing countries in the 1990s and 2000s, IMF policies are again much more restrictive than what IMF finds appropriate for the Western European countries. The credit line to Poland without conditionality is the only new tool used by the IMF. Otherwise Hungary, Romania, and Latvia have implemented a strongly pro-cyclical fiscal policy; fiscal discipline is still the norm, and cuts in public sector wages and pensions are significant ingredients in the recipe. In the fixed exchange rate countries the prevention of devaluation was the major aim to protect the foreign banks, which had extended the majority of the loans in foreign currency. The governments of these countries were also unwilling to push domestic firms and households indebted in foreign currency into bankruptcy through devaluation. Thus nominal devaluation was replaced by a brutal internal real devaluation via wage suppression. In Latvia as of the fourth quarter of 2009, average salaries had fallen by 12.1 per cent. Public sector wages were down by 23.7 per cent compared to a year earlier and pensions have been cut by 10 per cent. Together with increases in the VAT rate from 18 to 21 per cent, these were the conditions, which the government in Latvia had to agree to get the second tranche of the IMF package (Gligorov et al., 2009). The government has forced through spending cuts and tax rises worth a tenth of GDP (Ward, 2010). The cost of this internal devaluation has been a 25 per cent fall in GDP in two years and an unemployment rate of 22.9 per cent in 2009. Eventually, it also translated into a political crisis as the biggest party, the People's Party, broke from the ruling coalition because of its support for the tax cuts. In Estonia and Lithuania also at least 20 per cent cut in public wages and a reduction in social benefits was decided (Gligorov et al., 2009). Thus the current account imbalances are being corrected not through nominal but real devaluation and deep recession.

One difference during this crisis is that the IMF is now trying to bail in the banks to maintain the level of credits in the countries that have an IMF financial programme. The major difference compared to East Asia and Latin America was a reliance on parent banks in the mature markets with a longer-term strategy of expansion in the region rather than market finance via foreign capital flows. The parent banks' loyalty to the region did not happen automatically, however. For example, initially the Austrian government has said that it would only support its troubled Erste Bank, which was overexposed to risky loans in foreign currency in Eastern Europe, on condition that the money only went to loans inside Austria, and thus not to further expansion of loans in the East (The Economist, March 2010c). This approach would have led to each individual bank reducing its exposure by calling in loans and dumping assets, and a major currency crisis, which would have also hurt the banks themselves. The small number of large international players with a long-term investment in the region facilitated coordination, and the European Bank for Reconstruction and Development led the 'Vienna Initiative'. The ECB's liquidity provision to foreign banks in Eastern Europe encouraged them to continue to finance the subsidiaries outside the Euro area. The IMF support helped the central banks of Eastern Europe to provide liquidity to foreign-owned banks as well as the minority domestically owned banks. However, given the global crisis and the crunch in the wholesale credit markets, the ability of parent banks to maintain the credit booms in the region is exhausted, and even without further capital outflows, the region suffers from a deeper recession than in the West in the absence of former capital inflows. The speculation about the Greek sovereign debt is creating particular liquidity restraints for the Greek banks and their affiliates in Bulgaria and Romania; the funding problems of other European parent banks are also increasing. The currency depreciation or the recession will lead to increases in non-performing loans and further affect the parent banks' approach to the Eastern affiliates.

Another difference in this crisis in the Eastern MS compared to the former crises in the developing countries was the moderate scale and pace of depreciation. In countries with a floating exchange rate regime, there has been some contagion even in countries like Poland, but there has not been a total breakdown to date. The exchange rate only depreciated by some 20–30 per cent in Hungary, Poland, and Romania with some recovery afterwards, and the fixed pegs are still holding in the Baltic States and Bulgaria. The maintenance of the problematic pegs required rather large international rescue packages in comparison to the size of the economy. The Western European banks operating in the region, like the Swedish ones in the Baltic States and the Austrian ones in Bulgaria, have – in collaboration with the governments in the home country – exerted pressure to avoid devaluation for fear of high non-performing loan rates, which would erode their profitability. The local governments also stand behind the pegs. However, preserving this overvalued fixed exchange rate under the current policy framework came at the cost of a very deep recession and deflation to create a real devaluation, and the mechanism for that was massive wage cuts as can be seen in Latvia.

On the other hand, the consequences of an unmanaged devaluation following a market-made currency crisis would lead to also very severe distributional effects, as was the case during the Asian or Latin American crises. This is because of the inflationary effects of high devaluation rates following a currency crisis. In import-dependent developing countries, devaluation has a high pass-through effect to domestic prices as a result of the rise in the imported input costs, and during a severe recession and high unemployment, it is impossible for workers to index their wages to past inflation rates (Onaran, 2009). So far during the recent global crisis, not only has the depreciation rate been moderate, but also the pass-through effect to inflation has been restrained by the global deflationary environment and the falling commodity prices. However, any problem in the periphery in Eastern or Western Europe or other developing countries regarding speculative attacks to sovereign debt and capital outflows can easily trigger contagion effects and pressures on currencies in Eastern Europe again.

Capital controls on outflows or a managed devaluation are not even mentioned in the IMF or EU debates. The only recent revision has been a recent 'IMF Staff Position Note' about capital controls on inflows to moderate the effects on the exchange rate (Ostry et al., 2010); however, this does not help at this moment when the boom has already been followed by a bust.

4   There is an alternative!

Policies to address the major root of the crisis, the dramatic pro-capital shift in income distribution and hikes in managerial wages, cannot be found anywhere in the mainstream policy agenda. Although the costs of the rescue packages are clear, little effort is being made to extract payment from those either responsible or able to pay. The tax on bank bonuses in Britain only scratches the surface. With regards to current account imbalances or sovereign debt crisis, nothing is said about the wage dumping and stagnant domestic consumption in Germany or the lack of public investment programs to enhance productivity.

The struggles emerging across Europe can be turned into a lever for developing an internationalist alternative to the crisis. The existing wage suppression policies hurt all working people. The popular argument in Germany that Greece has a public spending crisis hides the fact that the German workers' loss of wages, unemployment benefits and pension rights over the past decade created part of the current situa-tion. Uncovering this is an important step towards building a working peoples' alliance for an alternative Europe. An internationalist solution might generate a more powerful front in the core and the periphery compared to national alternatives, for example, the exit of Greece from the euro based on an anti-capitalist agenda as suggested by Lapavitsas et al. (2010). A national solution in a small country is destined for isola-tion and a long-term persistence of the problems of underdevelopment. Moreover in the current situation, anti-European and anti-Euro policies are more likely to mobilise nationalist, right-wing currents. The left has more to gain from an internationalist alternative.

The economic crisis is intermingled with the ecological crisis, and showing that capitalism is economically, ecologically, and politically unstable and unsustainable. Any economic recovery plan must not imply a return to business as usual in economic as well as ecological terms. It is not possible to 'save capitalism from itself'. The major crisis calls for a major policy restructuring in the direction of a democratically planned, participatory economic model and the starting point is the urgent problems of employment, distribution, and ecological sustainability:

(a) Macroeconomic policy has to be centred on full employment and ecological sustainability. Public expenditures in labour-intensive services like education, child care, nursing homes, health, community and social services, as well as in public infrastructure, housing, and green investments are the areas to combine the target of full employment with sustainability, gender equality, and solidarity.

For the purpose of ecological sustainability, there is a need for a shift in the composition of demand towards investments in ecological maintenance and repair, renewable energy, public transport, the insulation of the existing housing stock and the construction of zero energy houses; this cannot be achieved without large strategic public investments.

To maintain full employment, a substantial shortening of working time (that is, in parallel with the historical rate of growth of labour productivity) is also required. This is not only a crucial answer to the problem of unemployment after the crisis, but also an answer to the ecological crisis: recovery efforts are all centred on maintaining growth through the restoration of business confidence. However, the ecological limits to growth are based on firm scientific principles. If the use of environmental resources is to maintain a certain 'sustainable' level, economic growth, in the long term, has to be zero or low, i.e. equal to the growth rate of 'environmental productivity'. However, for such a regime to be socially desirable it has to guarantee a high level of employment and an equitable distribution of income; i.e. full employment can only be achieved through shorter working time, not unsustainable growth. The income losses for the working masses can be prevented through substantial redistribution, i.e. an increase in hourly wages and a decline in the profit share.

In respect of employment in the private sector, it is important to prevent firms from making use of the crisis to implement their long-term downsizing strategies. An alternative would be legal measures to ban firing during the crisis and implement wage floors: if the firing ban leads to bankruptcy in certain firms, these firms can be re-appropriated and revitalised under workers' control, supported by public credits. In Argentina after the crisis there were many such examples.

In cases of sectors that are under the threat of mass layoffs, like the auto industry, nationalisation of the firms and restructuring of these public firms should be considered, e.g. in the auto industry a shift of focus towards the production of public transport vehicles, and a gradual transfer of labour towards new sectors.

(b) There is need for a fundamental correction of the wages to fully reflect the productivity gains of the past three decades. This was a crisis of distribution and a reversal of inequality is the only real solution. To limit the 'race to the bottom' it is necessary to introduce a minimum wage, which is to be coordinated at the EU level.

Higher productivity growth in poorer countries will help to create some convergence in wages, but regional convergence should be supported by fiscal transfers and public investments to boost productivity in poorer regions. Furthermore a European unemployment benefit system can be developed to redistribute from low unemployment regions to high unemployment regions. This requires a significant EU budget financed by EU-level progressive taxes.

(c) The full employment and green recovery plan should be financed through highly progressive income and wealth taxes, higher corporate tax rates, inheritance tax, and a tax on financial transactions. A progressive income tax mechanism could also introduce a maximum income with the highest marginal tax rate increasing to 90 per cent above a certain income threshold. This threshold should be set in relation to the median wage, and the income differential the society is willing to tolerate; this differential should be based on job-related risks and hardships as well as supply bottlenecks regarding particular skills, provided that the society offers equal opportunities for everyone willing to acquire sought-after skills.

This is also the just way to solve the debt crisis and to avoid budget cuts in social expenditures. In principle, the problem of the budget deficit can be solved through growth or tax or default/restructuring. There is a constraint to the higher growth solution due to the ecological limits on growth. This leaves tax and default/debt restructuring as the only solution of the debt problem. The restructuring of debt can be formulated as a progressive wealth tax on government bonds with the highest marginal tax rate reaching to 100 per cent for holdings above a certain high amount of bonds; this would make the banks, the private investment funds, and the high wealth individuals pay the costs of the crisis.

The Stability and Growth Pact and the conditions of the Maastricht Treaty for adopting the euro must be abolished. The ECB should be turned into a real central bank with the ability to lend to member states as well as European Bank for Reconstruction and Development.

(d) A redesign of the financial sector is also urgently required. Financial regulations are important but not sufficient. Finance is a crucial sector which cannot be left to the short-termism of the private profit motive. This sector has already been de facto nationalised, but without any voice for the society and with a commitment to privatisation as soon as possible. The crisis has shown us that large private banks are exploiting their advantage of being 'too big to fail'. Yet the challenge is the finance of socially desirable large new investments, e.g. in the energy sector. Instead what needs to be done is to build a public banking sector with the participation of the workers and other stakeholders to decision making and the transparence of the accounts.

(e) The crisis has indicated that, in addition to the banking sector, there are other critical sectors for the society, in which the ownership rights cannot be left to the private sector, e.g. the housing sectors. The energy crisis is indicating that the energy sector also requires substantial public intervention. The problems with the private pension funds as well as private supplies of education, health, and infrastructure are showing that social services are also too critical to be ruled by private profit motives. A democratic discussion should question, in which other sectors public ownership would produce more egalitarian as well as more socially efficient outcomes. This does not mean to praise the public sector as such, but calls for the participation and control of the stakeholders (the workers, consumers, regional representatives etc.) in the decision-making mechanisms. Such a shift in decision making also facilitates economy wide coordination of important decisions for a sustainable and planned development based on solidarity.

(f) In Eastern Europe the risk of a devastating devaluation can only be overcome with capital controls, debt restructuring and a managed devaluation with price controls. To avoid the negative effects of devaluation on indebted households and firms, the foreign currency-denominated debt must be converted to local currency at the current exchange rate, and the burden of devaluation must be shifted to the private banks of the core countries. Similarly in order to avoid the inflationary effect of devaluation, price controls should be introduced.

Notes

1. The author is grateful to Annina Kaltenbrunner, John Grahl, and the editors for comments.
2. Although guarantees in the financial packages might never be used, the ratios are still indicative.

3. The ratio of automatic and discretionary fiscal impulse cumulated over the period 2008–10 as a percentage of 2008 GDP.
4. The ECB had lowered the threshold for acceptable assets as collateral to triple-B-minus from A-minus in order to ensure that banks had access to sufficient amounts of ECB credit.

References

Arestis, P. and Sawyer, M. (2009) The Financial Crisis, Recession and the Future of Public Expenditures, mimeo.

Becker, J. (2007) 'Dollarisation in Latin America and Euroisation in Eastern Europe: Parallels and Differences', in J. Becker and R. Weissenbacher (eds), *Dollarisation, Euroisation and Financial Instability*. Marburg: Metropolis-Verlag, pp. 223–78.

Fitoussi, J.P. and Saraceno, F. (2010) 'Europe: How Deep is a Crisis? Policy Responses and Structural Factors Behind Diverging Performances', *Journal of Globalization and Development*, 1(1), article 17.

Gligorov V., Pöschl, J., Richter, S. (2009) 'Where Have All the Shooting Stars Gone?', *The Vienna Institute for International Economic Studies, Current Analyses and Forecasts* 4.

Goldstein, M. (2005) 'What Might the Next Emerging-market Financial Crisis Look Like?', Institute for International Economics, Working Paper 05-7.

Hunya, G. (2009) 'FDI in the CEECs under the Impact of the Global Crisis: Sharp Declines', The Vienna Institute for International Economic Studies Database on Foreign Direct Investment in Central, East and Southeast Europe.

ILO (2010) *World of Work*. Geneva: ILO.

Lapavitsas. C., Kaltenbrunner, N., Lindo, D., Michell, J., Painceira, J.P., Pires, E., Powell, J., Stenfors, A. and Teles, N. (2010) *Eurozone Crisis: Not Just a Greek Virus*, Research on Money and Finance Occasional Report, School of Oriental and African Studies, London.

OECD (2009) *Economic Outlook*, June.

Onaran, Ö. (2007) 'International Financial Markets and Fragility in Eastern Europe: "Can it Happen" here?', in J. Becker and R. Weissenbacher (eds), *Dollarization, Euroization and Financial Instability*. Marburg: Metropolis-Verlag, pp. 129–48.

Onaran, Ö. (2009) 'Wage Share, Globalization, and Crisis: The Case of Manufacturing Industry in Korea, Mexico, and Turkey', *International Review of Applied Economics*, 23(2).

Ostry, J.D., Ghosh, A.R., Habermeier, K., Chamon, M., Qureshi, M.S. and Reinhardt, D.B.S. (2010) 'Capital Inflows: The Role of Controls', *IMF Staff Position Note*.

The Economist (2010a) 'Greece's Sovereign Debt Crisis', 17 April, 66–8.

The Economist (2010b) 'Greece's Bail-out Maths', 27 March, 78.

The Economist (2010c) 'East European Economies', 20 March, 41.

Ward, A. (2010) 'Latvia Hacker Calls for Fat Cat Revolt', *Financial Times*, 4 March.

8
The Impact of the Subprime Financial Crisis on the Transition and Central Asian Economies: Causes and Consequences

Nigel F.B. Allington and John S.L. McCombie

1 Introduction

The subprime crisis precipitated the worst recession amongst the OECD countries since the Second World War. Although the value of subprime assets as a proportion of total financial assets was relatively small, the excessive leverage of many US and UK financial institutions, the marked revaluation of the risk associated with securitised assets, together with the collapse in world trade, meant that the 2008–10 crisis was the worst since the Great Depression of 1929. Moreover, contagion effects, especially those initiated through the freezing of the interbank and international financial loans markets, meant that the impact of the crisis extended far beyond those relatively few countries (especially the US and UK) whose banks were holders of the 'toxic assets'.[1] In this chapter the impact of the financial crisis on the European Union Transition Economies (TEs) and the transition Central Asian Economies (CAEs) is examined.[2] Particular attention is paid to the financial transmission mechanism that was crucial in determining the impact of the crisis on the TEs.

The result of the crisis in the euro zone was a decline in the average growth rate from 2.8 per cent per annum in 2007 to 0.6 per cent in 2008 and a negative rate of 4.1 per cent in 2009. Yet the impact was far more severe in the TEs, with all except Poland experiencing a rate of decline of over 4 per cent in 2009 (and with Estonia, Latvia and Lithuania having negative growth rates of over 13.9 per cent). Although the CAEs are also transition economies, moving since 1991 and the break-up of the Soviet Union towards market economies at various speeds, their experience has been markedly different. Throughout the 2000s until the crisis, they had achieved some of the fastest growth rates in the world. The crisis brought a slowdown in the growth rates of especially, Kazakhstan, the Kyrgyz Republic and Tajikistan, but nothing like to the degree of the TEs. Moreover, Turkmenistan and Uzbekistan were left relatively unscathed. The key difference is that Kazakhstan has one of the most sophisticated banking systems in the region and it is extensively integrated into the world financial system. It was thus badly hit by the virtual shutdown of the international credit markets. Kazakhstan has extensive holdings in the Kyrgyz Republic's banking system and so the latter also suffered. While Turkmenistan and Uzbekistan are open economies in trade terms, they have virtually isolated banking systems and were immune from the financial transmission mechanism of the crisis.

In this chapter, the various causes and consequences of the subprime crisis are traced and examined for the TEs and CAEs. Not surprisingly, the depth of the crisis depends upon the degree to which the TEs and CAEs are integrated into the world (especially the European) economy. This has occurred either through the TEs having their development financed through large capital flows (and hence running large current account deficits as a proportion of GDP) or having a high degree of financial integration, or both. As far as the last is concerned, many of the TEs have their banks owned or financed by Western European banks and this has been a mixed blessing. The dependence on foreign capital inflows has made the economies vulnerable to the credit crunch and capital flight, but this has been partially offset by the support that has been achieved through foreign ownership of their national banks. The TEs also suffered from a rapid decline of their export markets as the OECD countries moved into recession.

Given the distinctive characteristics of the TEs and CAEs, the two groups are largely treated separately in this chapter, but with a greater emphasis being placed on the former. In order to assess the effect of the subprime crisis the background to the recent economic performance of the TEs, notably their rates of growth during the preceding decade and their level of financial integration and their banking structure, are examined. The impact this had in transmitting the effects of the crisis to these countries is also considered. Finally, the very different experience of the CAEs receives attention.

2   The impact of the crisis on the economic growth of the European transition economies

Since 1995, when the TEs had begun to recover from the crisis induced by moving rapidly from planned to market economies, they have experienced rapid output and productivity growth as they began to catch up with the slower-growing Eurozone countries. The financial crisis has had a major impact on the key macroeconomic variables in the TEs. Just twenty years after their transition from command to market economies, the TEs ought to be growing rapidly as they catch up with the EU15 in terms of economic efficiency, technology and the capital-labour ratio. Consequently, it is somewhat ironical that they have sustained such dramatic falls in their GDP growth during the current financial crisis (see Table 8.1). Although the decline in growth rates are not as severe as those after 1989, the year of transition, when, for example, GDP in the Baltic States (Estonia, Latvia and Lithuania) contracted by more than 40 per cent and the other TEs registered falls of between 13 and 25 per cent, the current falls still pose a threat to social and political stability in the region (Svejnar, 2002).

After 1989 it took some of the TEs more than 15 years to regain the per capita income levels achieved immediately prior to the 'transition crises', but fortunately this time it will only be at most two or three years before pre-crisis growth levels are re-established. Nevertheless, the present downturn has produced severe economic problems that are comparable to those resulting from the Russian crisis of 1998.

The collapse in growth had occurred in the majority of TEs, albeit with some large differences. Poland was the least hard hit of all the TEs and often the disparity is large, especially between it and some of the

Table 8.1   Growth of real GDP: Transition economies (annual percentage growth rates)

	2003	2004	2005	2006	2007	2008	2009	2010ᶠ	2011ᶠ
Bulgaria	5.5	6.7	6.4	6.5	6.4	6.2	−4.9	0.0	2.7
Czech R.	3.6	4.5	6.3	6.8	6.1	2.5	−4.1	1.6	2.4
Estonia	7.6	7.2	9.4	10.6	6.9	−5.1	−13.9	0.9	3.8
Latvia	7.2	8.7	10.6	12.2	10.0	−4.2	−18.0	−3.5	3.3
Lithuania	10.2	7.4	7.8	7.8	9.8	2.8	−14.8	−0.6	3.2
Hungary	4.3	4.9	3.5	4.0	1.0	0.6	−6.3	0.0	2.8
Poland	3.9	5.3	3.6	6.2	6.8	5.0	1.7	2.7	3.3
Romania	5.2	8.5	4.2	7.9	6.3	7.3	−7.1	0.8	3.5
Slovenia	2.8	4.3	4.5	5.9	6.9	3.7	−8.1	1.1	1.8
Slovakia	4.8	5.0	6.7	8.5	10.6	6.2	−4.7	2.7	3.6
Eurozone	0.8	2.2	1.7	3.0	2.9	0.5	−4.1	0.9	1.5

Notes: ᶠ Figures are forecasts.
Sources: Eurostat and European Bank for Reconstruction and Development (2009).

worst affected TEs such as the Baltic States. Poland's exceptional position is due to its lower dependence on exports and imports, robust consumption and substantial EU-financed investment in infrastructure. The IMF also granted Poland a $20.6bn reserve credit line that pre-empted further investor flight.

Cerra and Saxena (2008) have shown that recessions accompanied by a financial crisis generally have a negative impact on the prospects for future growth. Capital scrapping occurs, consumption and investment levels fall and these possible sorts of responses are prominent in the TEs. The resulting increase in unemployment has a large structural component and as employees' skills atrophy, the duration of unemployment increases (Blanchard and Summers, 1986). Because this crisis was accompanied by a house price bubble in the Baltic States, these economies face even tougher post-crisis growth constraints than the other TEs (Claessen, Kose and Terrones, 2008). The flexible employment protection rules recently introduced as part of the Lisbon Agenda may reduce the effects on unemployment.

3   The process of integration between the TEs and the EU15

One of the major aspects of the economic development of the TEs just before, and then after, their accession to the EU, has been their progressive integration with the Western European countries. This has brought the benefits of increased inward investment and, with accession to the European Union (EU), access to the Structural and Cohesion Funds, but it has also made the economies more sensitive to international business cycles, as the subprime crisis has clearly shown. The level of integration between the TEs and the EU15 can be gauged by the extent of intra-EU trade. Between 1993, when articles of association were signed with the newly independent TEs and 2008, TE exports to the rest of the EU increased 2.5 times, with the level of exports accelerating after the TEs accession which was either in 2004 or 2007. At present, two-thirds of the TEs' trade is with the euro zone. Integration has also seen countries' business cycles in the EU15 and the TEs become more closely synchronised. In fact, correlations for the TEs are much higher than those between some of the EU15 countries, most noticeably Greece and Portugal (IMF, 2007).

While the TEs have a larger agricultural sector than the EU15 and a concomitant lower share of services, they are converging towards the EU averages and the most conspicuous area of integration is in financial services, where foreign banks from the EU15 and other emerging markets took advantage of the privatisation of TE banks to acquire partial or total stakes. Consequently, the rate of credit growth has increased in the TEs with increasing integration, particularly in the Baltic States, with considerable financial deepening. Equity markets are also more integrated (Cappiello, Gerard, Kadareja, and Manganelli, 2006) and bond prices are cointegrated particularly with those of Germany (Iorgova and Ong, 2008). Although the spectrum of interest rates had also been converging, with the current financial crisis they have started to diverge again because of the higher risk premium associated with investing in the TEs.

Despite considerable evidence in the literature that finance runs uphill from poor to rich countries (the so-called Lucas puzzle), Abiad, Leigh, and Mody (2009) show that Europe follows the textbook theory, with finance flowing from the rich EU15 countries to the poorer TEs, leading to faster convergence through financial integration. Borders in the enlarged EU have therefore become far less important. The consequence of this is that domestic savings are not the drivers of domestic investment, dispelling, at least in the case of the TEs, the Feldstein–Horioka puzzle (1985). Capital flows, especially in the form of FDI, also bring productivity benefits so that long-run per capita income grows at a faster rate, even if the benefits are 'time-limited'.

Eichengreen and Park (2003) contrasted the position of the TEs with that of Asia, noting that,

> one of the most striking aspects of Europe's recent development has been the growth and integration of financial markets. In Asia, in contrast, there has been less progress in financial integration. If anything, the countries of East Asia have developed stronger financial ties with Western Europe and the United States than with one another.

The capital inflows have also been reflected by large current account deficits (see Table 8.2), again in contrast with Asia and Latin America in the 2000s (although not in the lead-up to the 1997 Southeast Asian (SEA) financial crisis). Larger capital inflows have resulted in faster convergence, although the current financial crisis has illuminated the concomitant financial fragilities that accompany these developments.

Blanchard and Giavazzi (2002) showed that financial integration had a significant impact on the current account and the value of the beta coefficient in the Feldstein–Horioka equation that measures whether savings are internationally mobile or invested largely in the national

Table 8.2 Current account balances: transition economies (percentage of GDP)

	2003	2004	2005	2006	2007	2008	2009	2010[f]
Bulgaria	−5.5	−6.6	−12.4	−18.5	−25.2	−25.5	−11.4	−8.3
Czech R.	−6.3	−5.3	−1.3	−2.6	−3.1	−3.1	−2.1	−2.2
Estonia	−11.3	−11.3	−10.0	−16.9	−17.8	−9.3	1.9	2.0
Latvia	−8.2	−12.8	−12.4	−22.7	−21.6	−12.6	4.5	6.4
Lithuania	−6.9	−7.6	−7.7	−10.7	−14.6	−11.6	1.0	0.5
Hungary	−7.9	−8.4	−7.5	−7.5	−6.5	−8.4	−2.9	−3.3
Poland	−2.1	−4.0	−1.2	−2.7	−4.7	−5.5	−2.2	−3.1
Romania	−5.8	−8.4	−8.9	−10.4	−13.5	−12.4	−5.5	−5.6
Slovenia	−0.8	−2.7	−1.7	−2.5	−4.2	−5.5	−3.0	−4.7
Slovakia	−5.9	−7.8	−8.5	−0.7	−5.3	−6.5	−8.0	−7.8

Notes: [f] Figures are forecasts.
Sources: Eurostat and European Bank for Reconstruction and Development (2009).

economy.[3] As capital flowed from the richer EU15 countries to the poorer TEs, the estimated coefficient on per capita income in their current account equation increased, showing that richer countries ran current account surpluses while the poorer countries ran deficits. Abiad et al. (2009) are able to link this development to greater levels of financial integration in the EU. They estimated the relationship between the current account and a vector of explanatory variables, including financial integration that has a positive coefficient if poorer countries run larger deficits as capital flows increase. While the size of the effect is small in the whole sample of countries examined, when the authors consider the TEs, they are much larger and statistically significant, indicating a high degree of financial integration.

Although financial integration has increased enormously in the TEs, it has not yet reached the levels found in the EU15. Thus, the TEs have further to go, implying that current account deficits will remain large with some reduction as their incomes grow. The Structural Funds and Cohesion Funds are designed to facilitate convergence in the EU, but the empirical evidence as to their success is mixed at best (Esposti, 2008 and de Michelis, 2008). These funds now average about 3.5 per cent of a TE's GDP. Institutional quality receives some support in this empirical analysis (Abiad et al., 2009) with a threshold identified beyond which the institutional factors gain even greater importance. Finally, investors are found to be able to spread their risks through diversifying their investments where financial markets are highly integrated.

The EBRD (2009, pp. 64–5) employs a growth regression methodology for 55 countries to determine the relationship between average growth rates over the period 1994–2008 and the degree of financial integration, including the usual set of controls. Financial integration is measured by a number of alternative proxies; namely, the current account; the change in net foreign assets; and the level of gross foreign assets and liabilities, with all the preceding variables expressed as a proportion of GDP. A further measure is the degree to which foreign banks are embedded in the economy. The analysis compares the TEs with a group of other emerging market economies and the results suggest that financial integration is significant for the growth of the TEs, but not for the other emerging countries.

The analysis is extended to the sectoral level where it is hypothesised that those industries that rely on external finance (as opposed to retained earnings) should benefit more from overseas borrowing and greater financial integration. The results from using a reduced sample of 26 countries shows that this is indeed true for the TEs' industries, but there is little evidence that it has any effect for the non-transition industries.

Why has foreign capital stimulated growth in the TEs when this had not been the case in the other emerging countries? Three possibilities were explored by the EBRD (2009). First, the TEs have better financial capacity to use the finance more productively; secondly, they have better institutions resulting from their membership of the EU and, finally, they have a pre-existing higher level of financial integration which facilitates the benefits of integration. Extending the earlier econometric results, this research includes financial development, institutional quality and the level of integration as explanatory variables. The results suggest that the first two explanations are not important, but that the existing level of financial integration is. The authors speculate that this result might be due to the fact that foreign banks facilitate the allocation of capital inflows and/or foreign banks demonstrate a substantial commitment to their subsidiaries/branches. The latter position is borne out by the other studies reported in this chapter.

4   The transition economies, current account deficits and capital inflows

The variable which most distinguishes the TEs from most other emerging economies is the size of their current account deficits. The size of the deficits, as may be seen from Table 8.2, are substantial with five of the countries in 2007 having current account deficits as a percentage of GDP of over 10 per cent.

Shelburne (2009a) has addressed the question as to what accounts for the large size of these deficits. By definition, the current account (*CA*) deficit is related to either total (public and private) savings (*S*) being too small or investment (*I*) too big, as $CA \equiv S - I$. The twin deficit hypothesis suggests that a government budget deficit is a major cause of the current account deficit, but this is not true of the TEs with the exception of Hungary. From about 2000 until the crisis in 2008, the rate of investment has increased while savings have remained virtually constant (there was a very slight rise). Thus, the current account deficit, under this interpretation, was primarily investment driven. But from a comparison with other upper middle-income countries, the TEs' savings rate is significantly lower. Consequently, the current account deficit may be due to a combination of both high investment and low savings. Nevertheless, the pattern is not all that unique as the southern EU member states (Greece, Portugal, and Spain) also financed much of their borrowing from abroad and pursued a similar growth strategy. But it does differ from many other emerging countries.

The high investment rates are the result of lower wage rates, higher skills and substantial investment opportunities in the TEs. Moreover, given that their currencies are either pegged to the euro (directly or through a currency board) or that the euro is widely used, the borrowing costs in the TEs are considerably lower than those in other emerging markets. The low savings rate can be variously attributed to intertemporal smoothing effects (households expect faster growth rates to be permanent and are therefore borrowing against future earnings); an ageing population; a rapid increase in financial wealth resulting from the housing and financial asset bubbles that occurred in many of the TEs, or a combination of any of these (Shelburne, 2009a, p. 92).

Much of the banking system in the TEs is foreign owned and 'essentially, the west European parents have been loaning money to their eastern subsidiaries which then finance investment projects in the NMS [New Member States]' (Shelburne, 2009a, p. 93). One advantage of this is that although these are mainly short-term private bank loans, the parent banks have been particularly concerned with funding long-term investment projects. These loans are often denominated in euros with the consequence of severe liquidity problems if there is a substantial depreciation in the exchange rate (as firms have to find proportionally more domestic currency to pay back the euro-denominated loans). Thus, the TEs were directly exposed to the subprime crisis through their exposure to the international money markets and, in particular, financing from Western European banks. As the IMF reported, 'foreign bank lending funded by domestic deposits and denominated in local currency is likely to be more resistant to external financial shocks and indeed in Latin America acted as a firewall against the transmission of global financial shocks' (IMF, 2010). While this overseas borrowing could be an optimal growth strategy, the downside is that a severe currency crisis, such as repeatedly occurred in Latin America in the 1970s and 1980s or the 1997 SEA crisis, could undermine all the benefits of foreign investment-led growth. But, for reasons discussed below, this did not materialise.

One of the reasons the TEs have benefitted from financial integration and institutional arrangements to facilitate financial stability is their close links with Western European banks. Their regulatory regimes and system of supervision were brought into line with the EU15 and capital account restrictions were withdrawn, leading to financial institutions in the EU15 becoming major players in the TEs. The share of foreign-owned banking assets increased to 60 per cent of total banking assets in 2008 from 25 per cent in 1995. In the rest of the world the 2008 figure is a much lower 22 per cent and even in emerging markets (excluding the TEs) only 28 per cent of banking assets are in foreign ownership (BIS, 2009).

Between 2002 and 2007, net private capital inflows to the TEs were some US$515 billion, 30 per cent of the total going to Emerging Market Economies (EME) as a whole (when the TEs' output accounted for only 11 per cent of that in the EME) and the second highest after SEA. Some 46 per cent of the net inflows were loans to the banking and non-banking sectors, 47 per cent FDI and a mere 7 per cent portfolio investment in equities and bonds (BIS, 2009). The FDI inflows only partly paid for the current account deficit in the TEs and several economies, particularly the Baltic States and Hungary, had to rely on raising much larger sums from the international debt and credit markets. Those corporations that borrowed from foreign banks lent to households who bought real estate and invested in the non-tradable sector of the economy, but these activities greatly raised the level of imports. And many of the loans were denominated in foreign currencies such that by 2008 foreign currency debt had risen to 40–50 per cent of GDP in Bulgaria, the Baltic States and Romania, creating serious currency mismatches.

5   The benefits of foreign ownership and the strength of the banks

The effect of the crisis on risk premiums has been limited and, in fact, risk spreads have been lower in the TEs than in other emerging and advanced economies' financial markets. This is because unlike some emerging economies, government budget deficits in the TEs were relatively modest (except those in Latvia, Hungary and Romania). Even if the size of the budget deficits were important here, the explanation for investor confidence seems to be institutional quality, resulting from the close formal links the TEs have with the advanced EU countries. Membership of the EU gave overseas investors greater confidence that sovereign debt defaults by these economies, although entirely possible, were unlikely. It also meant policy advice would be forthcoming from the ECB and that various loans and other rescue measures would be possible; the EBRD and the IMF has since provided these (IMF, 2009c). In particular, the Vienna initiative set up in 2009 to coordinate the various policies of the international financial institutions, banks and other public and private stakeholders has proved to be very effective. The European Bank for Reconstruction and Development (2009, p. 18) argues that 'it (the Vienna initiative) has achieved its aim in avoiding a financial collapse in emerging Europe, notwithstanding the large shocks and output declines experienced in late 2008 and the first half of 2009'.

There are a number of major benefits from foreign banks: they can provide private sector credit in less developed economies and have access to funds from the parent bank; they raise the level of competition between financial institutions in the economy; they inject new knowledge and technology, thereby raising the efficiency and quality of the banking sector; and they can limit the worst effects of any banking crisis. However, there are some potential disadvantages: they may cherry pick the less risky and profitable lending; may reduce lending if the parent bank faces difficulties or suddenly stop lending and repatriate capital, leaving the country if political conditions change for the worst. Despite these possible disadvantages, however, the available evidence suggests that even partial ownership of the banking system by banks in advanced countries serves to mitigate the crisis (see Peek and Rosengren, 2000, Herrero and Peria, 2007, and de Haas and van Lelyveld, 2010).

This result has been confirmed most recently by Berglöf, Korniyenko, Plekhanov, and Zettelmeter (2009). The authors find that the increase in emerging market risk premiums when these are compared with the increased volatility of the S&P 500 stock index is low. Even after the intensification of the crisis, the risk premiums remained below those levels found during other financial crises and while risk premiums in the advanced countries reached historically high levels. Given that the TEs had higher external debt levels, experienced credit booms and were vulnerable to exchange rate risk, their relative immunity must be explained.

To test the significance of the presence of foreign banks, Berglöf et al. (2009) regressed net capital flows across borders following the collapse of Lehman Brothers (2008Q4 flows of lending as a percentage of 2008Q3 bank assets) against the extent of foreign bank ownership. They selected as controls country sovereign credit risk and per capita GDP. The effect of foreign bank ownership proved statistically significant for the TEs and insignificant if the sample was confined to the non-TE emerging countries. Thus, a 10 percentage point increase in the share of assets owned by foreign banks reduced capital outflows by 1.4 percentage points of the total asset stock. Since the average outflow from all emerging countries was about 6 per cent, this is a quantitatively important effect. Also, if the credit risk increased, then the outflow increased by an equivalent proportion, but adding a transition dummy revealed an increased mitigation effect from the presence of subsidiaries of foreign banks or wholly-owned foreign banks. Finally, Berglöf et al. (2009) report that the larger the pre-crisis credit boom and the higher the level of external debt then, *ceteris paribus,* the greater is the decline in output. This result is reinforced if a country has a hard currency peg.

An interesting question is the role played by credit creation in the run-up to the crisis. Maechler, Mitra and Worrell (2007) found that in the TEs a steady increase in lending, even at a rate of between 25 to 40 per cent, enhanced the 'soundness indicators' of the banks, whereas rapidly accelerating credit growth did not. Also, foreign-owned banks tended to have a higher risk profile than domestically-owned banks because of lower levels of capitalisation, even though they could rely on the parent banks for additional funding. But given the level of economic development in the TEs they identified plenty of unexploited opportunities for further financial deepening and non-speculative investments.

In a further study, Tamirisa and Igan (2008) could find no discernible difference in the rate of growth of credit by weaker and sounder banks in the TE during the 1990s. By the early 2000s, however, there had been a change in the situation. The weaker banks, especially those in the Baltic States, had credit growth that was as rapid, or sometimes more rapid, than the sounder banks. Much of this aggressive lending came from weaker foreign-owned, rather than weaker domestic banks, because of the greater resources available from the (foreign) parent bank. The authors argued that as a result, 'forward looking and risk-based supervision during credit booms' has now become essential. However, there is no evidence that the lack of prudence in the banking system, or the fact that credit had expanded too rapidly, was a major factor in the crisis in the TEs. Aydin (2008) also examined the role of foreign banks in the TEs in the years prior to the crisis and confirms that foreign banks have been a major source of credit for the TEs. In the 1990s the foreign-owned banks acted just like the domestically owned ones and sourced much of their loans from domestic savings, but by the early 2000s they were sourcing their loans from the parent bank or other large foreign banks, with the reputation of the parent bank acting as a guarantee for these loans. Aydin presciently warned that at the start of the crisis such borrowing on the inter-bank market could create problems during the credit crunch.

6   Was the growth of credit excessive?

In the crisis, financial integration seems to have pulled in opposite directions, while output sustained a large decline. On the one hand, the foreign ownership of many banks helped to mitigate the worst effects of the crisis, but, on the other hand, it contributed to 'excessive' credit expansion, housing and construction bubbles and growing foreign indebtedness accompanied by foreign currency mismatches. The subsequent collapse in house prices eroded bank capital and prolonged the recession. And governments were forced to contract aggregate demand to defend currency pegs, which compramised their necessary preparations for currency union. Hence, a crucial issue is whether or not the presence of foreign banks led to excessive levels of financing in foreign currencies beyond which the institutions could not cope realistically.

First, econometric work on excessive credit growth, defined as a rate greater than 2 per cent of GDP, considers two periods – 1996–2001 and 2002–07 – when the growth rate was higher than that (EBRD, 2009). Most TEs did not experience excessive growth during the first period, but Estonia, Latvia and Poland each had three years when credit growth could be described as excessive. During the second period, all TEs had at least one year of excessive credit growth while Bulgaria, Estonia, Hungary, Latvia, Lithuania, Romania, and Slovenia had a minimum of four years that could be so designated. Given the degree of financial integration and the varying degree of foreign ownership of the banks, the relationship between excessive credit growth and financial integration is far from simple. The authors argue that possible explanations for excessive credit growth in the second period include a simultaneous increase in global liquidity making borrowing easier; *changes* in financial integration rather than the *level* of integration as a positive contributory factor, while foreign banks' share of assets seemed to have no explanatory power.

The second issue concerns 'excessive' indebtedness, defined within a microeconomic framework as firms having debt levels greater than 40 per cent of their total assets (Hanson, 2000). The results of the statistical estimation show that financial development led to borrowing above the threshold, but that this depended on whether the borrowing was financed though FDI or debt. Excessive indebtedness turns out to be driven by debt and the share of assets attributable to foreign banks (rather than the number of foreign banks) and active domestic banks, but not by FDI. This leads to lower indebtedness.

7 Borrowing in foreign currencies

The level of foreign currency-denominated debt has been responsible for several financial crises including Mexico (1994), SEA (1997) and Argentina (2002), when the depreciation of the currency placed huge pressures on households, firms, financial institutions and government – pressures that were intensified by moral hazard. In the case of the TEs the desire, as well as the requirement, that they enter the euro zone as quickly as possible, led to the belief that the exchange rate pegs would be preserved whenever possible. The EBRD (2009) tests whether the trend towards foreign borrowing in foreign currencies in the TEs occurs because of financial integration, the presence of foreign banks, or simply through foreign funding, *per se*. Three data sets were used, the EBRD/World Bank Business Environment Performance Survey at the firm level, a quarterly macroeconomic data set (2002–05) and the annual version over a slightly longer period (2000–08) where the major difference is in the level of financial integration. The results show that weak institutions led to higher levels of foreign borrowing, that the volatility of inflation is important, but not robust in two of the studies and that hard currency pegs are significant in both macroeconomic models. The presence of foreign banks meant that borrowing in foreign currencies was more likely, but both of the macroeconomic models showed borrowing from banks (rather than the presence of foreign banks) determined the level of foreign borrowing. Financial integration appears not to have had an effect. Thus foreign borrowing and foreign banks have some limited effect, although the latter act as a channel for the loans rather than initiating the borrowing process.

The decline of capital flows into the TEs put pressure on their exchange rates to depreciate, which caused serious problems, especially for the Baltic States and Bulgaria that had currency boards, although they all avoided breaking the peg to the euro. Even the Czech Republic, Hungary, Poland and Romania which had more flexible exchange rate regimes found the situation difficult. But when the floaters found themselves short of liquidity the IMF provided three of them with balance-of-payments support. As most of the loans from abroad were denominated in euros and Swiss francs, devaluation would have markedly increased the cost of these loans in terms of the domestic currency. Loans denominated in foreign currencies ranged from 15 per cent of the total in the Czech Republic to over 50 per cent in Romania, Lithuania, Estonia and Latvia (IMF, 2009b). But, for example, the Polish zloty depreciated by about a third against the Swiss franc over a few months beginning on 1 July. The expectation of a currency depreciation led to the withdrawal of funds from the domestic banks and the deposit of them abroad. On the upside, however, depreciation led to a gain in export competitiveness. But this option was not open to Slovenia and Slovakia who were members of the euro zone. Nevertheless, the consensus of opinion is that being a member of the Eurozone was an advantage as it protected the country from currency speculation (Shelburne, 2009b, p. 16).

Given this background, the crisis of July 2007 might have been expected to generate a severe crisis along the lines of the SEA crisis of 1997. This, and other, postwar financial crises in emerging countries included a sudden cessation of capital inflows, followed rapidly by capital flight as foreign loans were not rolled over, a collapse of the currency, rapid contraction of credit, runs on the banks and, if western accounting standards had been in force, the bankruptcy of a large proportion of firms (Reinhart and Rogoff, 2009). This was often followed by political instability, sovereign default and the imposition of macroeconomic controls such as capital controls, which are not available to EU members.

There are, however, several notable differences between this crisis and the 1997–98 SEA crises. The 2007–10 crisis occurred against a backdrop of the most severe recession in post-war history, with trade flows falling by about 12 per cent in 2009. By contrast, in 1997 world trade was growing by around 10 per cent. While the falls in output in the emerging economies have been about the same in the two crises, the degree of capital flight in 2007–10 was, with the exception of Latvia (and beyond the TEs in Russia and the Ukraine), very much milder and so were the extent of currency depreciations. The degree of liquidity support for the TE banks was also generally much smaller than those required in the SEA crisis. The banks in the SEA economies lacked the benefits of foreign ownership and the size of support (as a proportion of GDP) received from the international financial organisations was generally less in the SEA crisis (just over 2 per cent of GDP compared with between 4 and 6 per cent for the TEs). These factors may explain why the impact of the crisis was less in 2007–10, even though the size of the shock was much greater (EBRD, 2009, pp. 12–13).

The other main route of contagion is through a collapse in the growth of the TEs' export markets, especially with the remainder of the EU and Russia in 2008Q4. The evidence suggests that when there is a collapse in world markets, even countries with floating exchange rates experienced a rapid decline in the value of their exports. Consequently, output growth falls more than just because exports are a component of GDP, through the action of the dynamic Harrod foreign trade multiplier and the Hicks supermultiplier (McCombie and Thirlwall, 1994). What is perhaps a little surprising is that Berglöf et al. (2009), in their core regression explaining the rate of output decline in emerging Europe, found that the fall in the growth of exports was not statistically significant (of the other two explanatory variables, the pre-crisis external debt-to-GDP ratio was statistically significant and an index of corruption was not). Two comments are in order here. First, this does not mean to say that *on average* the decline in exports was not important and secondly, the period covered by the regression 2008Q4 to 2009Q1 is very short.

The foreign banks caused the expansion of credit in the TEs and increased their financial vulnerability, but on the plus side they also helped to alleviate the worst effects of the crisis by continuing to lend when the crisis had already started elsewhere. (Moreover, the foreign lending also helped fuel the TE's rapid growth rates prior to 2008.) The foreign banks also extended credits when the recovery began. But there were limits to the aid given to the TE banks. The European governments did not want any assistance that they provided to their domestic banks to be passed on to their overseas subsidiaries. For example, 'the Greek government warned its multinational banks in January 2009 not to transfer funds provided by them in a $37 billion support package to their foreign subsidiaries in the Balkans' (Shelburne, 2009b, p. 9). The major contagion effect seems to have been through the collapse in the TEs exports markets as the advanced countries went into a deep recession, although further research is needed on this issue.

In summary, therefore, foreign banks help to foster faster economic growth and do have a stabilising effect on the economy, but there are some costs involved, including excessive borrowing and borrowing in foreign currencies as well as the higher costs associated with the actual process of financial integration. On balance, the evidence suggests that financial integration has more positive effects than negative, although there needs to be some control mechanism to deal with borrowing in foreign currencies and to deter excessive borrowing. The policy recommendations include the usual exhortation to macroeconomic stability, but also the use of equity finance so that borrowing becomes subject to shareholder scrutiny and tighter regulation, including stress testing the institutions and imposing greater counter-cyclical capital requirements, taking into account the associated risks (IMF, 2009a). The latter will undoubtedly follow at the EU level after the crisis is over, although any agreement needs to be multilateral if it is not to distort international capital markets. Following the Swedish banking crisis in the early 1990s, there has already been some correction to the terms applied to borrowing from foreign banks, whether or not they have subsidiaries and branches in the TEs.

8   The Central Asian economies

The CAEs have weathered the crisis much better than their transition counterparts in the EU. They are a landlocked group of countries that were formerly part of the Soviet Union and, as such, had been heavily dependent upon it, especially through bilateral trade. They gained independence in 1991 and the various countries adopted very different economic approaches, with, for example, the Kyrgyz Republic rapidly liberalising and, at the other end of the spectrum, Turkmenistan adopting few reforms. For a discussion of the development of these countries, post-independence see Pomfret (2006). All of the CAEs experienced dramatic collapses in income during the first decade, with the possible exception of Uzbekistan (although much of the data for Uzbekistan are dubious). However, from about 2000 onwards, the countries have experienced rapid growth largely on the back of the rapid exploitation of natural resources. Unlike the TEs, the balance of payments has never posed any serious problems for the CAEs.

Azerbaijan, Kazakhstan, and Turkmenistan have all benefitted from the substantial discoveries of oil in and around the Caspian Sea. Uzbekistan has a high dependence on cotton exports. The Kyrgyz Republic is the most resource-poor of the countries, depending upon a solitary gold mine. There are sharp differences in per capita income which are largely explicable in terms of whether or not the country has substantial energy reserves. There is not the space to present a detailed analysis of the effect of the credit crunch, but Table 8.3 reports their growth rates since 2003.

Table 8.3 Growth of real GDP: Central Asian economies (annual percentage growth)

	2003	2004	2005	2006	2007	2008	2009	2010f	GNP per capita $
Azerbaijan	11.2	10.2	24.3	30.5	23.4	10.8	9.3 (8.0)	(6.7)	7,770
Kazakhstan	9.3	9.6	9.7	10.7	8.9	3.2	1.2 (2.0)	(3.3)	9,690
Kyrgyz Republic	7.0	7.0	-0.2	3.1	8.2	7.6	2.3 (4.0)	(6.0)	2,130
Tajikistan	10.2	10.6	6.7	7.0	7.8	7.9	3.4 (3.0)	(4.0)	1,860
Turkmenistan	17.1	14.7	13.0	11.4	11.6	10.5	4.1 (10.0)	(10.0)	6,210
Uzbekistan	4.2	7.7	7.0	7.2	9.5	9.0	8.1 (7.0)	(6.5)	2,660
Russia	7.4	7.1	6.4	7.4	8.1	5.6	-7.9	n.a.	15,630

Notes: f Figures are forecasts. GNP is in international dollars at purchasing power parity. n.a. denotes data not available.
Sources: European Bank for Reconstruction and Development (2009), except for the figures in parentheses which are from *Asian Development Outlook* (2009).

There are three channels by which the contagion from the subprime crisis has affected these countries. The first is through trade. The net energy importers, the Kyrgyz Republic and Tajikistan, have been hit heavily through their trade links by the 7.9 per cent fall in Russia's output in 2009. More generally, the major impact has come from the reduced demand for the major commodities and falls in their prices (especially of oil and natural gas) with the world recession. Secondly, there is likely to be a fall in remittances from overseas workers. This will particularly hit the Kyrgyz Republic and Tajikistan who are heavily dependent on remittances from their workers overseas (amounting to 47 per cent of GDP in the case of Tajikistan and 25 per cent in the case of the Kyrgyz Republic, with over 90 per cent coming from Russia).

The final channel, which is the one that has had a major impact in the TEs, is through the financial links. Although the CAEs are open economies in terms of their share of exports in trade,[4] they have been reluctant (with the exception of the Kyrgyz Republic) to integrate into the world economy through tariff reductions and the implementation of agreed regional free trade areas. Moreover, only Kazakhstan has become integrated into the world financial system and this has posed a potential problem for the country.

From 2000 until the current crisis, Kazakhstan had been seen as one of the great success stories. With oil prices booming (they rose from $12 a barrel in 1998 to $91 a barrel in 2008),[5] Kazakhstan had been one of the fastest-growing countries in the world. (Azerbaijan's extraordinary growth has also been based on oil production.) It became progressively more financially integrated into the world economy and developed one of the most extensive and sophisticated banking systems of the CAEs. Kazakhstan's banks have extensive interests in the Kyrgyz Republic and account for just under half of all credit there as well as having a 70 per cent share in the Kyrgyz banking system. The Kazakhstan banks have also moved into Tajikistan. During the years of rapid growth, the demand for credit grew rapidly and there was a housing boom in the Kazakhstan cities of Almaty and Astana. Because this could not be satisfied by domestic credit growth, there was substantial recourse to the international financial markets. Moreover, the banks borrowed short, but lent long. The confidence that the exchange rate was stable, as in the SEA crises of 1997, led to a great deal of overseas borrowing to take advantage of lower interest rates. But, according to Pomfret (2009), there were growing concerns about the credit explosion, in particular about the creditworthiness of some of the borrowers purchasing real estate.

However, it should be emphasised that Kazakhstan had no direct exposure to the subprime securitisation. The banking system was hit by the rapid decline in lending in the international money markets. This led to a decline in lending both in Kazakhstan and in the Kyrgyz Republic. The government, through the Central Bank (NBK), was able to step in when there was a sudden halt of the inflow of capital funds, as it had built up considerable revenues in its Oil Fund. The fund is intended to generate income when the oil revenues have dried up. The foreign exchange reserves of Kazakhstan in 2010 are strong, with the NBK having reserves of $21 billion and the Oil Fund standing at $25 billion in 2008 (IMF, 2008). While there was concern expressed at using the Oil Fund as an emergency measure to prop up the banking system, as they were intended for the long-term development of the country, the indications are with the resurgence in the price of oil after the collapse in 2007/2008, the fund is rapidly being replenished. There was no exceptional pressure on the national currency, the tenge, and so the exchange rate remained relatively stable and foreign depositor confidence remained high.

The only Central Asian country that experienced political turmoil precipitated by the crisis was the Kyrgyz Republic. After President Akayev had been deposed in 2005, the increasingly dirigiste nature of Bakiyev's regime, including a corrupt privatisation programme that favoured his cronies and family, led to increasing tensions in the country. In 2010, the deterioration in economic prosperity resulting from the rapid fall in remittances from abroad (which had accounted for 30 per cent of GDP in 2008) and the rapid increase in energy prices contributed to the overthrow of Bakiyev. The IMF made available a US$100 million emergency standby in January 2010. All this has added another complicating dimension to the economic turmoil.

9 Summary and conclusions

An important issue in the context of the TEs is whether the financial crisis will presage a 'reform' or a transition crisis equivalent to the perceived crisis of capitalism in the developed western economies (Sen, 2009). There are two immediate possibilities: first, large non-performing loans and banking insolvencies might prompt political unrest and second, economic policy changes may be implemented to correct for institutional shortcomings. However, the crisis in the TEs is very recent so that any political changes are yet to emerge, although there have been some problems in Hungary, Latvia and Lithuania. The changes to macroeconomic policy on the other hand are no different from those implemented in the rest of the EU and in the short term should be no cause for alarm. While there has been a deceleration in the transition reforms as a direct consequence of the severity of the crisis, this situation is not expected to last very long (EBRD, 2009). Policymakers could not, in any case, have pursued structural changes when financial markets were in turmoil and the political climate hostile and the freezing of the loans markets precluded any further privatisations. Nevertheless the only downgrades recorded were in Latvia and Kazakhstan where banking reform and interest rate liberalisation regressed and both countries nationalised systemically weak banks despite the implied moral hazard. The private sector's share in GDP also fell in Kazakhstan. Surprisingly, there were upgrades too. In Latvia where improvements took place in the enforcement of competition and in the Slovak Republic where public-private partnerships were actively promoted.

Thus the institutional reforms that have already taken place were sufficient to militate against the crisis and the EU will continue to act as a powerful mechanism to keep the TEs on the reform path by reinforcing the single market programme to aid the recovery of growth. Exports are picking up and domestic demand has stabilised although the private sector's deleveraging remains incomplete. The TEs need to diversify away from non-tradables to manufacturing but not before competitiveness, that had deteriorated as unit labour costs rose before the crisis, has been addressed.[6] The main institutional changes will undoubtedly come in the financial services sector with greater regulatory scrutiny, but these changes will form part of a multilateral response to minimise the effect of future financial crises.

The crisis has had a much weaker effect on the CAEs. The main imperative for these countries to maintain their impressive growth record during the last few years is the continued implementation of reforms, which in some of the countries – for example, Turkmenistan and Uzbekistan – has been painfully slow. The CAEs need to promote greater regional cooperation and improve their transport infrastructure and reduce the formal and informal barriers to trade. It is with greater development and integration into the world financial system that they will become more exposed to international financial crisis, but that seems an inevitable concomitant of growth.

Notes

1. One of the worst-affected countries was Spain whose banks, paradoxically, had the greatest degree of prudential regulation of any country. Because of

the low risk of its securities, notably the Cédulas Hipotecarias, international investors had extensively purchased them and consequently Spain was particularly hard hit by international financial retrenchment and its failure to have the loans rolled over.

2. In this chapter the TEs are the Czech Republic, Estonia, Latvia, Lithuania, Hungary, Poland, Slovak Republic, and Slovenia (EU accession in 2004) and Bulgaria and Romania (EU accession in 2007). The CAEs are Azerbaijan, Kazakhstan, the Kyrgyz Republic, Tajikistan, Turkmenistan and Uzbekistan.

3. The key estimating equation is $I/Y = \alpha + \beta(S/Y) + \varepsilon$, where I/Y is the investment-output ratio, S/Y is the savings-output ratio and ε is the error term. Most studies find the estimate of β has a value close to unity indicating that savers prefer the less risky investment opportunity afforded by the national economy, but Blanchard and Giavazzi (2002) find a value of 0.14 for the Eurozone. Consequently, the elimination of exchange-rate risk makes savings more mobile within the zone.

4. Exports as a share of GDP in 2007 were Azerbaijan, 68 per cent,Turkmenistan, 63 per cent, Kazakhstan, 49 per cent, Kyrgyz Republic 45 per cent; Uzbekistan, 40 per cent and Tajikistan 21 per cent (*World Development Indicators*, 2009).

5. These are average values for the years.

6. Unit labour costs rose 90 per cent in Latvia, 40 per cent in Bulgaria and 30 per cent in Estonia and Romania in the run-up to the crisis.

References

Abiad, A., Leigh, D. and Mody, A. (2009) 'Financial Integration, Capital Mobility and Income Convergence', *Economic Policy*, 24, 241–305.

Asian Development Bank (2009) *Asian Development Outlook: Rebalancing Asia's Growth*. Manila: ADB.

Aydin, B. (2008) 'Banking Structure and Credit Growth in Central and Eastern European Countries', *IMF Working Paper 215*. Washington, DC: International Monetary Fund.

Berglöf, E., Korniyenko, A., Plekhanov, A. and Zettelmeter, J. (2009) 'Understanding the Crisis in Emerging Europe', *European Bank for Reconstruction and Development Working Paper 109*, November.

Bank for International Settlements (2009) *79th Annual Report*. Basel: BIS www.bis.org.

Blanchard, O. and Giavazzi, F. (2002) 'Current Account Deficits in the Euro Area: The End of the Feldstein–Horioka Puzzle?', *Brookings Papers on Economic Activity*, 1, 147–209.

Blanchard, O. and Summers, L. (1986) 'Fiscal Increasing Returns, Hysteresis, Real Wages and Unemployment', *European Economic Review*, 31, 543–66.

Cappiello, L., Gerard, B., Kadareja, A. and Manganelli, S. (2006) 'Financial Integration of New Member States', *Working Paper 683*. Frankfurt: European Central Bank.

Cerra, V. and Saxena, S.C. (2008) 'Growth Dynamics: The Myth of Economic Recovery', *American Economic Review*, 98, 439–57.

Claessen, S.M., Kose, A. and Terrones, M. (2008) 'What Happens During Recessions, Crunches and Busts?', *IMF Working Paper 274*. Washington, DC: International Monetary Fund.

de Haas, R. and van Lelyveld, I.V. (2010) 'Internal Capital Markets and Lending by Multinational Bank Subsidiaries', *Journal of Financial Intermediation*, 19, 1–25.

de Michelis, N. (2008) 'Regional Convergence: A Relevant Measure of Policy Success', *CESifo Forum*, 1, 10–13.

Eichengreen, B. and Park, Y.C. (2003) 'Why Has There Been Less Financial Integration in Asia than in Europe?' Paper presented to a conference on Financial Market Development in Asia, held in Honolulu, Hawaii, February.

Esposti, R. (2008) 'Regional Growth Convergence and EU Policies: Empirical Evidence and Measuring Problems', *CESifo Forum*, 1, 14–22.

European Bank for Reconstruction and Development (2009) *Transition Report 2009: Transition in Crisis?* London: EBRD.

European Commission (2009) 'The Impact of the Financial and Economic Crisis on Potential Output', *European Economy Occasional Paper 4*. Brussels: Director-General for Economic and Financial Affairs.

European Commission (2009) Klems database: http//www.euklems.net.

Eurostat: http://epp.eurostat.ec.europa.eu/portal/page/portal/eurostat/home.

Feldstein, M. and Horioka, C. (1985) 'Domestic Savings and International Capital Flows', *Economic Journal*, 90, 314–29.

Hanson, B. (2000) 'Sample Splitting and Threshold Estimation', *Econometrica*, 68, 575–603.

Herrero, A.G. and Peria, M.S. (2007) 'The Mix of International Banks' Foreign Claims: Determinants and Implications', *Journal of Banking and Finance*, 31, 1613–31.

Iorgova, S. and Ong, L.L. (2008) 'The Capital Markets of Emerging Europe: Institutions, Instruments and Investors', IMF Working Paper 103. Washington, DC: International Monetary Fund.

International Monetary Fund (2007) *World Economic Outlook: Spillovers and Cycles in the Global Economy.* Washington, DC: IMF.

International Monetary Fund (2008) 'Kazakhstan, Country Report', *Working Paper 288*. Washington, DC: IMF.

International Monetary Fund (2009a) *World Economic Outlook: Crisis and Recovery.* Washington, DC: IMF.

International Monetary Fund (2009b) *Creating Policy Space – Responsive Design and Streamlined Conditionality in Recent Low-Income Country Programmes.* Washington, DC: IMF.

International Monetary Fund (2009c) *Review of Recent Programmes.* Washington, DC: IMF.

International Monetary Fund (2010) 'A Tale of Two Regions', *Finance and Development*, March, 36.

McCombie, J.S.L. and Thirlwall, A.P. (1994) *Economic Growth and the Balance-of-Payments Constraint.* Basingstoke: Macmillan.

Maechler, A.S., Mitra, S. and Worrell, D. (2007) 'Decomposing Financial Risks and Vulnerabilities in Eastern Europe', *IMF Working Paper 248*. Washington, DC: International Monetary Fund.

Peek, J. and Rosengren, E.S. (2000) 'The International Transmission of Financial Shocks: The Case of Japan', *American Economic Review*, 87, 495–505.

Pomfret, R. (2006) *The Central Asian Economies Since Independence.* Princeton, NJ: Princeton University Press.

Pomfret, R (2009) 'Central Asia and the Global Economic Crisis' *Policy Brief, EUCAM EU-Central Asia Monitoring, No. 7*: www.eucentralasia.eu/publications/policy-briefs.html.

Reinhart, C. and Rogoff, K. (2009) *This Time is Different: Eight Centuries of Financial Folly*. Princeton, NJ: Princeton University Press.

Sen, A. (2009) 'Adam Smith's Market Never Stood Alone' *Financial Times*, 10 March.

Shelburne, R.C. (2009a) 'Current Account Deficits in the New Member States: Causes and Consequences' *Intereconomics*, March/April, 90–5.

Shelburne, R.C. (2009b) *The Global Economic and Financial Crisis: Regional Impacts, Responses and Solutions: Europe, North America and the CIS*. Geneva: United Nations Economic Commission for Europe.

Svejnar, J. (2002) 'Transition Economies: Performance and Challenges', *Journal of Economic Perspectives,* 16(1), 3–28.

Tamirisa, N.T. and Igan, D.O. (2008) 'Are Weak Banks Leading Credit Booms? Evidence from Emerging Europe', *IMF Working Paper 19*. Washington, DC: International Monetary Fund.

World Bank (2009) *World Development Indicators*. Washington, DC: World Bank.

9
The World Financial Crisis and the Implications for China

Shujie Yao and Jing Zhang[1]

1 Introduction

From September 2008, the failure of large financial institutions in the United States and the EU became visible. It then badly affected real economic activities, resulting in deflation, falls in the prices of shares and commodities, a shrinkage in the level of production and services, the failures of large firms in manufacturing and services, sharp rises in unemployment, and the collapse of people's confidence. The financial crisis spread quickly from the US and Europe into the developing and transitional economies, leading to the most severe global economic recession since the 1930s.

Many countries have adopted a set of monetary and fiscal policies immediately after the outbreak of the financial crisis. Some countries announced huge stimulus packages. However, it is still difficult to judge whether such rescue policies are effective in containing the crisis. In addition, 'the global crisis requires a global solution'.[2] Leaders of the Group of Twenty (G20) have met twice in Washington and London since the last quarter of 2008, aiming to bring the world economy out of recession.

In addition to the above-mentioned effects of the crisis on the world economy, another consequence of the crisis is a clear shift of economic and political importance from the west to the east. The biggest winner is China, which has been the greatest beneficiary of the current crisis.

In this chapter we first review the most recent studies on financial crisis and introduce a new theory of financial crisis, which is called 'asymmetric psychological reaction to gains and losses'. We then analyse the causes and consequences of the global financial crisis and evaluate governments' responses of major countries in the world to the crisis. We also discuss the long-term implications of the crisis on China before making some conclusions.

2 Assymetric reaction to gains and losses: a new theory of financial crisis

Since the outbreak of the financial crisis, there have been many reports, commentaries and studies on the causes, consequences and rescue efforts of the crisis. Reinhart and Rogoff (2008) present a historical analysis comparing the 2007 US subprime financial crisis with the antecedents of other banking crises in advanced economies since the Second World War. They found that standard indicators for the US, such as asset price increase, rising leverage, large sustained current account deficits and a slowing trajectory of economic growth, are all signs of a country on the verge of a financial crisis. Reinhart and Rogoff (2009) focus on the aftermath of systemic banking crises, including a number of recent emerging market cases and two pre-war developed country episodes to expand the relevant set of comparators. The aftermath of severe financial crises includes deep and lasting collapse of asset prices and profound declines in output and employment.

Claessens (2009) highlights the multiple causes of the financial crisis and recommends reforms of the national and international financial reforms to present any future crisis. Demigüç-Kunt and Serven (2009) use a large body of analytical research, econometric evidence and country experience to argue that the interventionist policy by some national governments, who offer almost blanket guarantees to their depositors and creditors, distorts the efficiency of the financial market and is not the most efficient method to solve the banking crisis. A handful of short papers have focused on the effectiveness/ineffectiveness of the monetary and fiscal policies during the financial crisis, including Mishkin (2009), Feldstein (2009), Taylor (2009) and Auerbach (2009).

However, none of these studies have developed a theory to explain why the economic crisis took place so suddenly after the world economy had enjoyed more than 15 years of successful growth. People were still arguing that the booming housing and stock markets would not end in tears as interest and inflation rates were low shortly before the crisis. Central bankers in the US, the UK and the EU were just busy focusing their monthly meetings on adjusting interest rates in order to meet inflation targets. Governments believed that low inflation and interest rates were the ultimate instruments of a free market economy to sustain growth without suffering from booms and busts, let alone a crisis. Unfortunately, this analysis proved to be mistaken.

In retrospect, it is not an easy task to come up with another new economic theory that can predict, let alone prevent the occurrence, or re-occurrence, of world financial crises. The authors firstly attempt to develop a theory of 'the asymmetric psychological reaction of market players to gains and losses' (Yao and Zhang, forthcoming). Different from traditional economic models, this theory assumes that many individuals, be they consumers, investors or firms, are irrational and markets inefficient. The asymmetric reaction of human economic psychology to gains and losses arise from the following fact (see Figure 9.1): the additional level of happiness derived from a certain unit of gains (e.g., $1,000) tends to be smaller than the additional level of unhappiness caused by the same unit of losses (also $1,000), i.e. The marginal happiness (MH) caused by 'one unit of gains' is significantly less than the marginal unhappiness (MUH) caused by 'one unit of losses'. More importantly, marginal happiness to successive units of gains diminishes but the marginal unhappiness to successive units of losses increases.[3]

To attain more happiness, driven by greed and speculation, investors need to invest aggressively once more and more gains are made. If the majority of investors behave in the same way, the market will be overheating. If no timely and decisive policies are taken to cool down the market, a crisis is likely to emerge. A crisis is like a market bubble, but it is different from a single market bubble in the sense that it may be caused by many market bubbles, e.g., housing, stock and financial markets, at the same time.

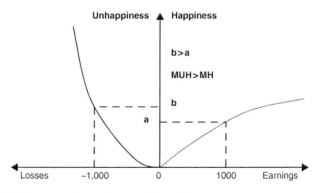

Figure 9.1 Asymmetric reaction to gains and losses

Once all of the bubbles burst simultaneously or in close succession, usually triggered by the weakest or most vulnerable market sector (for example, the US subprime mortgage market), individuals immediately start to run off the market once they are making losses. The speed they run off the market depends on how much losses they make and where the losses have come from. The asymmetric reaction to gains and losses, or to happiness and unhappiness, can be used to explain the occurrence of the current financial crisis and its prolonging recovery as shown in Figure 9.2.

When there is a relatively long period of gains in the market (from T_0 to T_1), investors may feel confident of price increases in the future and tend to take 'bigger risks' by investing more because they are not 'really happy' even though they may have made a lot of gains. It is also driven in part by greed and speculation on the future bullish market prospects (Yao and Luo, 2009).

As a result, the market bubble grows bigger and faster, driving prices to peak at point C in a relatively short time (from T_1 to T_2). As the bubble becomes too big and the prices too high, the prevalent market conditions suddenly fail to sustain the market bubble and prices at their high levels. At this point, even if there is a small event in the market system (e.g., the subprime mortgage market failure in the US) will trigger a massive bubble burst, causing the entire economic system to collapse as shown at T_2.

Once the bubble bursts, market prices, be they stock or housing prices, decrease dramatically within a very short time, say from C to D, or from period T_2 to period T_3, during which investors start to run away quickly from the market.

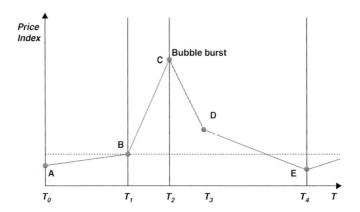

Figure 9.2 Evolution of market bubbles, crisis and recovery

Because most investors endured massive losses during the crisis, they are particularly sensitive to even a small amount of gain or loss. If most investors become excessively risk-averse, the entire market starts to collapse. The consequence is a long and painful process of an economic recovery, as seen from period T_2 to period T_4. When the confidence of investors comes back, the economy starts to pick up again, but due to the painful experiences during the crisis, investors are excessively cautious as to how quickly and how much will be invested not to miss the gaining opportunities while at the same time to avoid making large losses again.

According to the length of crisis, economic recovery can be broadly classified into three shapes: V, U and L.[4] A V-shaped recovery usually occurs if a crisis is caused by an unexpected shock, be it internal or external, or by sudden changes of macroeconomic policies so that the crisis represents a short-term structural adjustment in an economy or a particular market (e.g., stock or housing). A U-shaped recovery takes place if the crisis is triggered by several factors rather than a simple shock. A good example was the UK housing market downturn and the recession of the UK economy in the early 1990s. The L-shaped recovery usually takes place if the crisis is severe, rendering the economy or market into a long decline and stagnation. Factors causing this kind of crisis are complex and comprehensive. A typical example was Japan after its economy was hit by a crisis in 1989–90.

Based on the theory of asymmetric reaction to gains and losses, we suggest that the recovery of some industrialised economies from the current financial crisis will be U-shaped. For example, the UK's GDP contracted in the second and third quarters of 2009, marking the sixth consecutive quarterly decline from the second quarter of 2008.[5] Although the last quarter registered a 0.1 per cent rise, it will not be able to resume the normal annual growth rate of 2 per cent or more until 2012, implying that the economic recovery of the UK is likely to be U-shaped. The euro zone is similar to the UK and will endure a U-shaped recovery. There have been concrete signs that the US economy has continued its recovery from the third quarter in 2009, with real GDP growth of 3.2 per cent in the first quarter of 2010 thanks to strong levels of personal consumption. However, the recovery is still vulnerable. We forecast that the UK cannot regain a consistent growth at pre-crisis level until 2011 so that the recovery is probably also U-shaped.

In contrast, the two largest emerging economies, China and India, have not recorded negative growth in any quarter during the crisis. In addition, their growth is likely to demonstrate a V-shaped recovery.

China, in particular, had bottomed out from the second quarter of 2009 as its growth was 7.9 per cent, followed by 8.9 per cent in the third quarter and 10.7 per cent in the fourth quarter.

3 Causes of the crisis

The theory of asymmetric reaction to gains and losses explains why a single market bubble, or an economic crisis, may develop. An economic crisis is considered to be caused not by a single market bubble, but by a few market bubbles at the same time. The current crisis is a perfect example. Table 9.1 shows the evolution of the crisis. The housing, stock and banking bubbles were developed in the US and Europe but the whole world was affected because the US was the largest economy and the growth engine of the world economy.

The asymmetric reaction of individuals to gains and losses explains why a market bubble can be developed quickly. In good years when markets are high, most people tend to make financial gains through, for instance, rising house and equity prices. To derive more happiness, and in part driven by greed and speculation, they have to take more risk by investing more. As most people do the same, the market is inflated, or the bubble is formed.

The asymmetric reaction of individuals to gains and losses combined with the following elements explain how the collapses in subprime mortgage industry, asset values and credit market have caused the failure of the banking system in developed countries and thereafter have brought the world into depression.

The first element is the structural failure in the West. Over the past few decades, a number of developing countries have launched economic reform in quick succession. Some countries, including China

Table 9.1 Evolution of the financial crisis

Date	Events
2004–2007	Rising interests in US and Europe
2006 onward	Falling US house prices
August 2007	Subprime losses hit banks
2007–2008	Banking system meltdown
January–July 2008	Surging oil and commodity prices
2008	Contagion to all countries
September 2008	Stock market collapse on news of massive corporate losses
May 2008	Rescue action from the US, the EU, Japan and China
April 2009	G20 London

and India, have achieved great success. However, facing the changes in the developing world, most developed countries maitained their traditional economic growth paths with slow adjustment in industrial structure and gradually lost their competitiveness in world trade.

Some developed countries have experienced a large and persistent current account deficit before the financial crisis. The current account deficit of the US was modest before 1997, but increased substantially thereafter, reaching $788 billion (6 per cent of the country's GDP and 1.6 per cent of world GDP) in 2006. Such an enormous current account deficit was mainly caused by excess spending in the economy, which increased the total demand for imports and hence the huge trade deficit. The majority of the overheated demand was driven by the irrational behaviours of individuals to obtain more and more happiness which diminishes with successive units of gains. The government borrowing also contributed significantly to the excess spending. The negative current account balance requires a positive capital and financial account, which means that the holding of domestic assets by non-residents must increase. However, the US has had problems financing the current account deficit in the long term. A significant part of the US deficit was financed by Chinese and Japanese investors, as well as oil exporters, buying US Treasury Securities at relatively low interest rates (rather than the investment in manufacturing/production). US could borrow from abroad at a low interest rate because the US dollar is the world's reserve currency. The positive current account balances in China, Japan and oil-exporting countries and their willingness to purchase US debts have encouraged the further expansion of excess spending and the borrowing of individuals and government. A similar situation also existed in the UK and some European nations. Such expanded demands and consumption have sown the seeds of the crisis.

The second element of the financial crisis is the greed, complexity and opaqueness in the banking/financial system in developed countries including the intricate and highly-leveraged, high-risk financial contracts and operations, as well as low transparency and ineffective regulations. In order to pursue higher profits, financial institutions developed a range of products and derivatives. However, many banks and investors undervalued the level of the inherent risks involved in using economic pricing functions such as, for instance, the Gaussian copula model that was widely used for the pricing of collateralised debt obligations and calculating the co-association between multiple securities. Since none of the functions could reflect the real level of risk, the results were that financial institutions miscalculated prices and the investors took advantage of low interest rates to borrow tremendous amounts of money that they could only pay back if asset prices (e.g. housing) continued to rise.

Before the crisis, banking institutions became increasingly complicated over time. Numerous types of financial dervatives were created to increase market liquidities. Investment banks borrowed colossal amounts of money from the market and used them to lend to other financial institutions or to help firms making gigantic transnational, cross-sector mergers and acquisitions. The entire operation process and risk was totally obscured from outsiders and government regulatory bodies.

The third is the mismanagement of inflation and interest rates by central banks. In the late 1990s, falling interest rates led to the consumption boom and encouraged people to invest in the stock market and the property market. Between 2000 and 2002, in order to support the economic revovery from the early 2000s recession, central banks in most developed countries further reduced the interest rates and hence fuelled the consumption and investment in housing markets. From 2006, when the rising inflationary concerns promoted the US Federal Reserve, the Bank of England and the European Central Bank to engage in tighter monetary policies, the significant increases in interest rates reduced domestic demand and hurt consumers who have large amounts of debt, and hence resulted in a slowdown and crisis in the financial system.

The fourth is the rising prices of energy and materials. Figure 9.3 shows the changes of major commodity price indices. Oil price rose to over $140 per barrel in July 2008. The prices of metals and food also increased significantly. The bubble of commodity prices increased the costs of production and transportation, leading to a dramatic decline in global demand and damage to the world economy.

The current crisis shows the failure of free market capitalism, i.e., the invisible hand is no longer the panacea for economic growth and prosperity. For many years, the West believed that the market was self-correcting. The West often criticise state intervention in East Asian countries, especially during the 1997 Asian Financial Crisis. However, such an invisible hand became dysfunctional when a great number of financial institutions and big enterprises collapsed during the crisis.

4   Consequences of the crisis

The immediate consequence of the crisis has been the collapse of stock markets because of a continuous stream of depressing news

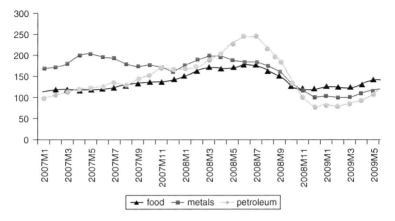

Figure 9.3   Monthly indices of primary commodity prices, 2007–2009
Notes: 2005 = 100, in terms of US dollars; petroleum index is average petroleum spot price of
UK, Brent, Dubai, and West Texas Intermediate, equally weighted.
Source: IMF.

about the colossal losses of some world-class financial institutions and
multinational corporations, including Lehman Brothers (the largest
bankruptcy in US history), Citigroup, American International Group
(AIG) and General Motors (GM) in the US, and Royal Bank of Scotland
(RBS) Group and Halifax Bank of Scotland (HBOS, now Lloyds) in the
UK. Table 9.2 gives two examples of AIG and RBS Group about their
huge losses. AIG lost $100 billion and RBS £28 billion in 2008. Their
share prices dropped more than 90%. These banks and insurers are
'*too big to fail*' as their failure would lead to serious market turbulence.
Therefore, the US and UK governments a huge amount of taxpayers'
money in a bid to avoid the collapse of these institutions and further
market upheaval.

The impact of the crisis on the world economy as a whole is a sharp
contraction in prices, production and services, leading to a dramatic and
consecutive slowdown of economic growth in many countries, including
the largest economies in the world. GDP growth rates in the major
developed countries slowed from the fourth quarter of 2007, turning
to negative growth from the first (some from the second) quarter in
2008. The latest IMF World Economic Outlook (April 2010) revealed
that in 2009 the economies in developed countries fell by 3.2 per cent,
with the US dropping 2.4 per cent, Germany 5.0 per cent, the UK 4.9
per cent and Japan 5.2 per cent (the strongest among OECD countries).

Table 9.2   AIG and the RBS Group

	AIG	RBS Group
Employees	116,000 (2008)	170,000 (2008)
Losses	Q4 2008: $61.7 billion 2008 in total: $99.29 billion	2008: total loss: £28 billion £325 billion toxic assets out of £1 trillion (80% overseas)
Market value	From $150 bn to $1.2 bn.	From £75 billion to £4.5 billion
Share price	$70.13 (09-10-2007) to $0.33 (27-03-2009)	£7.24 (20-02-2007) to £0.10 (19-01-2009)
Impact	$2 trillion financial products, $ 1 trillion insuring 12 large banks; 94% of Fortune 500 properties; 74 million customers in the world.	The second largest banking group in the UK and Europe (at its peak); the fifth largest in the world by market value.
Government rescue	$180 billion in total; could go to $250 billion	73% state ownership
Bonus	March 2009: $165 million in executive bonuses	Cutting from £2.5 billion in 2008 to £340 million in 2009

Although China's GDP still grew by 8.7 per cent in 2009, the growth rate was the lowest since 2000.

With the exception of China, industrial production in the major economies fell sharply (see Table 9.3). The US Federal Reserve reported that US industrial output in March 2009 fell to the lowest level observed since December 1998 and the UK ONS reported that UK industrial output had suffered its sharpest fall since 1968. China's industrial production grew by 5.3 per cent in the first quarter of 2009, the lowest growth rate for ten years.

The world's largest economies all showed a significant decline in trades and investments after September 2008. The volume of trade of developed countries levelled off in mid-2007, while trade in developing countries continued to expand until the third quarter of 2008. In the first quarter of 2009, the volume of world trade was 19 per cent lower than in the same period in 2008; and the value of trade was even lower because the prices of most primary commodities fell sharply (UNCTAD 2009b). UNCTAD data revealed that global FDI and cross-border mergers and acquisitions declined dramatically. Cross-border FDI flows dropped by 54 per cent during the first quarter of 2009

Table 9.3 Percentage changes in industrial production

Economy	Sep-2008	Oct-2008	Nov-2008	Dec-2008	Jan-2009	Feb-2009	Mar-2009	Apr-2009	May-2009	Jun-2009	Jul-2009	Aug-2009	Sep-2009	Oct-2009	Nov-2009
On a month-on-month basis															
US	-4.0	1.3	-1.3	-2.3	-2.2	-0.8	-1.6	-0.5	-1.1	-0.5	1.1	1.3	0.6	0.0	0.8
UK	0.1	-2.6	-2.2	-1.7	-2.6	-1.0	-0.6	0.3	-0.6	0.5	0.5	-2.5	1.6	0.0	0.4
Euro Area	-2.1	-2.2	-2.9	-3.1	-2.7	-2.6	-1.4	-1.9	1.1	1.0	0.4	1.1	0.3	-0.3	1.0
Japan	0.1	-3.4	-7.0	-8.4	-10.1	-9.4	1.6	5.9	5.7	2.3	2.1	1.6	2.1	0.5	2.6
China	N/A	N/A	N/A	N/A	N/A	N/A	N/A	N/A	N/A	N/A	N/A	N/A	N/A	N/A	N/A
On a year-on-year basis															
US	-6.4	-4.7	-6.5	-8.9	-10.9	-11.3	-12.5	-12.4	-13.1	-13.3	-12.3	-10.1	-5.9	-7.1	-5.1
UK	-2.8	-6.3	-8.3	-9.7	-12.2	-12.9	-12.6	-12.3	-12.4	-10.9	-9.7	-11.9	-10.8	-8.4	-6.0
Euro Area	-2.3	-5.9	-9.1	-12.4	-16.5	-19.1	-19.3	-21.6	-17.7	-16.7	-15.8	-15.1	-12.7	-10.9	-7.1
Japan	-4.0	-9.0	-14.1	-21.8	-30.0	-36.9	-35.1	-30.7	-27.6	-24.5	-22.7	-18.9	-17.3	-14.0	-5.2
China	11.4	8.2	5.4	5.7	N/A	11.0	8.3	7.3	8.9	10.7	10.8	12.3	13.9	16.1	19.2

Note: Year-on-year values for UK are constructed by authors based on the 'Index of Production', various months, ONS. Values for China are the percentage changes of industrial value added; seasonally adjusted.
Sources: Federal Reserve Statistical Release, US; Office for National Statistics, UK; Eurostat; Ministry of Economy, Trade and Industry, Japan; and National Bureau of Statistics, China.

compared with the same period in 2008 (UNCTAD 2009a). FDI inflows were likely to fall from $1.7 trillion to below $1.2 trillion in 2009 (UNCTAD 2009c).

The crisis had a substantial impact on the housing markets in the UK and the US. In the first quarter of 2009, US house prices dropped 7.14 per cent compared with the same quarter a year earlier (Figure 9.4). The situation in the UK was even worse. Average house price in the first quarter of 2009 dropped by 16.5 per cent.

The contractions in prices, production and services led to the collapse of many firms, leading to massive unemployment in all countries. By October 2009, the UK unemployment rate had risen to 7.9 per cent, up from just 6 per cent in one year. The US unemployment rate rose from 6 per cent in 2008 to over 10 per cent in December 2009.

The sequential flows of poor statistics in industrial production, GDP, employment, house prices and stock markets imply that many bubbles are bursting simultaneously, but the principal reason behind these collapses was due to the loss of confidence by all market players, be they investors, consumers, firms and governments.

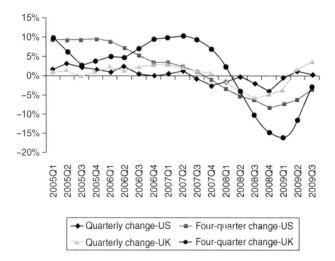

Figure 9.4 Housing price change in the US and the UK, 2005Q1–2009Q1
Note: Seasonally adjusted house price change; US: measured in purchase-only index; UK: measured in average house price.
Sources: Federal Housing Finance Agency (FHFA), US; Nationwide, UK.

5 Response to the crisis

Most countries' governments did not undertake any policy response to the crisis until the second half of 2008. Many countries used their monetary policies through successfully cutting their interest rates within several months, in order to lower the cost of credit for both financial and non-financial agents. The US Federal Reserve cut its Federal funds rate target to the historical low of 0.25 per cent by December 2008; the European Central Bank reduced its key policy rate to 1 per cent only in May 2009 from 4.25 per cent in October 2008; the Bank of England also cut the benchmark interest rate to record low, 0.5 per cent.

Although interest rates had remained at a low level of 0.5 per cent for seven years because of the stagnating economy, Japan cut interest rates on two further occasions to 0.1 per cent by the fourth quarter of 2008. China also cut the interest rates five times by 2.16 percentage points in total. Another measure adopted by central bankers is quantitative easing to expand the money supply. In March 2009, the US Federal Reserve announced that it would buy almost $1.2 trillion worth of debt, including $0.3 trillion of long-term government debt (US Treasuries), $0.75 trillion of mortgage-backed securities to boost mortgage lending, and $0.1 trillion of debt issued by government-sponsored agencies such as Freddie Mac. This announcement has achieved instant results, leading to a jump of the Dow Jones industrial average by 1.23 per cent (90.88 points), but also a depreciation of the US dollar. Similarly, the Bank of England announced an asset purchases programme of £125 billion in total, financed by the issuance of central bank reserves. China also increased the money supply to RMB60 trillion in 2009, a growth of about 28 per cent compared with 2008. ECB announced its intention of providing one-year financing for more than €440 billion to the euro-area banking system – the largest amount ever for a single ECB operation; the Bank of Japan also adopted a number of policies relating to the outright purchases of longer-term government securities.

However, the effect of monetary policy is usually limited. They are not sufficient to restore the confidence in financial markets. Therefore, many countries have adopted relevant fiscal policies. To provide state guarantees to large financial firms, the US and the UK adopted government bailouts for big firms and the partial nationalisation of large banks when the financial crisis became visible. Shortly after the mortgage leaders Fannie Mae and Freddie Mac were placed in deferral conservatorship, the US Congress passed the $700 billion bailout package to purchase non-performing collaterals and assets; and this could eventually reach

$1,000 billion. Eight firms (Bank of America, Citigroup, JP Morgan Chase, Wells Fargo, Goldman Sachs, Morgan Stanley, State Street, and Bank of New York Mellon) received $166 billion of public funds and AIG $180 billion – an 80 per cent stake in the company. The UK government initially announced a £500 billion bailout plan to inject capital into UK banks and then added £200 billion to buy up their toxic assets. The second bailout aimed to encourage the banks to increase lending to companies and homebuyers. The UK government currently owns 100 per cent of Northern Rock plc (nationalised in February 2008), 70.33 per cent of the Royal Bank of Scotland Group and 43 per cent of Lloyds Banking Group (the new group created by Lloyds TSB's takeover of HBOS).

Expansionary monetary policies and government bailout plans would help to prevent the further meltdown of financial sectors but have not been sufficient to restore the non-financial sectors. A recovery of the whole economy requires to stimulate global demand, rising employment, and rebuild the confidence of individuals. Therefore, it is necessary to adopt counter-cyclical fiscal policies that have a direct impact on aggregate demand.

Many countries have approved large economic stimulus packages, such as increases in government spending and tax cuts, to tackle the dramatic reductions in demand, production and employment. US President Barack Obama signed the $787 billion economic stimulus plan for 2009 and 2010, in order to save or create jobs, provide tax cuts, and boost consumer spending and rebuild infrastructure. UK announced a £20 billion fiscal stimulus consisting of an immediate cut in VAT and an increase of stamp duty exempt threshold, to boost consumer and house buyers' confidence. The German Parliament approved €50 billion stimulus plan, including investment in infrastructure, tax relief, reduction in health care contributions, and money for families with children and people with junk old cars to buy new vehicles. Japan's cabinet firstly provided ¥1.81 trillion ($17 billion) to cope with high energy and food prices at that time and cut taxes; and then another stimulus package of ¥20 trillion ($218 billion) in fiscal spending.

The stimulus package in China was RMB4 trillion ($586 billion) to be invested in infrastructure and social welfare by the end of 2010. China also proposed a budgeted fiscal deficit of RMB950 billion ($139 billion) for 2009, a record high in six decades, to increase government spending, which is recognised as the most active, direct and efficient way of expanding domestic demand. The 2008 financial crisis is the most serious one since the 1930s and its impact has spread across the globe.

The global economic recovery cannot be achieved successfully and rapidly without global efforts. The leaders of G20 met three times in 2008 and 2009 in Washington, London and Pittsburgh, exclusively to deal with the crisis. The aim of G20 summits was generally to enhance the cooperation among nations to restore global growth and reform the world financial system to prevent a future crisis like this.

The G20 has already delivered a number of signifcant and concrete outcomes. It committed to implement the unprecedented and most coordinated expansionary macroeconomic policies, including the fiscal expansion of US$5 trillion and the unconventional monetary policy instruments; significantly enhance financial regulations, notably by the establishment of the Financial Stability Board (FSB); and substantially strengthen the International Financial Institutions (IFIs), including the expansion of resources and the improvement of precautionary lending facilities of the IFIs.[6]

In 2010, the G20 Summits will be held in Toronto in June and Seoul in November.

By and large the above rescue efforts appear to have been successful. Stock markets seem to have recovered somewhat from their worst position in March 2009. Table 9.4 reports the improvements in major stock market indices in the first half of 2009. The Dow Jones and FTSE100 have both shown improvement since March 2009, while the Shanghai Stock Exchange had bottomed out in November 2008.

The rise of these stock indices, to some extent, has been driven by the recovery in bank shares. The share prices of most banks and resource companies hit their lowest points between January and March 2009 and have shown substantial increases since. For example, by the end

Table 9.4 Stock market prices (close price adjusted for dividends and splits)

	Lowest	Highest	Change (%)	30/June/ 2009	Change (%)
Dow Jones	6547.05 (09/March/2009)	8799.26 (12/June/2009)	↑34.4%	8447.00	↑29.0%
FTSE100	3512.10 (03/March/2009)	4506.20 (01/June/2009)	↑28.3%	4249.20	↑21.0%
Shanghai (Composite)	1706.7 (04/November/2009)	3124.67 (06/July/2009)	↑83.1%	2959.36	↑73.4%

Source: Yahoo! Finance.

of June 2009, comparing to the lowest points in early March 2009, in the US, Citigroup rose 191 per cent and Bank of America gained 320 per cent; in the UK, Lloyds Banking Group added 66 per cent, while Standard Chartered increased by 94 per cent. From March to May 2009, a so-called 'stress test' programme was launched by the US regulators for the 19 largest banks in order to see if they have sufficient cash reserves to cope with the recession. The results suggested that all the banks were solvent but 10 of them were urged to raise a total of $74.6 billion in capital to absorb additional losses if the economy weakeneed further (CNNMoney.com, 8 May 2009). In the UK, Barclays was subjected to a similar 'extreme stress test' and the report said that the UK bank would not need more money if it joined the Treasury asset insurance scheme (BBC News 27 March 2009).

6   China in the crisis environment

IMF recently reported that global growth in 2009 contracted by 0.6 per cent measured in terms of purchasing power parity (IMF World Economic Outlook, April 2010). The output of advanced economies decreased by 3.2 per cent and that of emerging and developing economies continued to expand by 2.4 per cent. The world economy is stabilizing with the help of unprecedented efforts to ease the credit strains and the expansionary fiscal and monetary policies. IMF revealed that global production and trade bounced back in the second half of 2009 as confidence rebounded strongly on both the financial and real sectors due to the extraordinary policy support.

In 2010, world output is forecast to rise by 4.2 per cent. However, the stabilization is uneven and the recovery is likely to proceed at varying speeds. The recovery is expected to be sluggish in advanced economies, whose real output may not regain its pre-crisis level until late 2011. The crisis in these countries, therefore, would be U-shaped (a recovery requires two to four years). Comparing with the recession in these advanced economies, China was not an exception but such negative influence was much less than its competitors. We affirm that China's economy bottomed out in 2009 and hence experienced a V-shaped crisis.

China's National Bureau of Statistics (NBS) reported that China has had contractions in terms of the country's trade, GDP growth, stock prices, foreign direct investment (FDI), production and employment (NBS, 2010). Although China has maintained positive growth, the growth rate in 2009 (8.7 per cent) was the lowest for a decade. China's industrial production growth in the first quarter of 2009 (5.3 per cent) was also the lowest for almost a decade, and the production of some major industrial products – such as sugar, air conditioner, crude oil and power equipment – experienced significant negative growth in 2009. External trade contracted by 13.9 per cent consisting of a 16 per cent reduction in exports and a 11.2 per cent reduction in imports. Inward FDI flows in 2009 was $90 billion, a decrease of 2.6 per cent compared with the previous year. The official urban registered unemployment rate also rose 0.1 percentage point. However, these contractions were much smaller than those in other large economies in the world. The reasons are as follows.

First, thanks to the bank reforms introduced from 1998 to 2006 the banking system has not been seriously affected by the financial crisis. From 1999, the Chinese government established four state asset management companies (AMCs) to strip off the non-performing loans (NPLs) of the four large state-owned commercial banks – the Industrial and Commercial Bank of China (IÇBC), the Bank of China (BOC), the China Construction Bank (CCB) and the Agricultural Bank of China (ABC). The Chinese government also directly injected huge amounts of the country's foreign exchange reserves to improve the balance sheets of these banks. By 2005, an amount of RMB 2.62 trillion of NPLs had been removed from the balance sheets of ICBC, CCB and BOC. All of these actions were intended to clear the obstacles to their initial public offering on the stock market. Therefore the huge toxic assets had been taken away from the largest Chinese banks prior to the financial crisis.

Second, China's economic fundamentals are strong. The current crisis only sharply affected China's external market, especially the sectors related to exports. China's domestic market is still stable and relatively strong. China had achieved an annual average economic growth at almost 10 per cent for almost two decades with a high savings/GDP ratio at about 50 per cent. China's national government revenue increased quickly, reaching RMB 6.1 trillion in 2008, and RMB 6.85 trillion in 2009 despite the crisis. In the mean time, the government maintained a relatively low fiscal deficit–GDP ratio at less than 1 per cent.[7]

On 5 March 2009 Premier Wen Jiabao announced a budget fiscal deficit of RMB 950 billion ($139 billion) for 2009, which still amounted to less than 3 per cent of national GDP, the internationally agreed risk level according to usual economic practice. China also accumulated huge foreign exchange reserves of $1.946 trillion by the end of 2008, rising to $2.4 trillion by the end of 2009 (People's Bank of China), making China the world's largest holder of foreign exchange reserves since 2006. The amount of China's foreign exchange reserves at the end of 2009 was equivalent to 2.4 times that of Japan's, or 30 per cent of the world's total.

Finally, in contrast to the reaction in the West, the Chinese political regime allows the government to adopt much swifter actions to restore its economy. For example, the government rapidly reached a decision on the cutting of tax, increasing the fiscal deficit, and introducing the RMB 4 trillion stimulus plan.

China's Premier Wen Jiabao pointed out many times that confidence is the most important factor – more important than gold or currency. The Chinese government has confidence in the stimulus package they are promoting and Chinese people have confidence in both the government and the economic outlook. The Chinese government supports domestic investment so that investors and entrepreneurs reap a harvest of hope at the time of crisis through taking risks to search profit opportunities. In contrast, many market players in the West would like to avoid any risks and hold cash in hand in order to avoid losing more money. Given such different circumstances of difference, the effect of government bailouts is limited. Thus, Chinese investors have moved to the curve of 'happiness' while those in the advanced economies still find themselves in the 'unhappiness' section of the curve. That is why China's economy revives quickly while the West will remain sluggish for a longer period.

Since the first half of 2009, there have been some positive signs of recovery in China. On 16 July 2009, the National Bureau of Statistics of China reported that China's GDP was RMB 13.986 trillion, growing at an annual rate of 7.1 per cent (7.9 per cent in the second quarter of 2009, 1.0 percentage point higher than the first quarter), indicating the positive results of the government stimulus package.

The total amount of public investment in fixed assets was RMB 9.1 trillion, an increase of 33.5 per cent compared with the same period in 2008; while the total amount of retail sales was RMB 5.8 trillion, 15 per cent higher than the same period in 2008. The year-on-year growth rate of industrial value-added was 7.0 per cent, a fall of 9.3 percentage points compared to the same period in 2008. However, the growth rate was 5.1 per cent in the first quarter and 9.1 per cent in the second quarter. The sales rate of industrial production was 97.2 per cent, indicating good connections between industrial production and sales. Between January and May 2009, national large-scale enterprises achieved a profit of RMB 850 billion, a fall of RMB 22.95 billion compared with the same period in 2008. Some industrial sectors experienced a rapid increase in profits, or transformed losses to profits, such as food manufacturing, textiles, garments, shoes and hat manufacturing, the ferrous and non-ferrous metal-smelting and sheet processing industries. The total amount of trade was $946.1 billion, a reduction of 23.5 per cent compared to the same period in 2008. However, imports and exports appeared to have hit their lowest levels in January and February 2009.

China's Shanghai Stock Exchange Composite Index gained about 75 per cent, making it the world's best-performing major market in 2009. It rose 1.4 per cent on 15 July 2009, sending the value of China's domestic stock market to $3.21 trillion, compared with Japan's $3.20 trillion, according to data compiled by Bloomberg. China

Table 9.5   China's economy in the first half of 2009

Indicators	Amount	% from the same period in 2008
GDP	RMB 13.986 trillion	+7.1% (6.1% Q1, 7.9% Q2)
Industrial value-added (large scale enterprises)		+7.0% (5.1% Q1, 9.1% Q2)
Profits (large scale enterprises Jan-May)	RMB 850 billion	–22.9% (–37.4% Jan–Feb)
Fixed asset investment	RMB 9.1 trillion	+33.5%
Sales on domestic market	RMB 5.8 trillion	+15.0%
Consumer prices		–1.1%
Trade	$946.1 billion	–23.5%
Exports	$521.5 billion	–21.8%
Imports	$424.6 billion	–35.4%
Trade surplus	$96.9 billion	–$2.1 billion
Exports Jun vs. Feb (lowest point)	$95.4 billion vs. $64.9 billion	+47.0%
Imports Jun vs. Jan (lowest point)	$87.2 billion vs. $51.3 billion	+69.8%
Exports Jun vs. May	$95.4 billion vs. $88.8 billion	+7.4%
Imports Jun vs. May	$87.2 billion vs. $75.4 billion	+15.6%
M2	RMB 56.9 trillion	+28.5%
M1	RMB 19.3 trillion	+24.8%
Loans of financial institutions	RMB 37.7 trillion	+RMB 4.9 trillion
Savings in financial institutions	RMB 56.6 trillion	+RMB 5.0 trillion

Source: National Bureau of Statistics, and General Administration of Customs, China.

then overtook Japan as the world's second-largest stock market in capitalisation for the first time in 18 months.[8]

On 7 July 2009 *China Daily* reported that the Chinese housing market was also showing a substantial recovery in demand in the first half of 2009, with more active transactions. Some cities (Beijing, Tianjin, Chongqing, Wuhan and Hangzhou) showed a 100% year-on-year jump in the rate of transactions, and the figure exceeds 150% in Shenzhen. The two main reasons for this boost in the market are the falling housing costs in 2008 and the added financial support to personal loans.

However, the current revival is not stable. China is still facing some challenges, including inactive domestic demand, the potential emergence of asset price bubbles, the pressure on exchange rate appreciation and the excess capacity in traditional industrial sectors. Proactive macroeconomic policy and industrial restructuring are still vital to strengthen the momentum of the recovery. After the 1997 Asian Financial Crisis, China changed the economic growth points to the automobile and real estate sectors. Today, China has to find new economic growth points and improve the quality of the recovery, for example, to support high-tech, environmentally-friendly industries for long-term sustainable development.

The current crisis provides China with a 'once in a century' opportunity to achieve a much speedier economic convergence with the world's largest industrialised economies, including the US, Japan, Germany and the UK. China has become the biggest winner from the crisis with the following opportunities.

First, China is rapidly catching up with Japan and the US. China's high growth rate over decades has pushed past Germany to become the world's third-largest economy in 2007 measured in terms of GDP at current prices (see Figure 9.5). It reinforced this position in 2008. As a result of the financial crisis, economic growth in these developed countries slowed down in the following few years and it is still not certain when the growth in these countries will return to its pre-crisis levels.

With a GDP growth of 8.7 per cent in 2009, China narrowly failed to overtake Japan as the world's second-largest economy thanks to the appreciation of the Japanese yen against the US dollar. There is every likelihood that China will surpass Japan by the end of 2010.

Second, China, alongside India, is rebalancing the global geo-ecopolitical power from the West to the East. Nowadays, China is not only the largest country in terms of population but also one of

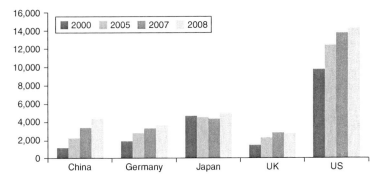

Figure 9.5   Nominal GDP of top five economies ($ billion)
Source: IMF.

the world's largest economies. China has been generally changing its foreign policies, playing its role in the United Nations and other global events, to exhibit its 'responsible great power' image. China tends to become more influential on the world economy and politics.

Third, China is likely to benefit from the low prices of oil and raw materials for its next stage of industrialisation and urbanisation.

Fourth, China may see the crisis as an opportunity to upgrade its industrial structure and move up the technological ladder. Excess capacities in some traditional sectors combined with increases in real wages in China will crowd out some unskilled-labour-intensive enterprises and industrial sectors that are characterised by low technology and low levels of efficiency. Those enterprises that aim to survive in the crisis have to improve their productive efficiency or innovate in their production using high and/or new technologies. These help the upgrading of China's industrial structure.

Regional inequalities are likely to be reduced during the crisis. Over the past thirty years, China's economic growth has been uneven. The coastal regions have significantly higher income levels than the inland regions. During the crisis, many enterprises in the coastal provinces collapsed because of the sharp shrinkage in exports, whereas inland regions maintained high growth rates because of the different economic growth modes.

Table 9.6 compares the regional economic performance in 2008 and early 2009. In 2008, of the 13 provinces that achieved regional GDP above 1 trillion RMB, four are located in central China, including Henan, Sichuan, Hubei and Hunan. In terms of GDP growth, Inner Mongolia grew at a rate of 17.5 per cent, the highest among of any province.

Table 9.6 Regional comparison, 2008–2009

Province	2008 GDP		January–May 2009 Industrial value-added	Urban investment			
	Value (RMB bn)	GDP growth	Annualized growth	Value (RMB bn)	Annualized growth	%	% in 2008
Total	30067.0	9.0	6.3	5352.03	32.9	100	100
Eastern regions				2654.91	24.9	49.6	52.8
Beijing	1000.0	9.0	-2.3	115.34	2.4	2.2	2.8
Tianjin	630.0	16.0	20.9	140.27	46.2	2.6	2.4
Hebei	1600.0	10.0	7.3	312.57	56.4	5.8	5
Liaoning	1345.5	13.0	12.1	263.28	49.4	4.9	4.4
Shanghai	1369.8	9.7	-6.6	148.84	5.2	2.8	3.5
Jiangsu	3000.0	12.5	11.7	478.97	24.9	8.9	9.5
Zhejiang	2100.0	10.0	-2	232.61	13	4.3	5.1
Fujian	1086.3	13.0	4.5	167.02	14.7	3.1	3.6
Shandong	3107.2	12.1	10.8	466.28	22.1	8.7	9.5
Guangdong	3569.6	10.1	3.1	302.09	14.1	5.6	6.6
Hainan	146.6	9.8	1.5	27.65	47.7	0.5	0.5
Central regions				1362.06	36.4	25.4	24.8
Shanxi	700.0	10.0	-22.5	84.73	27.4	1.6	1.7
Jilin	640.0	16.0	11.1	98.01	42.3	1.8	1.7
Heilongjiang	831.0	11.8	6.4	53.80	50.8	1	0.9
Anhui	887.4	12.7	15.8	253.67	32.2	4.7	4.8
Jiangxi	648.0	12.6	14.6	149.86	45.1	2.8	2.6
Henan	1820.0	12.0	5.3	325.37	33.8	6.1	6
Hubei	1133.1	13.4	11.9	214.16	36.6	4	3.9
Hunan	1100.0	12.8	17.6	182.46	37.5	3.4	3.3

(Continued)

Table 9.6 Continued

Province	2008 GDP		January–May 2009				
			Industrial value-added	Urban investment			
	Value (RMB bn)	GDP growth	Annualized growth	Value (RMB bn)	Annualized growth	%	% in 2008
Western regions				1258.04	47.4	23.5	21.2
Inner Mongolia	760.0	17.5	19.6	160.31	48.7	3	2.7
Guangxi	715.0	12.5	14.3	148.38	54.3	2.8	2.4
Chongqing	509.9	14.3	12.3	125.07	31.9	2.3	2.4
Sichuan	1250.6	9.5	20.7	315.10	55.2	5.9	5
Guizhou	335.0	10.0	6.1	56.23	36.6	1.1	1
Yunan	570.0	11.0	1.3	119.43	52.3	2.2	1.9
Tibet	39.2	10.1	8.2	5.17	25	0.1	0.1
Shaanxi	680.0	15.0	8.2	177.72	53.5	3.3	2.9
Gansu	310.0	10.0	-1.1	53.75	38.1	1	1
Qinghai	96.0	12.5	6.1	19.20	29.4	0.4	0.4
Ningxia	107.0	12.0	3.1	25.05	44.2	0.5	0.4
Xinjiang	415.0	11.0	3.7	52.33	27	1	1

Notes: GDP values and GDP growth rates are the estimated values in regional government reports (except Shanghai and Anhui, which are from regional bureaus of statistics);

Source: Xinhuanet, http://news.xinhuanet.com/local/2009-02/20/content_10853052.htm; National Bureau of Statistics, China.

Some inland regions, such as Jilin, Chongqing and Shaanxi, also had higher growth rates than the average level reported by the regional governments. From January to May 2009, industrial production in some coastal regions experienced negative growth measured in terms of industrial value added growth; while most of the central and western provinces achieved positive growth – some with a double-digit growth rate. In terms of urban investment, the growth rates in central and western regions were higher than in the eastern region; and the share of investment in the eastern region declined to 49.6 per cent compared with 52.8 per cent for the same period in 2008. Correspondingly, the share of the central and western regions increased. This shows that the coastal region was hit harder and the recovery speed was slower than the inland regions. Although considerable gaps still exist among the regions, the crisis to some extent has reduced their inequalities.

Finally, the crisis provides an opportunity for China to learn the lesson of developed countries and become aware of potential future crises that could possibly start in China. China has to learn how to prevent and cope with future crises in order to achieve its long-term goal of sustainable development.

7   Summary and conclusions

The current financial crisis was triggered by the credit crunch in the US from 2007 onwards and became apparent from the third quarter of 2008. It started in the developed countries but spread across the whole world. The scale and impact of the downturn have not been witnessed since the 1930s. Although the crisis has led to a global economic recession, the developed countries were hit harder than the developing world.

Governments in most affected countries adopted various rescure methods to prevent the worsening and then to pull the world economy out of recession. Leaders of a number of countries also tried to seek global collaboration via the G20 summits. Although it is not clear whether these rescue efforts are effective, a new global financial regulatory system is likely to emerge after the crisis.

According to our analysis based on the theory of asymmetric reaction of gains and losses and on the economic data, China has been the biggest winner in the crisis. It is projected that the economy in most of the developed countries will be sluggish for two years and taht it will probably take four years to return to its pre-crisis levels. By contrast, China continues to achieve high and positive economic growth and has shown strong recovery from the second half of 2009.

The crisis is an opportunity for China to catch up with the most advanced economies such as Japan and the US. By the end of 2010 it is almost certain that China will certainly overtake Japan as the second-largest economy in the world. It may take another 20 years to overtake the US to become the largest economy of the world. It can be concluded that the crisis has triggered a speedier shift of economic and political influence from the West to the East leading to the emergence of a new world order over the next two decades.

Of course, there is no guarantee that China will become the world's largest economy without encountering huge challenges and constraints. The Chinese economic and political systems have critical weaknesses and limitations. It has developed an industrial structure which depends heavily on energy- and material-intensive manufacturing, a political system that is still authoritarian and corrupt, and a social system that is highly divisive in terms of income distribution, and an environmental system that is highly polluting.

Notes

1. Shujie Yao, professor of economics and Chinese sustainable development, head of School of Contemporary Chinese Studies, internal fellow of the Leverhulme Centre for Research on Globalisation and Economic Policy (GEP), University of Nottingham, special professor of Xi'an Jiaotong University, e-mail, shujie.yao@nottingham.ac.uk. Jing Zhang, lecturer of contemporary Chinese studies, internal fellow of GEP, University of Nottingham, e-mail, j.zhang@nottingham.ac.uk. This paper was presented at the 2nd China Conference of GEP at University of Nottingham Ningbo, China, 10–11 November 2009. Financial support by the Leverhulme Trust is gratefully acknowledged (F00114AQ).
2. 'The Global Plan for Recovery and Reform', G20 London Summit Declaration, 2 April 2009.
3. Marginal happiness (MH) is positive but it tends to decline as successive units of gains are made; marginal unhappiness (MUH) with respect to losses is not only positive but also increasing in response to successive units of losses.
4. Yao and Zhang (forthcoming) defines that V-, U- and L-shaped crises respectively indicate the length of recovery to be less than two years, two to four years, and more than four years.
5. http://www.fin24.com/articles/default/display_article.aspx?Channel=Markets_Currencies&ArticleId=1518-1783_2545802&IsColumnistStory=False.
6. http://www.g20.org/.
7. To cope with the 1997 East Asian financial crisis, China increased its deficit–GDP ratio from less than 1 per cent in 1997 to 2.6 per cent in 2002 (RMB 319.8 billion). However, as the government revenue bulged on years of double-digit economic growth, the deficit–GDP ratio declined to 0.6 per cent in 2008 (www.news.xinhuanet.com).

References

Auerbach, A. (2009) 'Implementing the New Fiscal Policy Activism', *American Economic Review*, 99(2), 543–9.
BBC News (2009) 'Barclays Shares Jump after Test', 27 March, http://news.bbc.co.uk/1/hi/business/7967825.stm.
Blanchard, O.J. (1979) 'Speculative Bubbles, Crashes, and Rational Expectations', *Economic Letters*, 3(4), 387–9.
Brunnermeier, M.K. (2001) *Asset Pricing under Asymmetric Information: Bubbles, Crashes, Technical Anaysis and Herding*. Oxford, UK: Oxford University Press.
China Daily (2009) 'China's Housing Market Recovers', 7 July. http://www.chinadaily.com.cn/china/2009-07/07/content_8389574.htm.
Claessens, S. (2009) 'Lessons from the Recent Financial Crisis for Reforming the National and International Financial System'. A Keynote Paper Presented at the Annual World Bank Conference on Development Economics, Seoul, Korea. http://siteresources.worldbank.org/INTABCDESK2009/Resources/Stijn-Claessens.pdf.
CNNMoney.com (2009) 'Stress Tests: Banks need $75 Billion', 8 May, http://money.cnn.com/2009/05/07/news/companies/stress_test_announcement/index.htm.
Demirgüç-Kunt, A. and L. Serven (2009) 'Are All the Sacred Cows Dead? Implications of the Financial Crisis for Macro and Financial Policies', *Policy Research Working Paper 4807*. Washington, DC: The World Bank.
Feldstein, M. (2009) 'Rethinking the Role of Fiscal Policy', *American Economic Review*, 99(2), 556–9.
IMF (2009) 'Contractionary Forces Receding But Weak Recovery Ahead', 8 July 2009. http://www.imf.org/external/pubs/ft/weo/2009/update/02/index.htm.
IMF (2010) 'World Economic Outlook Update: A Policy-Driven, Multispeed Recovery', http://www.imf.org/external/pubs/ft/weo/2010/update/01/pdf/0110.pdf.
Mishkin, F.S. (2009) 'Is Monetary Policy Effective During Financial Crisis', *American Economic Review*, 99(2), 573–7.
National Bureau of Statistics of China (2010) 'Statistical Communiqué of the People's Republic of China on the 2009 National Economic and Social Development', http://www.stats.gov.cn/was40/gjtjj_en_detail.jsp?channelid=1175&record=15.
Odean, T. (1998) 'Volume, Volatility, Price and Profit When All Traders are Above Average', *Journal of Finance*, 53(6), 1887–934.
People's Daily Online (2009) 'Recession: V, U, or L-shaped?', 2 February, http://english.people.com.cn/90001/90778/90858/90864/6601782.html.
Reinhart, C.M. and Rogoff, K.S. (2008) 'Is the 2007 US Subprime Crisis So Different? An International Historical Comparison', *American Economic Revew*, 98(2), 339–44.
Reinhart, C.M. and Rogoff, K.S. (2009) 'The Aftermath of Financial Crises', *American Economic Revew*, 99(2), 466–72.
Shiller, R.J. (2000) *Irrational Exuberance*. Princeton, NJ: Princeton University Press.
Shleifer, A. (2000) *Inefficient Markets: An Introduction to Behavioural Finance*. Oxford: Oxford University Press.

Sydney Morning Herald (2009) 'China's Stock Market Overtakes Japan's', 16 July 2009. http://business.smh.com.au/business/chinas-stockmarket-overtakes-japans-20090716-dmfa.html.

Taylor, J. (2009) 'The Lack of Empirical Rationale for a Revival of Discretionary Fiscal Policy', *American Economic Review*, 99(2), 550–5.

UNCTAD (2009a) 'Global FDI Flows Halved in 1st Quarter of 2009, UNCTAD Data Show; Prospects Remain Low for Rest of Year', 24 June. http://www.unctad.org/Templates/Webflyer.asp?docID=11666&intItemID=2983&lang=1.

UNCTAD (2009b) 'Trade and Development Report, 2009'. http://www.unctad.org/en/docs/tdr2009_en.pdf.

UNCTAD (2009c) 'World Investment Report, 2009'. Available online: http://www.unctad.org/en/docs/wir2009_en.pdf. Accessed 20 March 2010.

Yao, S. and Luo, D. (2009) 'The Economic Psychology of Stock Market Bubbles in China', *The World Economy*, 32(5), 667–91.

Yao, S. and Zhang, J. (forthcoming) 'On Economic Theory and Recovery of Financial Crisis', *The World Economy*.

10
The 2008 Financial Crisis and Banking Regulation in Brazil

Luiz Fernando de Paula and Rogério Sobreira

1 Introduction

The Brazilian economy was severely affected by the 2008 crisis. At the beginning of the crisis, the overwhelming majority of economic agents and authorities thought that Brazil could face some sort of decoupling since many of its macroeconomic fundamentals were very good. What we saw, however, was that the Brazilian economy was not decoupled, and expectations faced a huge deterioration soon after the bankruptcy of Lehman Brothers on 15 September. Two aspects regarding the impact of the crisis in Brazil, however, deserve considerable attention: (i) although deep, the impact did not last long. Actually, the GDP growth experienced a good recovery in the second quarter of 2009, showing the reaction of the Brazilian economy (ii) the Brazilian banking system performed very well during the crisis, although we cannot say the system was not in danger at the worst time of the crisis. In this aspect, it is interesting to mention the fact that the system showed a great deal of resilience. In our opinion, the restructuring faced by the banking system in the aftermath of the Real Plan, the development of a solid banking supervision regulation and the government's management of public debt as part of the macroeconomic policy used to face the external crises was very helpful in allowing the system to avoid the systemic crisis that was a clear possibility to the Brazilian banking system in the beginning of 2009.

The chapter, thus, discusses the main policies implemented in the aftermath of the Real Plan in order to make the banking system more solid and the development of the prudential regulation that also allowed the system to behave very well during the 2008 crisis. More specifically, the prudential regulation and the fact that Brazil has one of the world's highest interest rates contribute to maintaining the level of domestic saving and helped the banking system to avoid the issuance of toxic assets, to embark on an banking internationalization that could harm it and to behave in a much more conventional way. The chapter is organised as follows. Section 2 presents the restructuring process faced by the Brazilian banking system starting in 1994, as well as the principal prudential regulation measures. Section 3 shows how the Brazilian economy was hit by the crisis and the main policy measures implemented to deal with the effects of the crisis. Finally, section 4 concludes the chapter.

2   The resilience of the Brazilian banking system

After several decades of high inflation, the Brazilian Finance Minister under President Itamar Franco, Fernando Henrique Cardoso, directed the implementation of the Real Plan in 1994. The Real Plan was an effort to stabilise the Brazilian economy by addressing the root causes behind Brazil's chronic inflation problem.[1] The plan, while meant to stabilise prices while introducing a new currency, the 'real', and to keep inflation under control, also had a great effect on the banking system. Brazil's banking sector depended to a great extent on high and chronic inflation in their profit schemes, and the end of high inflation under the Real Plan caused substantial turbulence in the banking sector. Following the Real Plan, fundamental changes were necessary in the banking sector in order to prevent a systemic crisis and also to foster profitability under new macroeconomic conditions.

Before the implementation of the Real Plan, many banks in Brazil attained substantial profits through 'floating' schemes. With an environment of high inflation, banks did their best when they were able to process transactions like deposits quickly. The speed with which Brazilian banks were able to process these transactions contributed to their technological innovation, which would in turn help Brazilian banks to maintain their competitiveness when faced with increased foreign competition. However, the speed with which transactions were processed was not used to transfer monetary resources efficiently from saving to investment units. This was only possible as a result of the existence of a broader domestically denominated indexed money and also the early development of a modern clearing system to support clients' demands for immediate information and the clearing of checks. As a result, the decrease in M1 (cash plus sight deposits) did not result in a loss of funds in the Brazilian financial system as happened in the Argentine high inflation experience. In the latter case, an extensive process of dollarisation was followed by an enormous decrease in financial deepening.[2]

Therefore, using deposit money, Brazilian banks bought government securities protected against high inflation, rather than extending credit to the private sector, and were able to make substantial profits in just one night. As can be seen in Figure 10.1 credit to the private sector under conditions of high inflation fell substantially – that is to less than 25 per cent of GDP in 1988–93 – and was constituted almost totally by short-term loans, because banks preferred to lend to the government since greater profits were available through 'floating'. That is, banks could apply sight deposits and money that circulated in the banking system in highly liquid public bonds indexed to Selic overnight interest rate,[3] so that they could extract advantages of the 'inflationary tax'.

With the Real Plan, inflation was dramatically reduced as well as the potential profits from 'floating'. In fact, 'floating' profits rapidly approached negligible levels. Indeed, the ratio inflationary revenues over net interest income banks' revenues (difference between interest gains and interest expenditures) was 38.5 per cent on average in 1990–93, and fell to almost zero in 1995 (IBGE, 1997). The Real Plan made the mid-1990s a crucial period for Brazilian banks, because they were either forced out of the market or pressured to find new ways to make money, such as the advance of credit. So, when inflation fell sharply after July 1994, its

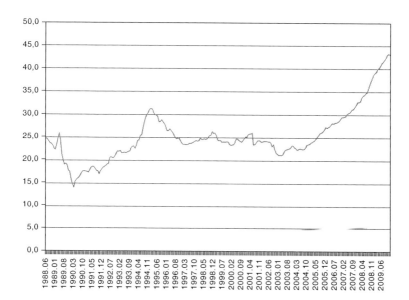

Figure 10.1 Total credit-to-GDP
Source: Central Bank of Brazil.

rapid decline eliminated these inflationary revenues to the banking sector. However, low inflation and re-monetization of the economy stimulated some increase in consumption spending, despite the increase in the Selic rate. In this new context, banks earned most of their profits from credit operations due to the rise in demand for loans and high interest rates.

Therefore, credit expansion was a viable option, as consumption expenditures increased with the price stabilization. With concerns that this could lead to a 'consumption bubble' such as had occurred in the Cruzado Plan (1986), the Brazilian government increased banks' reserve requirements in an attempt to prevent a rapid expansion of the advance of credit that could be risky,[4] but the supply of credit was greatly expanded regardless. This credit growth was positive for the banks in good times, but the situation deteriorated rapidly. Indeed, in April 1995 when the Central Bank of Brazil (BCB) sharply tightened monetary policy (short-term interest rate rose from 20 to 65 per cent per annum) in response to the Mexican financial crisis, banks came under severe pressure as the level of 'bad' loans increased rapidly. Defaults on loans increased substantially between the introduction of the Real Plan and the end of 1995, and this led to liquidity issues for banks. The 'tequila effect' threatened the banking sector as a whole, but in particular some of the domestic retail banks with problems that pre-dated the crisis, as in the cases of Banco National and Banco Economico. In 1995, the likelihood of a systemic crisis in the banking sector increased when the BCB, as regulator of the financial system, first decided to liquidate Economico (August 1995) and later Nacional (November 1995), which were, respectively, the seventh- and fourth-largest private banks. Public state-owned banks[5] in particular faced extremely difficult times as they experienced high rates of default on top of deteriorating state finances. The BCB was facing increasing pressure to intervene directly in the banking system, and with the deteriorating financial health of many institutions it was forced to address the issues within the system and to embark on a substantial reorganisation of the sector.

Early on the BCB decided that it could not let the system as a whole collapse as had occcurred in Venezuela. It would be better to spend public money injecting liquidity into the system and on a restructuring incentive programme than to bear the burden of rebuilding the entire system after a collapse. BCB relied on liberalisation, privatisation, and the restructuring of the banking sector in order to make the system more solid and prevent the devastation that could be brought about by a financial collapse. There was much to be accomplished in respect of foreign entry into the banking sector (made difficult by the 1988 Federal Constitution) and the privatisation of public state-owned banks in order to complete the restructuring sought by the BCB. The PROER and PROES programmes are two policy plans used to achieve BCB's objectives (Maia, 1999).

In November 1995, PROER (the Program of Incentives to the Restructuring and Strengthening of the National Financial System) was created as a set of preventative measures that the BCB could take in the instance of a troubled private bank. This programme aimed to preserve the solvency of the financial system by removing distressed banks and bolstering those that remained. One important feature of the programme was that the former controlling owners had to abandon their controls over the assisted bank. Furthermore, PROER provided a system of tax incentives and credit facilities to encourage the rapid consolidation of the banking system through mergers and acquisitions (M&As). It set up a special line of financial assistance targeted at financial and other reorganisations that resulted in the transfer of control or the modification of a financial institution's corporate objective. PROER was funded through compulsory deposits from financial institutions, meaning that in principle the programme had no impact on the fiscal budget. Participating institutions could defer their restructuring or modernisation expenses for ten semesters in order to be freed up temporarily to implement the operational limits of the Basle I Accord. In an effort to promote the rapid consolidation of the banking sector, which would ideally lead to greater stability, PROER advanced tax incentives and credit facilities to participating institutions. Banks that were acquiring troubled institutions were given a line of credit below the market interest rate, and they were allowed to absorb the financial losses of the troubled institution on its balance sheet through tax write-offs. Two of the prime instances of the use of PROER funds are the acquisition of Banco Nacional by Unibanco and the acquisition of Banco Econômico by Banco Excel. Later in 1997 the British bank HSBC acquired Bamerindus, at that time one of the greatest domestic private banks in Brazil. Table 10.1 gives a list of the acquisitions that were made with the support of PROER.

November 1995, a month of sweeping resolutions addressing the problems in the banking system, also saw the creation of the Credit Guarantee Fund (FGC). With the establishment of the FGC came the guarantee of up to R$20,000 for every deposit or investment titleholder in the case of a government intervention, out-of-court liquidation, bankruptcy, or perception on the part of BCB of a state of insolvency in any financial institution after the beginning of the Real Plan. All financial institutions were required to contribute 0.024 per cent of all balances in accounts covered by the FGC, and this guarantee had the effect of

Table 10.1   Mergers and acquisitions with incentives of PROER

Acquired bank	Purchaser	Official date
Banco Nacional	Unibanco*	18.11.1995
Banco Econômico	Banco Excel*	30.04.1996
Banco Mercantil	Banco Rural*	31.05.1996
Banco Banorte	Banco Bandeirantes*	17.06.1996
Banco Martinelli	Banco Pontual*	23.08.1996
Banco United	Banco Antônio de Queiroz*	30.08.1996
Bamerindus do Brasil	HSBC	02.04.1997

Source: Central Bank of Brazil.
(*) Domestic private banks.

increasing public confidence in the banking system and preventing runs on banks which were thought to be in a fragile state. Public confidence in the system was crucial to the restoration of its health, and the deposit insurance provided by the FGC created enough peace of mind to prevent crippling public runs on banks.

While PROER was used to deal with troubled private banks, the BCB created the PROES (Program of Incentives for the Reduction of the States' Participation in Banking Activities) in August 1996 (Provisory Measure no. 1514) with the aim of reducing public sector participation in the financial system under an overall strategy of forcing a fiscal adjustment of the states and the restructuring of their debt. There were a number of options for state banks under PROES. A public state-owned bank could use PROES to: (i) help transform the public state-owned bank into a non-financial institution of development agency; (ii) finance the restructuring of state banks with the end goal of subsequent privatisation; or (iii) finance up to 50 per cent of the cost of restructuring the state bank that is recapitalised by the state government (Baer, 2008, p. 145). In practice, the federal government offered to reschedule state governments' debts in order to persuade public state-owned banks to be 'federalised', at which point the federal government would either reorganize the bank for sale to a private institution or liquidate the institution. Under the PROER arrangements, a lot of state-owned banks were purchased by private domestic banks by foreign banks (Table 10.2).

With the use of PROER and PROES, and also as a result of the wave of banking mergers and acquisitions that followed these programmes, the period from 1995 to 2002 saw a clear reduction in the number of banks. Private and public banks alike saw decreases in the number of institutions (Figure 10.2).

Table 10.2 Privatisation of state-owned banks

Date	Acquired bank	Purchaser bank	Value (R$ million)	Ágio (%)
26.06.1997	Banerj	Itaú	311	0.4
07.08.1997	Credireal	BCN	121	0.0
04.12.1997	Meridional	Bozano, Simonsen	266	55.0
14.09.1998	Bemge	Itaú	583	85.7
17.11.1998	Bandepe	ABN Amro	183	0.0
22.06.1998	Baneb	Bradesco	260	3.2
17.10.2000	Banestado	Itaú	1625	303.2
20.11.2000	Banespa	Santander	7050	281.1

Source: Rocha (2001, p. 10).

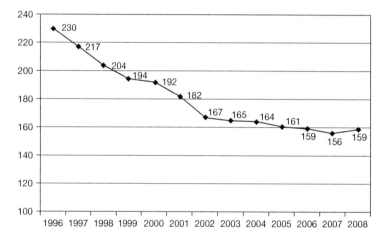

Figure 10.2 Number of banks
Source: Central Bank of Brazil.

During and after the 1994–95 period, many new national policies, apart from PROER and PROES, were implemented in an attempt to strengthen the Brazilian banking system. Many banks, including very large ones like Banco Nacional, were turning to BCB for assistance, and it was soon realised that in order to prevent a devastating systemic crisis, the system must be made more stable. One way to make the system more solid was for the BCB to provide more regulation and stricter guidelines to banking institutions. Up until the mid-1990s, financial regulation in Brazil was focused strongly on the liabilities of banking institutions, including a minimum capital and net equity requirement, a limit on the diversification of risks, a limit of immobilisation, and a limit on indebtedness. The aim of the BCB was to provide more liquidity for institutions facing problems with the end result of preparing them for tighter regulation and, in many instances, BCB intervention. By the time of the Real Plan, the focus on regulation had shifted from liability transactions to risk-weighted asset transactions.

While interventionist financial regulation measures were crucial in keeping the Brazilian banking system operating up until the early 1990s, Brazilian policymakers made a key shift to the idea of prudential regulation in the mid-1990s. The idea behind prudential regulation is to provide incentive measures to banks to operate in sustainable and profitable ways rather than to use direct intervention. Prudential regulation implies establishing policies for banks' behaviour and calling for the disclosure of information. This requirement of the disclosure of information, through quarterly statements and according to international reporting standards, as well as the presence of monitoring and supervisory bodies, deters banks from taking certain and great risks. The idea is to incentivise efficiency and financial innovation, thus making it in a banks' interest to operate according to prudential regulation standards. The rationale behind this new kind of regulation (the Basel Accord) was that the threat to a financial institution and to the system as a whole arises from the risks taken in the banks' investments, so it was necessary to link equity capital to the size of the risks the institution was taking.

One attempt to provide strength in the system through prudential regulation was in the promise of the implementation of the international standards of the Basel I requirements in 1994/1995, which stipulated that banks increase the amount of equity they are mandated to hold. The Basel Accord was incorporated to the Brazilian regulation by some National Monetary Council (*Conselho Monetário Nacional*) resolutions, which established the minimum capital requirements ratio weighted by risk of the bank's asset operations in 11 per cent. Basel I was implemented to strengthen the financial system, but the fragility of the system actually increased in Brazil after its implementation, because profits were already diminishing, becoming negative in some cases, and holding extra capital was a luxury that struggling institutions could not afford. This is where BCB intervention and liquidity provision, through measures like PROER, allowed for the continued restructuring of troubled banks. Brazil's banks surpass the level of capital requirement set forth in Basel I, and this level of capital requirements helped keep the Brazilian banking system afloat during a time of seemingly impending crisis. We can note in Table 10.3 that Brazil in the period 2003–08 has a very high Basel Ratio when compared to the other countries and far above the Brazil's minimum capital requirements ratio weighted of 11 per cent (Table 10.3). One of the reasons is that Brazilian banks portfolio is constituted partly by public bonds, that have zero risk. Anyway, one should consider that there was a credit boom in Brazil during 2004–08 that contributed to the reduction of the ratio, although it was kept in a very high level for international standards.

Prior to the 1990s, there were restrictions placed on foreign entry into the Brazilian banking system. The Federal Constitution of 1988 made foreign entry an unclear issue, but it kept open the possibility of foreign financial institutions having access to the domestic market through special Congressional or presidential decisions made in the interest of the Brazilian government. Within this legal context, Legislative Intent no. 311 of 23 August 1995 allowed the president to exceptionally authorise, on a case-by-case basis, the entrance of foreign banks in Brazil in response to the need to strengthen the financial system after the 1995 banking distress and also to help incorporate international experience of banking supervision into the domestic financial system. Because of the instability of the banking system in the 1990s, the Brazilian government decided it was in its interests to stimulate foreign entry and to adopt it as a policy.

With foreign entry would come increased competition, and it was believed that foreign institutions were more efficient than their domestic counterparts. Thus, foreign banks were supposed to help make Brazil's banks more competitive in order to reduce banking spread and to increase credit supply, but this did not happen as quickly as expected.

Table 10.3   Basel ratio in selected countries (%)

Country	2003	2004	2005	2006	2007	2008	2003–2008
Argentina	14.5	14.0	15.3	16.8	16.8	16.8	15.7
Australia	10.0	10.4	10.4	10.4	10.2	10.5	10.3
Brazil	19.0	18.5	17.4	17.4	17.3	17.5	17.9
Chile	14.1	13.6	13.0	12.5	12.2	12.4	13.0
Mexico	14.4	14.1	14.5	16.3	16.0	16.0	15.2
Spain	12.6	12.3	12.2	11.9	11.4	n.a.	12.1
Canada	13.4	13.3	12.9	12.5	12.1	12.3	12.8
South Africa	12.4	14.0	12.7	12.3	12.8	n.a.	12.8

Source: Central Bank of Brazil (2009, p. 61).

Although the evidence shows the foreign banks behaving even more conservatively in terms of portfolio allocation than the domestic private banks in Brazil (Carvalho, 2000; Paula and Alves Jr., 2003), evidence also shows that domestic private banks reacted the foreign bank entry increasing their operational efficiency (Faria Jr et al., 2007).[6]

Of notable interest was the high level of Merger and Acquisitions (M&A) activity on the part of some of the domestic private banks in operations that involved public state-owned banks and medium-sized domestic private and even foreign banks. For example, among others, Itau acquired the state banks Banerj, BEMGE, BANESTADO and BEG, and the private banks Fiat, BBA, BankBoston; Bradesco acquired, among others, BCN/Credireal, Boavista, Ford, Mercantil de Sao Paulo and BBV Banco; Unibanco acquired Nacional, Bandeirantes and Fininvest, and in 2008 mergered with Itaú, that became by far the biggest private bank in Brazil, disputing the leadership with Banco do Brasil, the federal government-owned bank. Some studies comparing efficiency (measured in terms of operational efficiency or profitability performance) between foreign banks and private domestic banks in the recent period show that, on the whole, the latter performed better than the former.[7]

We consider four factors that contributed to the reaction of domestic private banks to the entry of foreign banks into the Brazilian banking sector. First, the fact that the 1995 banking distress did not cause a banking crisis as had been the case for Argentina and Mexico, meant that the domestic private banks that had survived such distress – for example, Itaú, Bradesco and Unibanco – could take part actively in the wave of banking M&As in Brazil. Indeed, the rapid response of the BCB avoided banking distress becoming a systemic crisis. Second, the fact that such banks accumulated technological and management capabilities during the high inflation period so that they are used to dealing with unstable macroeconomic situations, as was the case with the effects of the 1997 Asian crisis, 1998 Russian crisis, and the 2002–03 Brazilian confidence crisis. Third, as we have already stressed, foreign bank entry was restricted in Brazil – that is, the permission for foreign banks was carried out on a case-by-case basis. Compared with Argentina and Mexico, the opening up of the banking sector was much less dramatic in Brazil. In this concern, Martinez-Diaz (2005, p. 34) concluded that

> one of the most important differences between the two cases is that Mexican policymakers had clearly articulated beliefs about the nature and degree of liberalization they saw as desirable, while Brazilian official were more improvisational and had few a priori expectations

of how liberalization should proceed. Brazilian policymakers also appeared less concerned with the ostensible long-term benefits of foreign bank presence and were far more interested in the short-term benefits of foreign participation, namely higher prices for privatized state banks and lower costs to the central bank for recapitalization.

Fourth, and more importantly, one should consider the way that public debt was managed in Brazil during the external crises: the Brazilian government offered the banking sector (which was the main buyer of public securities) hedges against exchange devaluation and interest rate changes, by offering them securities indexed to the exchange rate and the overnight interest rate. Consequently, notwithstanding severely restrictive macroeconomic conditions, the banks could adopt a conservative financial posture, i.e. a high proportion of government securities in their portfolio, low levels of mismatch between assets and liabilities and low leverage levels. On average, in the period 1998–2005 the share of public securities in total banking assets was around 40 per cent (Table 10.4). Therefore, banks were able to afford risk aversion strategies, thanks to the availability of high-yielding, relatively risk-free government securities as an alternative to private sector lending. The Brazilian banking sector did not face the classical liquidity-versus-profitability trade-off, as the institutional-macroeconomic

Table 10.4 Banks' portfolio (percentage share)

End of period	Loans-to-total assets				Securities-to-total assets			
	DP	FE	PB	Total	DP	FE	PB	Total
1998	42.25	38.77	54.52	44.94	35.90	38.48	32.90	39.48
1999	43.20	42.47	52.08	45.27	36.37	36.75	32.19	38.35
2000	47.17	43.00	53.95	47.87	35.96	43.34	29.22	37.79
2001	49.86	45.80	35.86	43.52	33.26	43.53	48.14	43.78
2002	47.43	47.74	32.33	41.18	35.43	39.04	48.01	43.47
2003	47.45	50.69	32.56	40.56	36.39	36.61	50.17	45.35
2004	50.07	50.12	36.60	43.48	31.37	36.84	45.09	41.50
2005	50.95	51.27	37.95	44.02	29.24	36.88	46.35	41.75
2006	48.67	54.64	41.46	46.06	30.82	35.18	43.70	39.82
2007	46.30	60.60	41.25	47.02	32.73	28.18	44.05	38.40
2008	46.68	56.49	46.43	49.39	34.26	28.45	43.95	37.27

Notes: DP: domestic private banks (Bradesco, Itaú, Safra and Unibanco); FE: foreign banks (ABN Amro, BankBoston, Citibank, HSBC, Santander); PB: public banks (Banco do Brasil, CEF and Nossa Caixa).
Source: Central Bank of Brazil.

context afforded an environment with the scope for banks to combine liquidity *and* profitability. This is the explanation of why the external crisis did not cause a banking crisis in Brazil, at the costs of public finance deterioration in terms of increasing public debt.[8]

Finally, we should consider the credit boom of 2004–08 under the environment of economic growth that benefited from the benign international context (a commodities boom and high liquidity levels in the international financial market) (Figure 10.3). Credit-to-GDP increased from 21.8 per cent in March 2003 to more than 40 per cent in 2009. Indeed, although the bank spread reduced in the period as the result of some decline in the Selic interest rate, it was very high by international standards (more than 30 per cent in 2000–09), so that banks could take advantage of an environment that combined an increase in the volume of credit with high bank spread – a combination that resulted in high banks' profitability.

As a result of these factors (the privatisation of public state-owned banks, the entry of foreign banks, the reaction of domestic private banks, and the way in which macroeconomic policies have been managed in Brazil) in the Brazilian banking sector there were significant changes in the market share by shareholder control in Brazil: government-owned banks

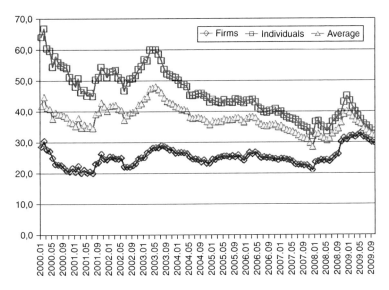

Figure 10.3 Bank spread (%)
Source: Central Bank of Brazil.

Table 10.5 Market share by shareholder control (in percentage of total assets)

Banking segment	Dec/96	Dec/97	Dec/98	Dec/99	Dec/00	Dec/01	Dec/02	Dec/03	Dec/04	Dec/05	Dec/06
Public banks*	21.9	19.1	11.4	10.2	5.6	4.3	5.9	5.8	5.5	5.1	4.5
Banco do Brasil	12.5	14.4	17.4	15.8	15.6	16.8	17.1	18.4	17.4	15.4	14.5
Caixa Econômica Federal	16.5	16.6	17.0	17.1	15.4	11.0	11.7	13.0	11.5	12.1	10.7
Government-owned banks	50.9	50.1	45.8	43.0	36.6	32.0	34.7	37.2	34.4	32.5	29.6
Domestic private banks	38.3	36.8	35.3	33.1	35.2	37.2	36.9	40.8	41.7	43.1	47.1
Foreign banks	10.5	12.8	18.4	23.2	27.4	29.9	27.4	20.7	22.4	22.9	21.7
Credit cooperatives	0.3	0.4	0.5	0.7	0.8	0.9	1.0	1.3	1.4	1.5	1.5
Total	100.0	100.0	100.0	100.0	100.0	100.0	100.0	100.0	100.0	100.0	100.0

Source: Central Bank of Brazil.
(*) Except Banco do Brasil and Caixa Economica Federal.

(at both the federal and state levels) reduced the relative share in total banks' assets from 50.9 per cent in 1996 to 29.6 per cent in 2006; foreign banks increased their share from 12.5 per cent in 1996 to 29.9 per cent in 2001, reducing since then to 21.7 per cent in 2006; domestic private banks reduced their share from 38.3 per cent in 1996 to 33.1 per cent in 1999, and increased steadily to 47.6 per cent in 2006 (Table 10.5).

Summing up our analysis in this section, we have seen that the end of high inflation following the implementation of the Real Plan in 1994 was a solution to one of the most long-standing problems in the Brazilian economy. At the same time, it had the effect of bringing the banking sector to the brink of a systemic crisis. The BCB could no longer rely on its older regulatory measures, which were more interventionist, to fix the situation of the mid-1990s. In addition to using programmes like PROER and PROES to intervene directly in troubled banks and to provide liquidity to the system, that avoided the spread of a banking crisis in 1995–96, the government quickly developed policies in accordance with the new international idea of a prudential regulation apparatus. Using prudential regulation, incentives were used rather than interventions, and preventative actions could be taken to avoid future systemic crises. At the same time that prudential regulation took hold in Brazil, foreign entry also began to increase in the banking sector. The regulated and limited entry of foreign banks provided an increased level of competition, which helped Brazilian banks to decrease their operational costs and increase efficiency under the new macroeconomic conditions. However, the penetration of foreign banks was limited in Brazil so that the banking sector did not experience such severe problems related to the internationalisation of the domestic market as had been experienced in Argentina in 2002–03. The Brazilian banking system effectively avoided a systemic crisis in the mid-1990s, and it developed a solid framework of prudential regulation that has allowed it to weather financial shocks fairly well since this time. More importantly, the management of the public debt under the context of external contagions allowed the Brazilian banks to compose their portfolio combining liquidity with profitability.

Regarding specifically the changes in banking supervision that were implemented during the restructuring process, it is important to notice that the Brazilian Central Bank and the Ministry of Finance suggested that the fragility could not be considered to be solely a feature of the banks. The supervisory laws could also be considered inadequate during a period of price stability (Moura, 1998). Thus, we may say that the restructuring introduced by the Brazilian banking system in the aftermath of

Table 10.6 Return on equity (%)

End of period	Return on equity (ROE)			
	DP	FB	PB	Total[1]
1999	20.8	16.6	11.1	17.0
2000	20.5	11.7	12.6	11.1
2001	23.3	−24.8	−23.6	−1.4
2002	18.8	31.3	22.3	20.7
2003	16.6	10.7	22.5	15.9
2004	23.4	10.1	20.9	17.6
2005	26.9	14.0	25.8	21.5
2006	21.7	14.5	27.3	20.9
2007	22.5	23.6	20.9	22.7
2008	21.3	8.7	29.1	17.9

Source: Central Bank of Brazil.
Notes: DP: domestic private banks (Bradesco, Itaú, Safra and Unibanco); FB: foreign banks (ABN Amro, BankBoston, Citibank, HSBC and Santander); PB: public banks (Banco do Brasil, CEF and Nossa Caixa).
1. Total is related to the banking sector as a whole.

the Real Plan helped to create a more resilient system that was able to deal with changes in the nation's financial sector.

3 The contagion effect of the 2008 financial crisis on the Brazilian economy

In the final quarter of 2008, following the bankruptcy of Lehman Brothers, the financial crisis spread around the world, and reached the Brazilian economy. The contagion effect of the crisis to the Brazilian economy was mainly by the external accounts and credit market.[9]

Concerning the external accounts, the contagion from the financial crisis hit Brazil through a number of transmission channels. The most immediate channel was through the capital flows related to the portfolio investments and other investments that changed sharply from a high surplus up to September 2008 to a deep deficit in the fourth quarter of 2008, under an environment of increasing risk aversion on the part of foreign investors and banks. There was an enormous reversal in the flow of foreign capital in the fourth quarter of 2008, as a result of portfolio investments and other investments; FDI remained high in this quarter (US$14.2 billion), but fell sharply in the first quarter of 2009 – to US$5.4 billion. The transmission of capital flight to the stock market (BOVESPA) was immediate, with a sharp fall in equities prices traded on the secondary market, in consequence of the significant participation of foreign investors (institutional investors) in this market. Concerning the portfolio investments, as can be seen from Figure 10.4, there was a deficit in foreign investments in equities of US$6.1 billion in October 2008, and a deficit in debt securities abroad of US$4.9 billion in December 2008, as a result of the risk aversion and increase in the liquidity preference around the world. On the other hand, other investments (foreign loans and finance) changed from a surplus of US$8.4 billion in the third quarter of 2008 to a deficit of US$19.6 billion in the fourth quarter of 2008. The reduction in foreign credit had a particular effect upon the financing of exports.

Secondly, the 2008 financial crisis also affected the performance of the current account because of its impact on investment income which, as we have already stressed, had an increased tendency since 2005, due to the increase in the stock of foreign liabilities, which resulted from the structural characteristics of the Brazilian economy (a high degree of internationalisation of the manufacturing sector and financial openness) and some conjectural reasons (the overvaluation of the Brazilian currency). Following the spread of the financial crisis, this tendency was accentuated in consequence of the rise in the remittance of profits and

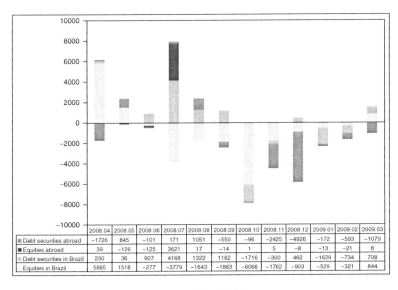

	2008.04	2008.05	2008.06	2008.07	2008.08	2008.09	2008.10	2008.11	2008.12	2009.01	2009.02	2009.03
Debt securities abroad	−1726	845	−101	171	1051	−550	−96	−2425	−4926	−172	−593	−1079
Equities abroad	39	−126	−125	3621	17	−14	1	5	−8	−13	−21	8
Debt securities in Brazil	230	36	907	4168	1322	1182	−1716	−300	462	−1629	−734	708
Equities in Brazil	5865	1518	−277	−3779	−1643	−1863	−6066	−1762	−903	−529	−321	844

Figure 10.4   Portfolio investments in 2008–2009
Source: Central Bank of Brazil.

dividends by the subsidiaries of firms and banks to their headquarters in order to compensate for the losses in other markets, as well as to provide financial resources to the corporations because of the difficulties related to the rollover of the credit operations (IEDI, 2009). This former trend had begun to operate since the beginning of the subprime crisis in EUA. As a consequence, income investments increased from US$29.7 billion in 2007 to US$41.1 billion in 2008. A further determinant of the deterioration of current account was the decline in the price of commodities since the middle of 2008 as a result of the fall in world demand. Following the bankruptcy of Lehman Brothers, which threatened the stability of the entire world economy, there were also effects on manufacturing exports. Indeed, exports declined from US$60.2 billion in the fourth quarter of 2008 to US$47.1 billion in the third quarter of 2008 and US$31.2 billion in the first quarter of 2009.

The reversal in capital flows exerted strong pressure on the exchange rate, which depreciated by 42.6 per cent from 1 September to 31 December 2008. In the final quarter of 2008 BCB sold US$23 billion of its international reserves and offered foreign exchange swaps in order to provide a hedge against the depreciation of the currency. According to Hoff (2009, p. 129), BCB sold a volume of around US$10 billion up to the deficit of the foreign exchange market, providing the necessary supply for the banks cover their purchaser position. Furthermore BCB also provided an special line of credit for exporters (in dollars), using foreign exchange reserves as funding for this operation. One further factor that contributed to the pressure on the foreign exchange market was the existence of 'toxic derivatives', the name given to the foreign exchange derivatives operation carried out by exporters that placed a bet on the continuity of the appreciation of the exchange rate. When Brazil suffered from the contagion of the financial crisis, they were affected adversely by the sharp depreciation that took place in September–October 2008; on that occasion it was announced the losses of two big exporters with 'toxic derivatives', Aracruz and Perdigao, and the Brazilian press also divulged that large numbers of average firms was involved in such operations, with a total volume estimated by R$ 60.5 billion.[10] According to OECD (2009, p. 26): 'Central-banks intervention in the foreign-exchange markets were aimed essentially at enhancing liquidity, rather than defending a particular level of the exchange rate. Most interventions focused on the sale of foreign exchange swaps to support enterprises and banks in their efforts to liquidate positions in foreign-exchange derivatives.' From January 2009, however, capital outflows began to reduce, and at the same time the foreign exchange fluxes associated with the commercial segment were retaking; consequently, the exchange rate stopped to rise and retook its appreciation trend (Figure 10.5).

According to IEDI (2009), Brazil was assisted by some actions of the federal government that were carried out before the international financial crisis. These resulted in some mechanisms that reduced the extent of contagion from the crisis: (i) Trade balance still high, although declining in 2008; (ii) Foreign exchange reserves up to US$200 million in 2008; (iii) The combination between the previous government's reduction of its external debt and the increase in foreign exchange reserves resulted in government's net credit position in foreign currency, so that a exchange rate devaluation benefited public finances. For the first time since the 1980s an external crisis did not result in a fiscal deterioration in Brazil. Therefore, these mechanisms prevented the contagion from the international financial crisis bringing about a balance of payments crisis.

In addition to the effect of the contagion on the balance of payments, another important transmission channel of the international financial crisis was the domestic credit market. The most immediate effect was the reduction in the volume of international credit operations, which had an impact on the modalities of corporate credit that are supplied, backed by foreign funding, as export finance. A further mechanism of contagion was the reduction in the cross-border credit

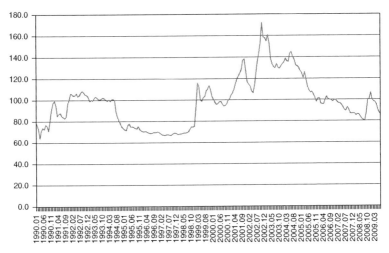

Figure 10.5   Real effective exchange rate[11] (1994=100)
Source: IPEADATA.

operations as a result of the reallocation portfolio of international banks. This mechanism affected, in particular, the direct credit operations of firms on the international financial market. On the other hand, the overall deterioration of expectations related to the future as a result of the spread of the financial crisis combined with the uncertain environment in relation to the volume of losses and the firms involved in foreign exchange derivatives increased the liquidity preference that contributed to the slowdown in the interbank market and the reduction of domestic credit.[12] As a consequence of the shortfall in capital inflows to the Brazilian economy, the banking system – principally the banks in the middle market – faced increased difficulties in borrowing money from abroad to fund their credit operations. The credit squeeze placed those banks in danger as they faced increasing difficulties borrowing money on the Brazilian interbank market since the liquid banks had increased their levels of risk aversion and, thus, decided to ration the credit to less liquid middle institutions. Accordingly, despite the fact that the Brazilian banking system did not – either directly or indirectly – trade securities linked to the subprime market, one may say that this system entered in a liquidity crisis that almost led to a confidence crisis.

The reduction in the growth rate of the credit supply was more marked in the case of firms compared to individuals' credit. According to IEDI (2009), the growth rate of firms' credit reduced from 45.0 per cent in September 2008 (compared with September 2007) to 39.2 per cent in December 2008 (compared with December 2007). The reduction in the growth of the credit supply was led by non-channelled credit, while channelled credit (agricultural credit, BNDES' long-term credit for investment, real estate credit, and so on) provided principally by public federal-owned banks increased after the contagion of the financial crisis.[13] Indeed, state-owned banks (BNDES, Caixa Economica Federal and Banco do Brasil) exhibited counter-cyclical behaviour, expanding channelled credit and also buying up the credit portfolios of some small to average-sized banks, which were experiencing funding difficulties during the contagious phase of the financial crisis: the state-owned banks total credit-to-GDP ratio increased from 12.5 per cent in August 2008 to 17.3 per cent in July 2009, while domestic private banks' total credit-to-GDP and foreign banks; total credit-to-GDP increased only from 16.2 per cent and 7.7 per cent to 17.6 per cent and 8.3 per cent, respectively, in the same period (Figure 10.6). Therefore, the increase in loans by public federal-owned banks compensated – at least in part – for the deceleration in the credit supply by private banks.

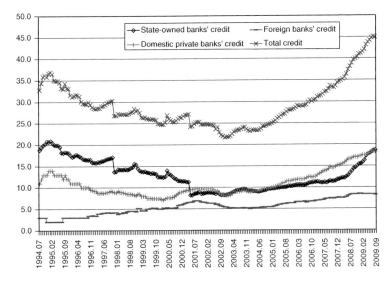

Figure 10.6 Domestic credit-over-GDP (%)
Source: Central Bank of Brazil.

The drop in economic activity after the contagion effect of the global economic crisis was driven principally by the industrial sector, which experienced average negative growth of 7.0 per cent in IV/2008–III/2009 (Figure 10.7), resulting in both declines in the level of final consumption (household consumption and government consumption) and the gross formation of capital (which includes investment and stock levels), and since the first quarter of 2009 also by a reduction in the exports of manufacturing goods (Figure 10.8). GDP growth (measured in comparison to the former trimester) had a negative performance in the fourth quarter of 2008 (–2.9 per cent) and in the first quarter of 2009 (–0.9 per cent), and then shows signs of recovery in the second quarter of 2009 (1.1 per cent). However, when GDP growth is measured in comparison to the same quarter in the previous year, the recovery has been sluggish. In 2009 almost all of determinants of demand contributed to the reduction in GDP growth, with the exception of final consumption which contributed positively and increasingly to the growth of the economy. Final consumption was encouraged by government measures oriented towards stimulating the consumption of durable goods and also by the increase of 3.9 per cent in the average of real income in 2009 compared with the average in 2008.[14]

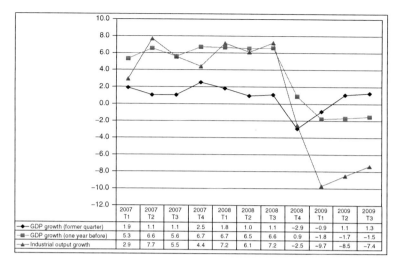

Figure 10.7 GDP growth in 2007–2009
Source: Central Bank of Brazil.

	2007 T1	2007 T2	2007 T3	2007 T4	2008 T1	2008 T2	2008 T3	2008 T4	2009 T1	2009 T2	2009 T3
GDP growth (former quarter)	1.9	1.1	1.1	2.5	1.8	1.0	1.1	−2.9	−0.9	1.1	1.3
GDP growth (one year before)	5.3	6.6	5.6	6.7	6.7	6.5	6.6	0.9	−1.8	−1.7	−1.5
Industrial output growth	2.9	7.7	5.5	4.4	7.2	6.1	7.2	−2.5	−9.7	−8.5	−7.4

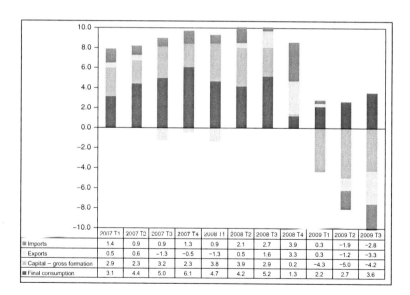

	2007 T1	2007 T2	2007 T3	2007 T4	2008 T1	2008 T2	2008 T3	2008 T4	2009 T1	2009 T2	2009 T3
Imports	1.4	0.9	0.9	1.3	0.9	2.1	2.7	3.9	0.3	−1.9	−2.8
Exports	0.5	0.6	−1.3	−0.5	−1.3	0.5	1.6	3.3	0.3	−1.2	−3.3
Capital – gross formation	2.9	2.3	3.2	2.3	3.8	3.9	2.9	0.2	−4.3	−5.0	−4.2
Final consumption	3.1	4.4	5.0	6.1	4.7	4.2	5.2	1.3	2.2	2.7	3.6

Figure 10.8 Contribution to GDP growth in 2007–2009
Source: Central Bank of Brazil.

Brazilian authorities responded to the financial crisis by adopting a number of counter-cyclical measures:[15]

(a) The BCB adopted a number of liquidity-enhancing measures, principally between October 2008 and January 2009, which included a reduction in the level of compulsory reserve holdings by banks, and also the creation of incentives for larger financial institutions to purchase the loan portfolios of smaller banks, which were affected by worsening credit conditions.[16]

(b) As we have stressed already, the BCB did intervene in the foreign exchange markets that aimed principally to enhance liquidity in the banking sector, rather than defending a particular level of exchange rate.

(c) After the increase in interest rates to 13.75 per cent in September 2008, left unchanged for the remainder of the year,[17] monetary policy began to be relaxed in January 2009, with a cumulative reduction of 450 basis points in January–June 2009 – that is, a reduction until 9.25 per cent.

(d) As we have seen, public federally owned banks were encouraged to expand their credit operations, performing a counter-cyclical policy in the credit market.

(e) The Ministry of Finance have introduced a number of fiscal measures in order to stimulate aggregate demand. These include a reduction in the industrialized products tax (IPI) burden on motor vehicles and on a wide range of consumer durables and construction items, and also an increase in the duration of unemployment insurance and in government support for housing.

Liquidity-enhancing measures were expected to increase the supply of money in the economy by US$22 billion. In fact, the Brazilian Central Bank promised to increase the supply of money by US$50 billion through the introduction of these measures. In this respect, of particular note is the decision of the government to allow the two largest public commercial banks (Banco do Brasil and Caixa Econômica Federal) to acquire stakes in private financial institutions without any need for public bid. The aim of this measure was not principally to support small financial institutions, but to ensure a greater supply of credit. Another incentive to increase the supply of credit to private financial institutions was a penalty on the reserve requirement of time deposits. The reserves that depositary institutions should hold against time deposits consisted of public securities that pay interest on required reserve balances.

The new measure led the Brazilian Central Bank to cease to pay interest on 70 per cent these funds as long as the biggest institutions avoid to advance credit and/or to acquire credit operations of smallest banks (and other financial institutions).

Together with those incentive measures, the government also decided to increase directly the credit supply of the economy through new credit lines at the Brazilian National Development Bank (BNDES) and the Banco do Brasil. Those lines were advanced to fund investment expenses and to finance working capital. At the same time, the government created new credit lines at Caixa Econômica Federal to finance the acquisition of consumer goods.

By the end of 2008, the government had turned its attention to the performance of GDP. As a consequence, some fiscal measures were implemented, in order to incentivise the consumer and investment expenses such as the reduction of the financial operations tax to finance the acquisition of consumer goods from 3.38 per cent to 0.38 per cent. One of the main measures was the reduction in both income tax and the tax on manufactured goods (IPI). On the other hand, the primary surplus target was reduced to 2.5 per cent of GDP against the previous 3.8 per cent, giving more fiscal room to increasing government spending to offset the negative impact of the financial turmoil.

Finally, in the middle of 2009 the government decided to reduce the annual long-term rate of interest (TJLP) from 6.25 per cent to 6 per cent, helping to facilitate the advance of long-term credit supply by the Brazilian National Development Bank (BNDES).

In summary, the Brazilian government had instruments to face the effects of the global financial crisis that contributed to the rapid recovery of the economy, although the contagion of the crisis had been sharp and deep. According to CEPAL (2009), in a survey of Latin American countries, Brazil was one of the few to make use of a wide variety of tools to face the effects of the financial crisis.

5   Conclusion: lessons to be learned

The main lessons to be learned from the 2008 crisis regarding the behaviour of the Brazilian banking system are:

(a) A strong prudential regulation seems to be very important, although too much prudential regulation could harm the system, affecting negatively its efficiency;

(b) The entry of foreign banks, at least in the case of the Brazilian banks system, did not seem to play a decisive role;

(c) Public federal-owned banks played a decisive counter-cyclical role during the contagious period of the financial crisis on the Brazilian economy, showing that their presence can be decisive in coping with adverse situations in the credit markets;

(d) A high degree of openness is not necessarily good. In fact, since the Brazilian banking system has been strongly domestically oriented and has a low degree of openness, it has avoided becoming engaged in financial operations with a high risk/return relationship;

(e) The 'too big too fail' philosophy leads to the moral hazard problem, but the alternative is not to let the bigger banks fail. It is definitely necessary to avoid a systemic crisis;

(f) The relaxation of prudential regulation does not seem to be positively related to the increase of credit supply. Actually, banks seem more prone to be engaged in more risk operations as a consequence of the relaxation in the regulation.

Notes

1. In Brazil, the Real Plan (1994–99) was conceived on the same basis as stabilisation programmes with an exchange anchor that have been applied in Latin America since the late 1980s, using a fixed or semi-fixed rate of exchange in combination with more open trade policy as a price anchor. It differed from Argentina's Convertibility Plan by adopting a more flexible exchange anchor; that is, a typical currency board system, rather than pegging the domestic currency at one-to-one parity with the US dollar. At the outset of the Brazilian programme, in July 1994, the government's commitment was to maintain an exchange rate ceiling of one-to-one parity with the dollar. Moreover, the relationship between changes in monetary base and foreign reserve movements was not stated explicitly, allowing some discretionary leeway. Following the effects of the Mexican crisis, the exchange rate policy was reviewed and in a context of a crawling exchange rate band the nominal rate began to undergo gradual devaluation. In early 1999, however, after six months of speculative pressure, the *real* was devalued and, some days later, the Brazilian government adopted a floating exchange rate. For a general analysis of the origins and development of the Real Plan, see Ferrari-Filho and Paula (2003).

2. According to Bresser-Pereira and Ferrer (1991, p.10), in Argentina both M1 and M4 (which includes M1 plus financial assets) have decreased since the late 1970s. In February 1990, M1 was less than 3 per cent of GDP, while M4 was less than 5 per cent of GDP, because economic agents reallocated their portfolios to the dollar. Alternatively, in Brazil, accelerating inflation decreased M1 from the early 1970s, but M4 remained stable as a consequence of the supply of domestically denominated indexed money. According to data from BCB, the ratio M1/GDP and the ratio M4/GDP were 9.2 per cent and 25.1 per cent in 1980, respectively, while in 1993 they were 1.3 per cent and 23.1 per cent, respectively.

3. Selic rate is the interest rate for overnight interbank loans, collateralised by those government bonds that are registered with and traded on the 'Sistema Especial de Liquidação e Custodia' (Selic). It serves as the short-term prime interest rate of the Brazilian economy, and for this reason it is used as the reference – that is, as the operational variable – for monetary policy purposes by the BCB.
4. Firstly, the Brazilian government implemented a reserve requirement of 100 per cent over sight deposits; later 30 per cent over time deposits and 15 per cent on all types of bank credit operations.
5. For 'public state-owned banks' we are referring to those banks that are controlled by the states. It differs from 'public federal-owned banks' that are controlled by the federal government.
6. Table 10.6 shows that domestic private banks have had a greater return on equity (ROE) than foreign banks in Brazil.
7. See, for instance, Guimarães (2002).
8. Public debt-to-GDP ratio increased from 31.8 per cent in 1997 to 44.5 per cent in 1999, and 52.4 per cent in 2003. It has fallen since this time – for example, to 38.8 per cent in 2008.
9. For a more detailed analysis of the contagion from the financial crisis on the Brazilian economy, see IEDI (2009).
10. Cristiano Romero, 'BC avalia o tamanho do estrago com câmbio', *Valor Econômico*, 15 October 2008, p. A2.
11. Real effective exchange rate (REER) is defined as a nominal effective rate index (index of the period average exchange rate of the currency in question to a weighted average of exchange rates for the currencies of selected countries) adjusted for relative movements in national price of home country and selected countries. It should be stressed that REER in Brazil and other Latin American countries is calculated differently from the most conventional way; that is, REER is calculated by multiplying the nominal exchange rate by the inflation rate of the home country and dividing it by that of a partner country, while, most frequently, REER is calculated by multiplying the nominal exchange rate by the inflation rate of a partner country and dividing by that of the home country. As a result in the case of Brazil when REER increases this results in undervaluation and when it declines results in overvaluation.
12 IEDI (2009) reports that the reduction of the credit supply in Brazil cannot be seen clearly in the data, as the credit-to-GDP ratio increased from 36.4 per cent in September 2008 to 40.0 per cent in January 2009 (data from BCB) the devaluation of the currency increased in domestic currency the foreign credit operations. Furthermore, as the credit supply in the international financial markets 'closed' with the spread of the international financial market, firms' domestic credit demand increased substantially in order to compensate the reduction in overseas markets. Indeed, the total credit-to-GDP ratio increased from 36.4 per cent in August 2008 to 43.3 per cent in July 2009.
13. Total channelled credit-to-GDP increased from 10.5 per cent in September 2008 to 13.7 per cent in August 2008, an increase of almost 3.0 per cent of GDP in just one year.
14. The increase in the average income in 2009 is consequence of a large number of factors, including the real increase in the minimum wage (a basic reference

for salaries and pensioning in Brazil), and increase in the wages of civil servants.

15. For further details, see OECD (2009).

16. Banks were allowed to deduct (up to 70 per cent against an original 40 per cent) from their compulsory time deposits the resources used to purchase loan portfolio from small banks.

17. The BCB increase in the Selic interest rate in September 2008 and the delay in reducing it later in the year was criticised by some analysts, as it contributed to the fall in the overall liquidity of the Brazilian banking sector. This had a negative effect on the credit supply, and, consequently, on the performance of the industrial sector since this was the most affected by the credit constraint (see Oreiro and Araújo, 2009).

References

Baer, W. (2008) *The Brazilian Economy: Growth and Development*. Boulder, CO: Lynne Rienner.

Belaisch, A. (2003) *Do Brazilian Banks Compete?* IMF Working Paper 03/113.

Brazilian Central Bank (2009) *Relatório de Estabilidade Financeira*, 8(1), May.

Bresser-Pereira, L.C. and Ferrer, A. (1991) 'Dolarização crônica: Argentina e Brasil', *Revista de Economia Política*, 11(1), 5–15.

Carvalho, F. (2000) 'New Competitive Strategies of Foreign Banks in Large Emerging Economies: The Case of Brazil', *Banca Nazionale Del Lavoro Quarterly Review*, 213, July.

CEPAL (2009) *Estudio Económico de America Latina y el Caribe 2008–2009*. Santiago del Chile: CEPAL.

Faria Jr, J.A., Paula, L.F. and Marinho, A. (2007) 'Eficiência do setor bancário brasileiro: a experiência recente das fusões e aquisições', in L.F. Paula and J.L. Oreiro (eds), *Sistema Financeiro: Uma Análise do Setor Bancário Brasileiro*. Rio de Janeiro: Campus/Elsevier.

Ferrari-Filho, F. and Paula, L.F. (2003) 'The Legacy of the Real Plan and an Alternative Agenda for the Brazilian Economy', *Investigación Econômica*, 63(244), 57–92.

Guimarães, P. (2002) 'How Does Foreign Entry Affect the Domestic Banking Market? The Brazilian Case', *Latin American Business Review*, 3(4), 121–40.

Hoff, C.R. (2009) *Aprendizado e Desafios do Regime de Câmbio Flutuante no Brasil*. Unpublished doctoral thesis. Rio de Janeiro: UFRJ.

IBGE (1997) *Sistema Financeiro: uma análise a partir das contas nacionais, 1990–1995*. Rio de Janeiro: IBGE/DECNA.

IEDI (2009) 'A crise internacional e a economia brasileira: o efeito-contágio sobre as contas externas e o mercado de crédito em 2008'. São Paulo: IEDI.

IEDI (2010) 'Emprego, setor externo e crédito: uma visão de 2009', *Carta IEDI* no. 399. São Paulo: IEDI.

Maia, G. (1999) 'Restructuring the Banking System – The Case of Brazil', *BIS Policy Papers* 6, 106–23.

Moura, A. (1998) *A Study of the Banking Supervision in Brazil*, Relatório de Pesquisa no. 19. São Paulo: FGV/EAESP/NPP.

OECD (2009) *OECD Economic Surveys: Brazil*. Paris: OECD.

Oreiro, J.L. and Araujo, E. (2009) 'Sim, o Banco Central errou, e muito, na condução da política monetária durante a crise financeira mundial'. Paper presented in the VI Fórum de Economia de São Paulo, FGV-SP, 21–2 September.

Paula, L.F. and Alves Jr., A.J. (2003) 'Banking Behaviour and the Brazilian Economy after the Real Plan: a Post-Keynesian Approach', *Banca Nazionale del Lavoro Quarterly Review*, 227, 337–65.

Puga, F. (1999) The Brazilian Financial System: Recent Restructuring, International Comparisons, and Vulnerability to a Foreign Exchange Crisis. Mimeo.

Rocha, F. (2001) 'Evolução da concentração bancária no Brasil: 1994–2000', Banco Central do Brasil. Brasília. *Notas Técnicas*, no. 11.

11
Exchange-Rate Derivatives, Financial Fragility and Monetary Policy in Brazil during the World Financial Crisis

José Luis Oreiro and Flavio Basilio

1 Introduction

The crisis of subprime mortgages in the United States, which began in mid-2007 and intensified in the last months of 2008 following the bankruptcy of Lehman Brothers, brought an end to the internationally favourable situation the Brazilian economy seems to have taken advantage of in the past few years. Since September 2008, there has been a significant decrease in the level of international liquidity. Credit lines for exports shrank dramatically, slowing down export expansion, while a generalised increase in risk aversion produced an outflow of liquid capital from Brazil of the order of US$11 billion in the months of October to December 2008. Because of capital movements, between July (the valley of the exchange rate series) and December (the peak of the series) 2008, the Brazilian currency was devalued by 50 per cent against the US dollar; the depreciation in the year was 34 per cent. Panic has spread throughout the country's banking system as a combined result of all such factors, leading to a further drastic reduction in credit to families as well as to firms. A consequence of this sort of credit evaporation was a strong deceleration in the growth pace of consumption and the otherwise already announced hold on a number of investment projects. As an overall result, the Brazilian economy experienced a 0.2 per cent fall in its GDP in 2009.

The objective of this chapter is to show that a Minskian crisis occurred in Brazil in the last quarter of 2008 as the result of the burst of a speculative bubble on the exchange rate market in a setting characterised by the widespread use of exchange-rate derivatives by non-financial firms. This speculative bubble was the result of growing confidence about the external robustness of the Brazilian economy in the face of the high level of international reserves, macroeconomic stability and the adoption of a floating exchange rate regime that was supposed to isolate the economy from external shocks. This growing confidence produced a huge exchange rate appreciation which induced non-financial firms to look for alternative sources of income in order to compensate losses in external competitiveness. One of these sources was the use of exchange-rate derivatives as a device for obtaining loans from the banking sector at lower rates. After the bankruptcy of Lehman Brothers, the nominal exchange rate suffered a devaluation of 50 per cent in just a few weeks, causing large losses for non-financial companies in Brazil because of the widespread adoption of these kind of contracts.

Estimates of these losses by the BIS suggest that they could have reached around 2 per cent of Brazilian GDP. Although foreign reserves in Brazil were more than sufficient to achieve the stabilisation of the nominal exchange rate (some US$200 billion just before the crisis), the Brazilian Central Bank allowed a sudden and huge devaluation of the domestic currency, which had destabilising effects on the private sector. As a consequence of these losses, Brazilian banks reduced the rate of credit expansion, producing a large fall of money supply (high powered money and M1). Because of the substantial contraction of money supply and banking credit, industrial output fell by 30 per cent in the last quarter of 2008, bringing about a contraction of almost 14 per cent of GDP.

But the financial fragility caused by exchange-rate derivatives is only one part of the story of the Brazilian crisis. Another important element is the unjustifiable delay of the Brazilian Central Bank to reduce short-term interest rates in an environment of a catastrophic fall in industrial output. Indeed, the Brazilian Central Bank only began the process of reducing short-term interest rates in January 2009, three months after the bankruptcy of Lehman Brothers. This time delay of monetary policy was an important cause of the contraction of liquidity in the Brazilian banking sector in the last quarter of 2008, contributing to the severity of the crisis in Brazil. This behaviour by the Brazilian Central Bank is a consequence of the extremely rigid Inflation Targeting Regime adopted in Brazil in 1999. The excessive rigidity is clearly shown by the fact that the Brazilian Central Bank behaved in an *asymmetric way* in relation to the risks of target loss and the fall in the level of output. In December 2008, or even in October, the balancing of risks between inflation and recession showed clearly that the risk of output contraction was much higher than the risk of missing its inflation target. So the Central Bank could have reduced the short-term interest rate in the meeting of October of COPOM (the Comitê de Política Monetária). However, on this occasion the Central Bank adopted a strategy of 'wait and see'. They were holding for new information about the fall of output before making decisions about any reduction of interest rates. When the Central Bank finally decided to reduce the short-term interest rate, it was too little (just 100 base points) and too late (Serra, 2009).

The chapter is organised into seven sections, including the present introduction. In section 2, we present a brief outline of the theory behind derivatives and an analysis of the specific case of reverse exchange rate swaps in Brazil. In section 3, we analyze how exchange-rate derivatives created a Minskian financial fragility for Brazilian firms and the responsibility of the Brazilian Central Bank for aggravating the impact of the world financial crisis in Brazil. Section 4 is dedicated to an empirical analysis of the Central Bank of Brazil's reaction function in order to show the excessive rigidity of the Inflation Targeting Regime in Brazil. Section 5 presents a brief proposal for the regulation of derivatives and section 6 presents a proposal for a more flexible monetary policy in Brazil. Finally, section 7 concludes the chapter.

2 Exchange rate derivatives: theory and the Brazilian case

2.1 An overview on derivatives

Derivatives are financial instruments whose value derives from a market value of a security or pool of securities. An important feature of these instruments is called contingent claims. As the asset value is derived from the performance of other underlying assets, changes in base asset prices change the market value of the derivative. The right is contingent because the owner of the asset has the right to exercise it. Thus, if the holder of the derivative has, for example, a call option on a stock, it will exercise its right by a certain date if the market value of this action is greater than the value set by the option. If the market value is less than the contracted amount it will be more advantageous for the agent to buy such assets in the market. To establish this right and to gain the flexibility to buy this asset at a predetermined price one has to pay a price for this freedom. Another important feature that differentiates derivatives from other financial instruments relates to the high leverage that exists in these markets, which may result in losses greater than the contracted amounts. Moreover, the speed of transactions with derivatives is extremely high (the agents can quickly discard their positions).

The main reason for the existence of derivatives is uncertainty about the future price of assets. In most models of derivatives pricing such as, for example, in the Black–Scholes model, the concept of uncertainty used is probabilistic, which differs radically from the vision of strong uncertainty established by Keynes and Knight (see Schmidt, 1996). In this model, for example, the data needed to evaluate the price of an option are exactly the current price of the asset, the exercise price of the option, the remaining time to maturity of the option, the interest rate risk-free (in the case of Brazil CDI[1]), the standard deviation of the annualised rate of return of the price of the asset base and the table of normal distribution. For this approach, as the model for pricing options based on probability distributions, the agent has, for example, a perfect contingency plan. All possible outcomes are considered by the model and have an associated probability. Furthermore, the rate of return on risk-free assets is assumed to be independent and identically distributed in time, giving the estimates of variance past good forecasting tools. In particular, models based on risk evaluation assume, ultimately, a methodology similar to those established by Arrow–Debreu (1954) and McKenzie (1959). In other words, market participants share the same information so that the competitive equilibrium is always guaranteed. Moreover, the information held by an individual or firm is not affected by the information available on the market and cannot be changed for any actions taken, including those related to the acquisition of more information (Stiglitz, 1993).

The big problem with this approach is that the stock price and other financial assets exhibit more complex behaviors than those that arise from geometric Brownian motion. According to Dixit and Pindyck (1993), a Brownian motion or Wiener process is a stochastic process in continuous non-stationary time subject to three key properties: (i) it is a Markov process; (ii) changes at any moment at a finite interval of time assume a normal distribution, in which the variance grows linearly with time; and (iii) it has independent increments of change over time. The big problem with this, according to the authors, is to find variables in the real world that can be modeled according to those assumptions.

2.2 The economic reasons for using derivatives: a review of the literature

In the perfect world of Modigliani and Miller (1958) there is no reason for economic agents to use derivatives since capital structure is irrelevant for firms' investment decisions. However, in the real world it can be seen that there is a huge increase in the use of this type of financial instruments.

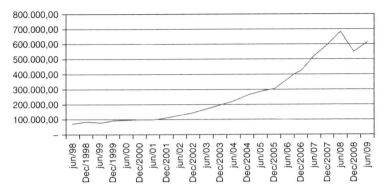

Figure 11.1 Amounts outstanding of over-the-counter (OTC) derivatives in billions of US dollars
Source: BIS Semiannual OTC derivatives statistics at end-June 2009.

According to BIS (Bank for International Settlements) data the amount of operations with derivatives increased 838 per cent in the period between June of 1998 to June of 2009, reaching a value of US$ 605 billion. Figure 11.1 shows the evolution of derivatives operations around the world.

Conventional theory of finance states that firms use derivatives in order to reduce potential losses and expected costs generated by changes in the price of assets, increasing the coordination between cash flows and inflows. The volatility in the prices of assets can produce situations where firms are not able to meet their financial commitments. In this setting, risk management can reduce the probability of these states of nature to happen, reducing the expected costs associated with these events (Smith and Stultz, 1985; Stulz 1996).

To get the argument more precise, let us define $V(S)$ as the value of a firm that does not carry out hedge operations, where S describes the vector of state variables that can change the market value of the firm. In this setting, two identical firms, a and b, may have different market values depending on their hedge policies. Firm a will be more protected against state variable i than firm b if the absolute value of covariance of market value of firm a with state variable i is lower or equal to the one held by firm b. This means that hedge operations reduce the dependence of market value of the firm to state variables. To be more precise, firm a will be more hedged that firm b if the absolute value of the covariance of the market value of firm a compared to a firm without hedge but with the same portfolio, capital structure and production is lower or equal than the one exhibited by firm b.

Smith and Stulz (1985) show that with risk management, the expected utility of wealth of a risk-averse manager is significantly affected by the variance of firms expected profits. In this setting, a risk manager will buy derivatives contracts if he/she believes that is less costly to buy a hedge contract than to fully take the risk of changes in the price of assets. This means that there is a positive relation between portfolio management and the decision to buy derivatives. Froot et al. (1993), in turn, show that if capital markets are imperfect then there is a relation between investment opportunities and hedge activities. A similar result is reached by Geczy et al. (1997).

Brown (2001), based on a sample of small, medium-sized and large corporations in the United States, showed that the costs of maintaining and operating a structure of derivatives are substantial, especially regarding the management of exchange-rate risks. According to him, the annual cost of holding hedge positions in the exchange-rate market for the biggest corporation in the sample was US$3.8 million, consisting of US$1.5 million resulting from operational costs and $2.3 million due to transactional costs. The author also pointed out that the net benefit of this derivative program for the firm under consideration was US$5 million. Finally, he concluded that standard theories of risk management are insufficient to explain the real motivations of the firms to adopt derivatives. Gauzy et al. (1997), in turn, based in a sample of 372 non-financial firms listed by Fortune in 1990, concluded that firms with high growth potential but low access to internal and external finance were more likely to use derivative contracts. According to the authors, this result is consistent with the hypothesis that hedge operations can reduce the costs of investment decisions under uncertainty. More precisely, hedge operations can reduce or even eliminate problems related to underinvestment (Myers, 1977; Garven and MacMinn, 1993).

2.3 The reverse exchange swap contracts of the Central Bank of Brazil

The exchange market is without doubt the largest financial market in the world and has the largest number of traders. In general, the main currency derivatives are futures, options, swaps and forwards. The foreign exchange market in Brazil is divided into three main vectors. The first one is the primary market exchange in which agents buy and sell currencies, especially the exporters and importers to honour its commitments in foreign currency. This market includes unilateral money transfers from abroad. In this situation, the position of banks is always passive in relation to the agents since they only guarantee the supply and demand of foreign exchange for these operations. The second is the interbank market in which banks transact foreign exchange among themselves. In this sense, the operations may be hedging, arbitrage or speculation. Indeed, banks can take both long positions in foreign currency (when betting on the devaluation of domestic currency) but also sold (when betting on the appreciation of local currency). Finally, there is the derivatives market: futures, options, swaps and forwards, which may also be hedging, arbitrage or speculation.

As we know, the monetary authority performs exchange market interventions both to regulate the level of the exchange rate and also to reduce its volatility. This intervention can occur in either the primary or the derivatives market, particularly in relation to the supply of swaps. A *swap* contract is a derivative transaction in which there is trade of rates. In a *foreign exchange swap* the Central Bank commits itself to pay the variation of exchange rate to financial institutions in exchange for the receipt of the change of inter-bank interest rate. In other words, in these operations the Central Bank buys foreign exchange swap contracts (tip exchange coupon) and the institutions that acquired such a contract takes a 'sold position' in DI.

In periods of substantial appreciation in the value of the Real – the Brazilian currency – the monetary authorities have reversed this process and started to adopt the so-called *reverse exchange swap* transactions. In these reverse contracts financial institutions receive the change in interest rate and the central bank receives the results of changes of currency values. Thus, when conducting auctions of reverse swaps, the Central Bank is in fact forcing a depreciation of the domestic currency.

Given this scenario, a very pertinent question to ask is the following: Why make interventions in the foreign exchange market through derivatives if these interventions can take place through the primary market? Since 1999, Brazil has adopted an Inflation Targeting Regime with a floating exchange rate. Under this framework, direct interventions in the exchange rate market will generate a high cost for the Treasury for conducting the so-called sterilisation operations that are required to hold the short-term interest rate at a level compatible with the target for inflation. In an intervention in the spot market for a foreign currency, the Central Bank injects *Reais*, thereby expanding the monetary base. To keep the short-term interest rate constant, it is necessary to conduct a second operation – the sale of bonds to the private sector. Therefore, instead of adopting capital controls inflows to avoid the adverse effects of currency appreciation on the Brazilian economy, the Central Bank chose to adopt the expedient of selling reverse currency swaps. In practice, these operations are equivalent to a purchase of US dollars in the futures market and thus ultimately push up the price of future dollars, preventing a fall of the forward premium and high foreign exchange coupon. As result, this operation, at least in theory, does not stimulate the inflow of additional dollars, but has a fiscal cost associated with the return of DI and also the exchange rate appreciation.

Indeed, in September 2008, reverse contracts held in Brazil amounted to R$40 billion, and the exposure of the country in US dollars at the end of January 2009 was approximately R$28 billion. Until July 2008, the result of foreign exchange swap operations was negative from the standpoint of the Central Bank, amounting to losses of R$6 billion from January to July 2008. Since the derivative contract is a bilateral one, the loss of the monetary authority translates into earnings of the counterpart, constituted of both banks and also exporting firms who have just endured sizable losses with the devaluation of the height of the crisis.

For these reasons, it is possible to answer some questions that have most intrigued Brazilian economists over the past three years, namely: how were exporting companies surviving during the period of strong exchange rate appreciation between 2005 and 2007? They were offsetting operating losses with financial revenues from foreign exchange derivative contracts facilitated by a friendly environment evidenced in the domestic market. Exporting companies conducted excessive forward target operations, making a double bet on appreciation. In the first bet, companies sold US dollars to banks through an instrument called forward. In other words, in this operation firms undertake a classic operation to sell US dollars in the forward market, betting on currency appreciation in order to gain the interest of the operation, and thereby receiving a financial income. In the second operation (bet) firms sells US dollars to banks again in the future market through the sale of call options short, giving banks the right to buy US dollars in the future at a predetermined price.

According to data from the Brazilian Central Bank, between January and August 2008, the flow of dollars into the country was positive at $14.38 billion. In just the first nine days of October 2008, for example, the balance shown was positive at US$1.604 billion, resulting in a surplus in trade of US$1.304 billion and a balance, also positive, of US$299 million in financial transactions. Faced with these data, we cannot say that in the first months of the crisis (August–October 2008) there was a capital flight from the country. What was revealed was a huge demand for dollar by Brazilian companies with the goal of honoring the positions taken in the forex market.

The mechanism behind this depreciation is extremely perverse. If we imagine that there is a *continuum* of options for market sales, as the dollar depreciates, new companies are forced to buy US dollars in the spot market to fulfill contracts for the sale of uncovered options, exerting strong pressure on the demand for dollars. As the Central Bank has not exercised – in time – the role of regulator of the monetary system through dollar sales on the spot market in order to contain the process of price increases, the banks again exercised its right to purchase the US currency, still pressing over the dollar. This process only subsided following the return of the auctions of foreign currency. Indeed, at the height of the crisis (August–October 2008) the Brazilian Central Bank earned about R$12 billion, behaving like a private bank rather than a regulatory agent.

3 The arrival of the world financial crisis in Brazil

In the last quarter of 2008 and the first quarter of 2009, the effects of the world financial crisis began to affect the Brazilian economy. In the United States the financial crisis had its origins in the bursting of the speculative bubble in the housing market, fed mainly, but not solely, by subprime mortgages. In Brazil, however, the financial crisis had its origins in the burst of a speculative bubble in the exchange rate market following the bankruptcy of Lehman Brothers and in the successive errors in the conduct of monetary policy by the Brazilian Central Bank. Contrary to what was expected by the advocates of the floating exchange rate regime, the sudden and fast devaluation of the nominal exchange rate after the bankruptcy of Lehman Brothers produced destabilising effects in the Brazilian economy. Many firms in the industrial sector, principally those dependent upon export operations, suffered huge losses following the devaluation of the real.

As we have already seen in the previous section, many Brazilian firms engaged in *target forward* operations, making a double bet in exchange rate appreciation. These highly speculative operations in the exchange rate markets had the objective of compensating the losses experienced by export firms following the overvaluation of the exchange rate in the period 2005–07. In fact, as is shown by Figure 11.2, in the third quarter of 2007, the real effective exchange rate in Brazil showed an overvaluation of 25% in respect of its equilibrium value.

In this setting we can see the first error of the Brazilian Central Bank in the conduction of monetary policy during this period. Instead of using the device of *capital controls* to avoid the exchange rate overvaluation,

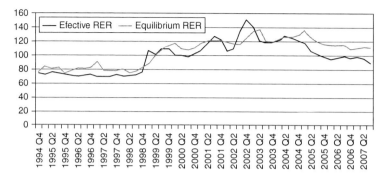

Figure 11.2 Effective and equilibrium values of the real exchange rate (indexed –
average value of 2000 = 100)
Source: Oreiro et al. (2009).

monetary authorities in Brazil chose to use an exotic financial instrument (the *reverse exchange rate swap*), which only increased the financial
fragility of the private sector since it induced firms to become involved
in highly speculative operations in exchange rate markets.

It is important to emphasise that the substantial depreciation of
the nominal exchange rate after the bankruptcy of Lehman Brothers
was not the result of *capital flight* or the reduction of international
credit lines for Brazilian firms, but the consequence of an increase in
the precautionary demand for foreign currency in order to face the
debt commitments of exchange-rate derivatives. In fact, according to
Central Bank data, between January and August 2008, the flow of external currency to Brazil was positive to the extent of US$14.38 billion.
In the first nine days of October, the currency flow to Brazil continue
to be positive, reaching US$1.604 billion, as a result of a surplus of
US$1,304 billion in trade operations and US$299 million in financial
operations.

Given these data, we can state that in the first months of the crisis
(August to September) there was no capital flight from Brazil. What
happens was a huge increase in the demand for foreign currency by
residents in order to fulfill their commitments in the future and deriva
tive markets. As we can see in Figure 11.3, in September there is a huge
depreciation of the exchange rate but the exchange rate market had
exhibited a positive surplus of more than US$2 billion. This dynamics
of the exchange rate and the surplus on exchange rate operations can
only be explained as being the result of a strong increase in the demand
for foreign currency by residents in the spot market.

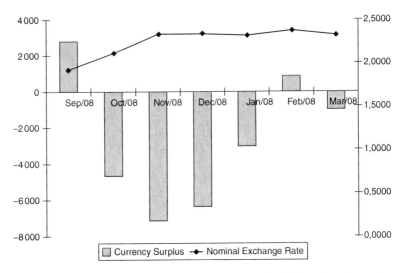

Figure 11.3 Nominal exchange rate and currency surplus/deficit from September 2008 to March 2009

The stubborn refusal of the Brazilian Central Bank to intervene in the exchange rate market in the first days of the crisis allowed monetary authorities in Brazil to profit US$6,507 billion in September with exchange rate derivatives. However, private firms such as Aracruz and Sadia incurred heavy losses[2] from these financial instruments.

As a result of these losses, there was a significant increase in the credit risk of firms in the productive sector. This situation, worsened by the uncertainty generated by the world financial crisis, caused Brazilian banks to reduce the supply of credit, mainly for the finance of working capital of firms and the consumption expenditures of households in durable goods, like automobiles. This credit crunch produced a sharp increase in the *banking spread*, as we can see in Figure 11.4.

Between September and October 2008, the Brazilian Central Bank committed another mistake in the conduct of monetary policy as a result of its incapacity to deal with the systemic effects of the increase in the liquidity preference of banks. We have already seen how the huge losses caused by the exchange rate depreciation have increased the credit risks of productive firms. The standard reaction of banks – and, indeed, of any economic agent – to an increase in the level of uncertainty is to increase the liquidity preference; i.e. the position of highly liquid assets, easily convertible in means of payments. In the case of banks,

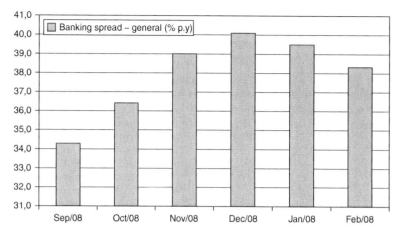

Figure 11.4   Evolution of banking spread – general (% p.y)
Source: Central Bank of Brazil.

reserves are the most highly liquid assets. In this setting, it led to a simultaneous contraction of credit and an increase in the level of bank reserves, which jumped from R$39.232 thousand in September to R$40.134 thousand in October – that is, a 2 per cent increase in just one month.

The Brazilian Central Bank decided to deal with the problem of the increased liquidity preference of banks by means of a partial liberation of reserve requirements over demand deposits. In September, the total amount of reserve requirements of banks was R$117.971 thousand. This value was reduced to R$96.923 thousand in October. In adopting this policy the intention of the Brazilian Central Bank was to induce banks to return to the pre-crisis level of credit by means of a considerable increase in the level of liquidity of the banking sector as a whole.

This policy could have been successful in increasing the aggregate level of liquidity of the banking sector if it was carried out in conjunction with a major reduction in the level of short-term interest rates. As is well known to any undergraduate student of monetary economics, for the banking sector as a whole, banking reserves can only increase if the central bank decides to increase its balance sheet, buying foreign currency or bonds from the private sector (Carvalho et al, 2000). When the central bank buys bonds in the secondary market (or foreign currency in the spot market), it increases the monetary base, which allows banks to expand their credit operations due to its effects over the level of banking reserves. However, the side effect of an increase in the monetary base is a reduction in the level of short-term interest rate.

From this reasoning we can conclude that for the central bank to increase the level of liquidity of the banking sector as a whole, what is necessary is not a reduction in reserve requirements, but an increase in the monetary base, which demands a reduction in the short-term interest rate. However, the Brazilian Central Bank refused to reduce short-term interest rates until January 2009, three months after the arrival of the world financial crisis in Brazil! This ignorance of an elementary principle of monetary economics by the Brazilian Central Bank resulted not only in the ineffectiveness of the reduction of reserve requirements as an attempt to restore the level of liquidity of Brazilian banks, but also to a destruction of liquidity. In fact, the total amount of banking reserves (including reserve requirement in the Central Bank) was R$157.294 thousand in September 2008. The following month, the level of total reserves had been reduced to R$137.057 thousand – that is, a fall of 12.86 per cent in just one month. The liquidity of the banking sector as a whole was reduced dramatically in a very short period of time.

The liquidity reduction of the Brazilian banking sector was the consequence of the realisation of non-sterilised interventions of the Central Bank by means of selling of international reserves in the exchange rate market after October 2008 (see Figure 11.5). It is well known that every time that the monetary authority sells foreign currency in the spot market, it produces a contraction of the monetary base. To avoid this effect, the Central Bank must buy bonds from the private sector in order to sterilise the contraction of the monetary base. The problem is that the Brazilian Central Bank has not carried out this second operation to the required magnitude to avoid a contraction of the monetary base, since banking reserves showed a clear reduction in the period between October 2008 and January 2009, as was shown in the figures below.

In the context of a huge decrease in the liquidity of the banking sector as a whole how could banks be expected to increase their credit operations to its pre-crisis levels? The reaction of Brazilian banks to the change in the liquidity conditions were precisely what could be expected based on elementary principles of monetary economics; that is, the contraction of banking credit.

The credit crunch, together with the negative effect of a tight monetary policy on the expectations of entrepreneurs and households, had catastrophic effects on the time path of industrial production. As can be seen in Figure 11.7, industrial output showed a contraction of 2 per cent in

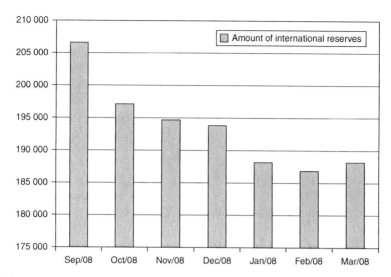

Figure 11.5 Evolution of international reserves
Source: Central Bank of Brazil.

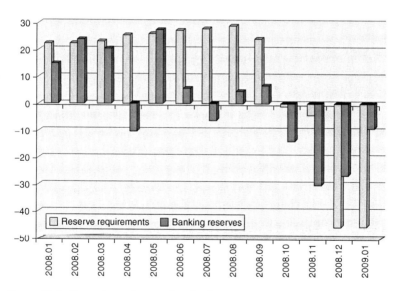

Figure 11.6 Percentage change (p.m) of reserve requirements and banking reserves in Brazil (2008.01–2009.01)
Source: Central Bank of Brazil.

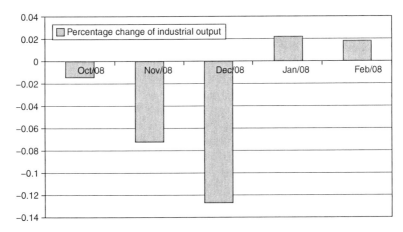

Figure 11.7 Percentage change of industrial output (compared to the same month in 2007)
Source: IPEADATA.

October, 7 per cent in November and more than 12 per cent in December compared to the same period in 2007.

Although these data had only been published in January 2009, the Brazilian Central Bank surely had a previous knowledge of them before the final meeting of the Monetary Policy Committee (COPOM) of 2008, which was held in the first days of December. However, instead of beginning a huge reduction of the short-term interest rate in order to minimise the effects of the financial crisis on the Brazilian economy in 2009, COPOM had decided to hold interest rate constant at 13.75 per cent per year, based on the argument that there were still some risks of inflation acceleration due to the pass-though effect of exchange rate devaluation over domestic prices. This was the third error committed by the Brazilian Central Bank. Since October 2008, inflation expectations collected by the Central Bank in *Boletim Focus* had been continuously revised downwards. At the beginning of 2009, all of the data showed that the actual inflation rate could be lower than the target of 4.5 per cent per year pursued by the monetary authority. In fact, the actual inflation rate recorded for 2009 was 4.3 per cent.

In the first meeting of COPOM in 2009, the Central Bank of Brazil had finally decided to reduce the level of short-term interest rate by one percentage point. The magnitude of this reduction, rare in the recent history of monetary policy in Brazil, was a clear recognition of the Brazilian Central Bank of the errors it had committed in terms of the operation of monetary policy in the last quarter of 2008. It was significant that a few days before the bankruptcy of Lehman Brothers, the Central Bank of Brazil had increased the short-term interest rate from 13 per cent per year to 13.75 per cent per year. During that period, the fall in commodity prices (Figure 11.8), initiated two months before the bankruptcy of Lehman Brothers, showed that the effect of exchange rate devaluation over inflation will be less than zero, but the Brazilian Central Bank insisted on pursuing a route of monetary tightening. As a consequence of the error committed in September, the Central Bank became morally incapable of reducing the short-term interest rates in its meetings held in October and December. The persistence of this error meant that the short-term interest rate was kept at an extremely high level given the context of a liquidity crisis, the credit crunch and a contraction of output throughout the world.

The evaluation errors about the effects of the crisis on the Brazilian economy by the Central Bank were caused, however, by the excessive rigidity of the Inflation Targeting Regime in Brazil. This excessive rigidity is shown clearly by the fact that the Brazilian Central Bank behaves in an *asymmetric way* in relation to the risks of target loss and the fall in the level of output. In December, or even October, the balancing of risks between inflation and recession showed clearly that the risk of output

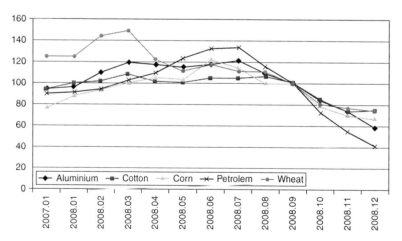

Figure 11.8 Evolution of the international prices of five commodities (2007/
12–2008/12)
Source: IPEADATA.

contraction was much higher than the risk of missing its inflation target. So the Central Bank could have reduced the short-term interest rate in the October meeting of COPOM. Instead, the Central Bank adopted a strategy of 'wait and see', delaying for new information about the fall of output before deciding to reduce the interest rate. However, a 'wait to see' strategy is not only a good policy for inflation control, but also for output stabilisation, which is an element of objective function of *policy-maker*, even under an ITR.[3] The monetary authority must anticipate movements of inflation and output in order to minimise the volatility of the short-term interest rate and increase the welfare of society.[4] In the case of Brazil, the Central Bank, however, always acts promptly in order to avoid the risk of output loss, but chooses to 'wait and see' if output would fall or not. This shows an excessive rigidity of ITR in Brazil, a rigidity that is demonstrated by the low level of attention given to the effects of monetary policy on the levels of economic activity.

4 Why is the Brazilian Central Bank so conservative in its conduct of monetary policy?[5]

In the final section of this chapter we argue that the Brazilian Central Bank appears to be excessively concerned about the rate of inflation, which caused an excessive delay in the loosening of monetary policy in the context of the global financial crisis. We will now argue that empirical evidence points out that the Brazilian Central Bank utilises the short-term interest rate as a tool against inflationary pressures originating, finally, from cost pressures that derive from changes in the nominal exchange rate. Our estimation of the reaction function of the Central Bank, while exhibiting this pattern of behaviour of the monetary authority, also highlights the existence of a *high degree of aversion to inflation*, something that further increases the level of interest rate required to ensure the convergence of inflation to its long-run target values.

To support such an interpretation, we will now estimate the relevance of the exchange rate in the reaction function of the Central Bank, using an Autoregressive Vector (VAR) model. To do this we have to identify the causality relation between the principal variables that are used to determine the interest rate. These variables will be: interest rate (Selic) set by the Central Bank; the Extended Consumer Price Index (IPCA), calculated by the Brazilian Institute of Geography and Statistics (IBGE); the exchange rate Real/US Dollar as results from Institute of Applied Economics (IPEADATA); the inflation expectations that are monitored in the *Boletim Focus* of the Central Bank; finally, the monthly value of the degree of capacity utilisation from IPEADATA.

With this we will be able to estimate the dynamics of the determination of the Selic rate in the period July 2001 to April 2008, trying in particular to quantify the relevance of exchange rate for monetary policy. Our choice of time period was determined by the aim of discarding the earlier two years of the inflation targeting regime, and analysing the behaviour during a time interval characterised by an already consolidated regime with monetary anchor.

4.1 The estimation of the dynamics of determination of the Selic rate

The VAR methodology used hereafter is also utilised by the Central Bank to estimate the expectations of IPCA and industrial production. It can also be used to support decision making in monetary policy.[6]

First, tests for stationarity of the time series were applied, taking into account the degree of integration, the lagged structure of the series and the specification of the intercept and trend, to avoid problems of spurious results leading to incorrect interpretations. The ADF test was once again implemented, as it permits to incorporate extra lagged terms of the dependent variable as a way to eliminate autocorrelation in residuals.

Based on the econometrics tests, certain inferences can be made about the dynamic interaction between variables. The diagram of causality between variables, reported below, is instructive as it synthesises all significant relations derived with Granger causality test.[7]

Its analysis yields the following results. The Selic is *caused* by the exchange rate variable, IPCA and the inflation expectations; the IPCA by inflation expectations and exchange rate; expectations on their turn are caused by the exchange rate and this latter is exogenously determined. Finally, the level of capacity utilisation is caused by the IPCA, expectations and SELIC. Figure 11.9 shows such relationships.

From Figure 11.9 we see that the exchange rate causes the Selic, both directly, and indirectly through expectations and IPCA. Through its impact on the Selic, the rate of exchange also causes the level of capacity utilisation. In fact, the exchange rate is treated here as an *exogenous* variable, being the principal determinant of all other variables. This is further confirmed by the test for endogeneity. As can be readily ascertained, the level of capacity utilisation, the Selic, the IPCA, and expectations, follow, in this order, the exchange rate in terms of increasing degrees of exogeneity.[8]

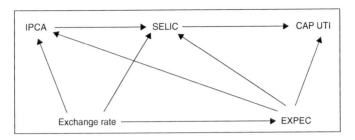

Figure 11.9 Causality diagram

On the other hand, from the decomposition of variance, the impact of the Selic rate onto the IPCA and the utilisation level of productive capacity, is considerably modest. This seems to imply the necessity of resorting to 'overdosing' interest rates in order to attempt at curbing aggregate demand and to control inflation pressures.

From the variance decomposition it can be ascertained that, with a 6-month lag, approximately 47.51 per cent of the changes in expectations taking place are due to movements in the exchange rate. In the same way, a change in the rate of exchange and inflation expectations explains, with a 5- and 2-month lag, 37.7 per cent and 37.54 per cent, respectively, of the change in IPCA. Moreover, with a 12-month lag, about 22.6 per cent of the change in the SELIC rate can be explained by the change in the exchange rate. Finally, with a 12-month lag, some 11.81 per cent of the change in the capacity utilisation rate can be explained by a change in the Selic.

5 Derivatives and financial fragility: how to regulate?

The difficulties in monitoring the financial risks are especially important in the case of a derivative contract for a variety of reasons. One important reason occurs when the monitoring process is not well designed and the principal is set in an advantageous position to speculate in the market. '*Whenever outside principals cannot fully monitor, an agent may find it optimal to speculate*' (Dow and Gorton, 1994).

This question shows clearly the existence of a dilemma. On the one hand, derivatives are an important instrument for protection and risk transfer; but, on the other hand, its widespread use could generate severe financial crises as the Brazilian experience with exchange-rate derivatives had shown. Moreover, as a result of its amplitude and capacity to penetrate in the entire economic system, local problems such as those exhibited in the subprime market in the United States could spread across the entire economy, generating catastrophic effects over the real sector, despite the comparatively small magnitude of this particular market.

Another problem relates to Basel II. When a crisis occurs, asset values fall and banks are obliged to allocate more capital to cover the *downgrading* of their assets, generating a vicious cycle of credit contraction and liquidity destruction. In other words, Basel II established a pro-cyclical capital allocation. At the exact moment that more liquidity is required to re-establish the working of the financial system, capital requirements restrict banks' credit operations.

To solve this dilemma, two policiy measures are required. The first is to separate bonds and titles that banks hold in portfolio for speculative reasons from the ones that they hold until maturity. The first ones must be registered in the balance sheet of banks by their market value and the others must be registered by their cost of acquisition. In addition, the weighting factors must be anti-cyclical. In boom periods, more capital will be required by banks, reducing liquidity levels and increasing the buffer stock of capital of the banking system. This procedure has the additional advantage of reducing banks' incentives to 'clean up' their balance sheets by means of securitisation, since higher weights reduce the profits that can be obtained from that kind of financial operation. During a crisis, however, the buffer stock of liquidity is liberated in order to allow banks to increase their credit operations, increasing the liquidity of the economic system as a whole. Obviously the operation of a system such as this will require expertise on the part of the monetary authorities and a 'learning-by-doing' process, as occurred with the setting of short-term interest rates.

6 A proposal for a more flexible monetary policy in Brazil

Interest rate policy can be an efficient instrument for controlling demand inflation, but it is certainly not efficient to control inflation caused by supply shocks. For this reason, the Brazilian Central Bank must react through interest rate changes only to inflation pressure caused by situations of excess demand. This objective could be accomplished through the use of inflation rate measurement by means of an inflation index that excludes those products that are more sensitive to supply shocks, such as food and energy. This means the selection of a core inflation index instead of a headline inflation index as the measure of inflation to be targeted.

Furthermore, the Brazilian Central Bank should react only to situations of permanent excess demand. A temporary excess demand, resulting from a high rate of growth of effective demand that induce an increase in investment, must be accommodated by monetary authorities through a more passive monetary policy. In order for the Central Bank to improve the chances for economic growth, interest rate increases must be considered only in situations of excess demand that are not followed by an increase in the rate of capital accumulation. So, if investment expenditures are increasing at a higher rate than the overall level of aggregate demand, then, *ceteris paribus*, capacity output growth will be increasing in the medium term, signalling the temporary nature of a situation of excess demand. Under such conditions, a larger horizon of convergence (more than one year) to the inflation target is desirable in order to smooth the effects of temporary demand shocks over the measured rate of inflation.

Some empirical studies, for instance Sarel (1996), show the existence of a minimum inflation rate below which the growth rate is reduced. The reason for that is the nominal wage rigidity that prevails in labour markets. As we have stressed already, according to Tobin (1972) when there is downward nominal wage rigidity, inflation can help grease the wheels of labour market adjustment by facilitating relative wage and price adjustment in sectors with substantial unemployment. So, a positive, although small rate of inflation is necessary for the achievement of robust economic growth. Padilha (2007), using a sample of 55 developed and underdeveloped countries in the period 1990–2004, replicated the methodology used by Sarel (1996) for a larger time span and showed that for emerging countries the minimum rate of inflation is 5.1 per cent per year and for the developed countries it is around 2.1 per cent per year. The difference between the minimum level of inflation in emerging and developed countries is the result of the fact that a higher rate of output growth in the former generates a higher rate of increase of prices of non-tradable goods relative to the observed in developed countries. This means that in order for emerging countries to have the same rate of inflation as developed countries, the rate of increase of prices of tradable goods has to be higher in the latter. This requires a nominal exchange rate appreciation of emerging countries' currency relative to developed countries' currency, which can be done only by means of a tight monetary policy which has harmful effects over investment and growth. Based on this reasoning we can state that the catching-up of emerging countries to developed countries demands, among other things, different target levels of inflation. For Brazil, this means that long-run inflation target can not be lower than 5 per cent per year.

As we have seen in section 4, the devaluation of the exchange rate is one of the main sources of cost-push inflation in Brazil. Empirical works show that interest rates have been one of the instruments used to deal with exchange rate movements, as they affect the capital account and thereby affect the real and nominal exchange rate. For this reason economic authorities should have a more active role in relation to the exchange rate, avoiding its volatility and seeking somehow to affect its long-term trajectory (for instance, avoiding excessive depreciation or appreciation).

One possibility is the use of official intervention in the foreign exchange market, which may exert a direct influence on the nominal exchange rate as it alters the relative supply of domestic and foreign currency assets. On the one hand, the countries' ability to resist currency depreciation is limited by its stock of foreign exchange reserves and its access to potential credit lines. Reserve accumulation can be seen as an insurance against future negative shocks and speculation against domestic currency, as emerging economies like Brazil have limited access to the international capital market. On other hand, the ability to avoid currency appreciation may require the use of sterilised intervention. The increased monetary reserves can place downward pressure on the short-term interest rate in case of no-sterilised intervention, so that bank credit would tend to expand and inflationary pressures would eventually arise. However, if central banks have a target for the short-term rate, then they would attempt to offset increases in bank reserves selling domestic assets or issuing their own securities, an operation known as sterilised intervention (Mohanty and Turner, 2006).

Another possibility to help the management of the exchange rate regime (that is, not excluding official intervention) in Brazil is the use of 'capital management techniques' which include 'capital controls', that is norms that manage volume, composition, the allocation of international private capital flows, and/or 'prudential domestic financial regulations', that refer to policies, such as capital-adequacy standards, reporting requirements, or restrictions on the ability and terms under which domestic financial institutions can provide funding to certain types of projects (Epstein et al. 2003: 6–7). Prudential controls can include: (i) limiting the opportunities for residents to borrow in foreign currency and to monitor them when they do, and (ii) keeping very tight constraints on banks' ability to have open foreign exchange positions or indirect exposure through foreign exchange loans.

For economies that are operating domestic interest rates higher than offshore interest rates, such as Brazil, reserve requirements on capital inflows can be used as a complementary tool for monetary and exchange rate policies. For countries where domestic interest rates are lower than offshore interest rates – as has been the case in China, Malaysia and South Korea since the end of the 1990s – there is no need for capital controls on inflows as there are no arbitrage gains involved.

7   Final remarks

This chapter showed that a Minskian crisis had occurred in Brazil in the last quarter of 2008 as a result of the widespread existence of exchange-rate derivatives among Brazilian companies. These financial instruments increased the financial fragility of the private sector in Brazil since it increased the potential losses from a sudden depreciation in the exchange rate, what finally happened between September and October of 2008. In addition to the financial fragility caused by derivatives, the magnitude of the crisis was severely aggravated by the unjustifiable delay of the Brazilian Central Bank in loosening monetary policy in the context of a catastrophic fall in industrial output. Indeed, the monetary authorities in Brazil only began to reduce short-term interest rates in January 2009, three months after the bankruptcy of Lehman Brothers. But at that time, the reduction was too little and too late. Those events highlight the importance of a better regulation of exchange-rate derivatives and a reform of the Inflation Targeting Regime in Brazil in order to avoid another financial crisis in Brazil.

Notes

1. Brazilian interbank interest rate.
2. Many Brazilian companies showed significant losses due to foreign exchange derivative transactions in 2008, among them: Sadia annual losses of R\$2.48 billion; Aracruz annual losses of R\$4.20 billion. CSN, despite not having registered losses, lost US\$1.3 billion in a single derivative operation that has reduced its profit by 94 per cent to R\$40 million. Another group of companies that suffered severe losses were the alcohol plants, reaching a record R\$4 billion. For more details, see Aracruz (2009), Sadia (2008) and Financial Web (2008).
3. See Blinder (1999).
4. See Gali (2008).
5. This section relies largely on Oreiro et al. (2007).
6. As is the case with the *Relatórios de Inflação* (Inflation Reports) by the BCB.
7. The ADF test shows that all variables being considered are first difference stationary. With the exceptions of expectations and the exchange rate, showing a

lag of 3 and 2 periods, respectively, all other variables have a 1-lag as the best lag structure, according to Schwarz criterion. The best phase structure for the model as a whole has 2 lags, as for the time period the LM test (the Lagrange Multiplier Test) does not show significance in terms of serial correlation of residuals. With that lag structure, we applied the Granger causality test, estimated the error variance decomposition and the order of endogeneity of the variables by means of the *VAR Pairwise Granger Causality*. Finally, with the view of checking for the existence of a long run relationship between variables, Johansen cointegration test was applied, from which at least two cointegration vectors at a 5 per cent significance level were identified.

8. VAR Pairwise Granger Causality/Block Exogeneity Wald Tests.

References

Aracruz (2009) *Aracruz Resultados*. Available at: http://aracruz.infoinvest.com.br/ptb/2500/4Q2008release_BRGAAP.pdf.

Arrow, K.J. and Debreu, G. (1954) 'Existence of an Equilibrium for a Competitive Economy', *Econometrica*, 22, 265–90.

Banco Central do Brasil *Circular n. 3.068, de 08/11/2001*, and *Circular n. 3.082 de 30/01/2002*. Available at: http://www.bacen.gov.br.

Banco Central do Brasil. *Nota para a imprensa – Política Fiscal. Brasília*. Available at: http://www.bcb.gov.br/htms/infecon/notas.asp?idioma=p&id=ecoimphist.

Banco Central do Brasil. *Nota para a imprensa – Setor Externo. Brasília*. Available at: http://www.bcb.gov.br/htms/infecon/notas.asp?idioma=p&id=ecoimphist.

Blinder, A. (1999) *Bancos Centrais: teoria e prática*. São Paulo: Editora 34.

Brown, G. (2001) 'Managing Foreing Exchange Risk with Derivatives', *Journal of Financial Economics*, 60, 401–49.

Canal do Produtor (2009) *Perdas com Derivativos nas Usinas atingem até R$ 4 bi*. Available at: http://www.canaldoprodutor.com.br/noticias/perdas-com-derivativos-nas-usinas-atingem-at%C3%A9-r-4-bi.

Carvalho, F.C. et al. (2000) *Economia Monetária e Financeira*. Rio de Janeiro: Campus.

Dow, J. and Gorton, G (1994) 'Noise Trading, Delegated Portfolio Management, and Economic Welfare', *Working Paper No. 4858*. Cambridge, MA: National Bureau of Economic Research.

Dixit, A.K. and Pindyck, R.S. (1993) *Investment Under Uncertainty*. Princeton, NJ: Princeton University Press.

Epstein, G., Grabel, I., and Jomo, K.S. (2003) 'Capital Management Techniques In Developing Countries: An Assessment of Experiences from the 1990s and Lessons For the Future', *G-24 Technical Paper*.

Financial Web (2008) 'Derivativos Reduzem Lucro da CSN em 94%'. Available at: http://www.financialweb.com.br/noticias/index.asp?cod=52981.

Froot, K., Scharfstein, D. and Stein, J. (1993) 'Risk Management: Coordinating Corporate Investment and Financing Policies', *Journal of Finance*, 48, 1629–58.

Gali, J. (2008) *Monetary Policy, Inflation and the Business Cycles*. Princeton, NJ: Princeton University Press.

Hull, J.C. (1997) *Options, Futures, & Other Derivatives*, 3rd edition. Englewood Cliffs, NJ: Prentice Hall.

IASB – International Accounting Standards Board. IAS – 39 Financial Instruments: Recognition and Measurement – Technical Summary. Available at: http://www. iasb.org.

Garven, J.R. and MacMinn, R.D. (1993) 'The Underinvestment Problem, Bond Covenants, and Insurance', *The Journal of Risk and Insurance*, 60(4), 635–46.

Geczy, C., Minton, B.A. and Schrand, C. (1997) 'Why Firms Use Currency Derivatives', *The Journal of Finance*, 52(4), 1323–54.

Magud, N. and Reinhart, C. (2006) 'Capital Controls: An Evaluation', *NBER Working Paper*, No. 11973.

McKenzie, L.W. (1959) 'On the Existence of General Equilibrium for a Competitive Market', *Econometrica*, 27, 54–71.

Modigliani, F. and Miller, M.H. (1958) 'The Cost of Capital, Corporation Finance, and the Theory of Investment', *American Economic Review*, 48, 261–97.

Mohanty, M. and Turner, P (2006) 'Foreign Exchange Reserves in Emerging Countries', *BIS Quarterly Review*, 24, 39–42.

Myers, S. (1977) 'The Determinants of Corporate Borrowing', *Journal of Financial Economics*, 5, 147–75.

Oreiro, J.L., Paula, L.F., Jonas, G. and Quevedo, R. (2007) 'Por que o custo do capital no Brasil é tão alto?', *Papers and Proceedings of XXXV Meeting of Brazilian Economic Association*, Recife.

Oreiro, J.L., Punzo, L., Araújo, E. and Squeff, G. (2009) 'Macroeconomic Constraints to the Growth of the Brazilian Economy: Diagnosis and Some Policy Proposals', *Working Paper* no. 001/09, Universidade de Brasília.

Padilha, R. (2007) *Metas de inflação: experiência e questões para os países em desenvolvimento*. Masters Dissertation. Curitiba: Federal University of Paraná.

Sadia (2008) Demonstrações Financeiras Padronizadas. Available at: http:// ri.sadia.com.br/ptb/1602/DFP2008Completa.pdf.

Saunders, A. (2000) *Administração de Instituições Financeiras*. São Paulo: Atlas.

Sarel, M. (1996) 'Nonlinear Effects of Inflation on Economic Growth', *IMF Staff Papers*, 43, 199–215.

Schmidt, C. (ed.) (1996) *Uncertainty in Economic Thought*. Cheltenham, UK and Brookfield, VT: Edward Elgar.

Serra, J. (2009) 'Só com palavras não se criam empregos', *O Globo*. Rio de Janeiro, 26 January.

Smith,W.C. and Stultz, M.R. (1985) 'The Determinants of Firms Hedging Policies', *Journal of Financial and Quantitative Analysis*, 20, 391–405.

Stiglitz, J. (1993) 'The Role of the State in Financial Markets', World Bank Research Observer. Annual Conference on Development Economics, Supplement, 19–61.

Stiglitz, J. and Weiss, A. (1981) 'Credit Rationing in Markets with Imperfect Information', *American Economic Review*, 71(3), 393–410.

Stulz, R. (1984) 'Optimal Hedging Policies', *Journal of Financial and Quantitative Analysis*, 19, 127–40.

Stulz, R. (1996) 'Rethinking Risk Management', *Journal of Applied Corporate Finance*, 9, 8–24.

Tobin, J. (1972) 'Inflation and Unemployment', *American Economic Review*, 62, 1–18.

Index